A STRATEGIC GUIDE TO CHURCH CAMPUS DEVELOPMENT

THE NEXT STEP

How to Discover the Right Solutions to Plan, Design, & Build Your Church

BUILD UP, BUILD UP,

PREPARE THE ROAD!

REMOVE THE OBSTACLES

OUT OF THE WAY OF

MY PEOPLE.

– ISAIAH 57:14

BILL CHEGWIDDEN

THE
NEXT
STEP

BILL CHEGWIDDEN

RIVERSTONE GROUP
PUBLISHING

CONTENTS

Gratis

114134

NEHEMIAH'S JOURNEY

NEHEMIAH'S JOURNEY

The Old Testament book of Nehemiah provides an excellent model for the prayer, planning, preparation, and perseverance required for the journey that many of our churches are undertaking today. It is a *journey* of growth, development, and expansion, and while it can prove to be exciting and full of adventure, it also can be challenging and something that requires a strong, steady faith.

This is one of the reasons why I believe the lessons we can glean from Nehemiah's life will keep us on the right path. Nehemiah understood how to plan for a project. Likewise, he knew what it was like to remain faithful during trying times. He realized that if he kept his heart and mind fixed on the goal set before him, the project would be successful and used by the people of God. Can you and your church have the same experience? I believe you can.

Several years ago, after completing a study of this favorite Old Testament book, I assembled the following thoughts—not as a theological interpretation, but as a compilation of the steps Nehemiah took on his journey. These steps have been assembled from years of experience and a desire to provide a systematic method of helping churches grow and fulfill their mission statements. If you are currently working on a church building project or plan to begin this process in the near future, then you may want to take the time to reread the book of Nehemiah with a set of fresh eyes and an open mind to strategic planning. My sincere desire is that this Old Testament book will come alive to you and help you and your church discover the right path to follow on your journey to a lifetime of growth and expansion.

Give Your Servant Success Today

Since I have used portions of Nehemiah to introduce the steps in this book, I thought that it would be helpful to explain why I chose his life and work as an example. In the first chapter, we find that Nehemiah is leading a rather comfortable lifestyle as a cupbearer to the king. However, this is about to change.

The Bible says that when Nehemiah had an opportunity to inquire about his former hometown of Jerusalem, he took it. The news, however, was not good. The walls surrounding the city had been broken down and lay in ruins, and Jerusalem was open to enemy attack. When he heard this, Nehemiah sat down and cried. He was so overwhelmed by the report that he prayed and did not eat for several days.

These steps have been gathered from years of experience and a desire to provide a systematic method of helping churches grow and fulfill their mission statements.

When Nehemiah heard the news, he realized that he had a great passion for God's people and their condition.

Truthfully, this same information was available to many other people. In fact, many knew the condition of Jerusalem, but had chosen to do nothing to remedy the problem. No one had stepped forward to take up the challenge of reconstruction.

However, when Nehemiah heard the news his heart was stirred, and he realized that he had a great passion for God's people and their condition. He mourned over the city's condition and spent time in prayer before the Lord. Then he responded in faith to the situation by asking the Lord to allow him to do something to help. Like Nehemiah, many today know about the plight of God's people. Some choose to leave the problems for others to solve. However, others discover they have a passion to be used by God and want to be equipped for His service. We may wonder, "How could a cupbearer be used to change a situation as great as this one?" God had a plan and Nehemiah had the passion to discover it and carry it out.

Over the years, I have observed that God often uses ordinary people to do extraordinary things. The only requirements are a willing heart and availability. If you feel as though you have little to offer in the area of design and construction, then you are in good company because Nehemiah probably felt the same way.

Whenever we ask God for an opportunity to serve Him, we had better be prepared to begin a great journey. Nehemiah could have stayed where he was and remained the cupbearer to the king. Instead he committed himself to helping God's people.

He chose to leave the court of the king and to go to Jerusalem. After he made this decision he prayed again, "Oh Lord, let your ear be attentive to the prayer of this your servant and to the prayer of your servants who delight in revering your name. Give your servant success today by granting him favor in the presence of [the king]" (Nehemiah 1:11).

In the second chapter of Nehemiah, we find that four months had passed, but the time had not been wasted. Nehemiah was planning how he would approach the project. His concern for the city of Jerusalem grew to be so great that soon King Artaxerxes noticed a change in his demeanor and asked what was wrong.

Nehemiah had anticipated this day and answered with honesty and conviction. He also did not hesitate to ask the king for help. He wanted to return to Jerusalem so that he could help in the reconstruction of the city's walls. He had taken time to think through every aspect of the project and knew how long it would take and how much help he would need.

Those months of waiting had been spent in sincere preparation. Now, Nehemiah was ready to ask for permission to move ahead with the project. He also requested the resources that would be needed for the journey. The journey that you are considering may not be to a far away place, though in this case Nehemiah had to travel some distance to reach his hometown. For Nehemiah, it was a journey back to Jerusalem and working through the process of redesigning and rebuilding the walls of the city of Jerusalem. This was his journey and although your journey is not the same it is mirrored in his prayer and faith. Your journey also is one that will lead you through the necessary stages of planning, designing, and building in order to address the needs of your church.

Speaking of faith—Nehemiah's faithfulness paid off. God answered his prayers by prompting the king to respond with support—more than Nehemiah had requested. Chances are, it did not take long for Nehemiah to pack his bags and head out on the road to Jerusalem.

Momentum was on his side. However, as soon as he arrived in the city, he met his first detractors. Even before he surveyed the problem and could organize the people for the work, he found that there were others whose main goals were to stop him from completing his mission. More than likely, the same will hold true for you as you begin your project. God never told us that the road laid out before us would be easy to travel. However, He has promised that He will walk each step with us and ultimately grant us the victory. This promise was the foundation of Nehemiah's faith and courage, and it should be ours, too.

As soon as possible, Nehemiah selected a few men to ride with him as he surveyed the broken-down walls. Yet, he kept the plans that God had placed in his heart to himself. At this point, he did not share what he believed the Lord wanted him to do. Instead, he personally reviewed the situation. He didn't just take a quick glance or a short overview. That was not his style. Instead, he viewed the project from many different vantage points, while taking time to consider its depth and scope. How many others had seen the same view of the city? Perhaps in their mind's eye, they saw only piles of rubble and destruction. However, Nehemiah saw the potential for hope, a possibility for growth and development, and an opportunity to help prepare a place for God's people to live again.

Nehemiah saw the potential for hope, a possibility for growth and development, and an opportunity to help.

The Sharing of a Vision

After Nehemiah had personally reviewed, analyzed, and decided how to solve the problem, he began to share the plan that God had given him. He told the people about his passion and desire to see the city's walls reconstructed. He also laid out the evidence of God's involvement through the provision of the resources that would be used to complete the work. When the people heard his plan, they began to catch his vision and agreed to work alongside him.

Nehemiah organized this huge project by dividing it into small, manageable steps. Looking at a plan of this magnitude can be overwhelming. However, when it is broken down into achievable goals, it is easier to stay on task. This also helps the people to remain encouraged as they reach smaller goals on a consistent basis.

Different groups took the responsibility of completing each one of the smaller goals. The reconstruction of the walls became a team effort that was completely successful. Good planning and progress, however, do not prevent our enemies from causing conflict. Nehemiah had plenty of conflict—a group of people were committed to stopping the work. His detractors told the workers that the task was too great for them. They stressed that the resources were far too limited and that the reconstructed walls would not stand the test of time. With the hope of dealing a final discouraging blow, the cynics charged that the work being done would not make a difference and that any effort spent on Jerusalem's walls would not change the city's condition.

From their view-point, the situation seemed hopeless, but from God's vantage point, it was a formula for success.

From a human perspective, the situation may have seemed hopeless, but from God's vantage point, it was a formula for success. How many times do we hear the same type of statements coming from our detractors? They are not necessarily against us, but they are against the work we feel called to do.

Nehemiah did not yield to their negative comments. Instead, he turned to prayer, sought God's strength and encouragement, and kept his eyes set on the goal—which was to finish the work God had given him to do. He refused to believe these men's lies or to become discouraged. Instead, he continued to lead the effort until the walls were halfway completed.

Reaching this milestone gave the workers a renewed sense of hope, but it also brought even more disdain from detractors. As the project continued, the leaders and the workers began to grow weary. The journey they began with great excitement now seemed formidable. It was here that Nehemiah realized the workers needed a time of rest. However, before they left, he made sure that they were guarded from the enemy's tactics and that all the completed work was securely protected.

Review and Renewal

Nehemiah reviewed his plans along with the progress that had been made. After his assessment, he did something that made a difference in the outcome of the project. He reassured the people that God was fighting for them and that they should not be afraid. Nehemiah admonished his leaders and workers to remember the Lord their God, their friends, their family members, and their homes. (Nehemiah 4:14-20)

He also asked them to remember why they agreed to begin the project, and to recall how they felt when the work first began. There is a tremendous excitement that goes along with the beginning of any project. Recalling this moment can bring fresh strength and encouragement. The leaders and workers listened to Nehemiah's words and responded by returning to their work.

Following Nehemiah's example, the workers continued at a steady pace.

Worthwhile goals are not reached without effort. Every journey requires enough commitment and dedication to last through many different seasons. As the work continued, Nehemiah noticed that the leaders and workers had become spread out along the walls. He knew this could pose a threat and provide an opportunity for enemy attack. The successful completion of the project depended on keeping the team together. This also meant keeping the lines of communication open and everyone informed.

Following Nehemiah's example, the workers continued at a steady pace. They knew that what they were doing would truly make a difference. In fact, they were so energized that they worked from sunrise to sunset, trusting in God for the outcome of the project, while keeping their swords at their side. (Nehemiah 4:18) They believed that they would succeed. However, they also were fully prepared to fight the enemy if necessary.

Nehemiah also had to deal with some of his own leaders—men who were taking advantage of their workers. They were profiteering from their own people and *not* doing all that they were capable of doing. Once again, he prayed, reviewed the situation, decided what needed to be done, and then spoke honestly and courageously. He told them that they were not doing their share and that they were being unfair to their workers. Then he asked them to sign an agreement stating that what they had done was wrong and that they were committed to

Nehemiah was setting an example by his leadership. He did not take advantage of his calling or his position.

changing their ways. This was done in public so that everyone would be aware of the promised changes.

Nehemiah was setting an example by his leadership. He did not take advantage of his calling or his position. Instead, he remained a servant throughout the entire project—obeying God, continuing to work right beside his men, and requiring his officials to do the same. In doing this, he was demonstrating what many call today *leadership by example.*

He also understood the intent of his enemies. He knew their goal, which was to stop the work at any cost. Therefore, he was under no illusion of their intent and knew that they were against the plans of God. When challenged by one of his enemies, he remained faithful and steady and refused to be distracted. He said, "I am doing a great work and I cannot come. Why should the work stop while I leave it and come down to you?" (Nehemiah 6:3 NASB). He understood his position, his priorities, and his potential to help God's people.

We also learn that Nehemiah understood the importance of wise counsel and was quick to discern the ploys of his enemy. Even though there were dangers on all sides as men tried to persuade him to leave the work and to compromise his beliefs, he refused to waver.

As news about the work that was being accomplished spread, many local leaders continued to support this project. In fact, even before Nehemiah fully understood God's plan and purpose, the king had been moved to provide the resources to underwrite the effort. His provision set an example for others. This project could not have been completed without the help of many people—all doing what they could. Some gave financial resources, some gave physical resources, and some gave both.

Nehemiah understood the importance of wise counsel.

Joy in the Journey

At the completion of the project, a time was set for great celebration. However, in the light of God's faithfulness and provision, the people became aware of their sin and began to weep. A project like this often draws people closer to the Lord where they experience the reality of His love and grace. Journeys like this often lead to spiritual rededication and recommitment, and this is what God's people experienced. But Nehemiah instructed them not to cry on "such a day as this." It was a time to celebrate—a day of holy joy and *not* sadness. He explained that it was a time of celebration because the people of God would now be able to hear God's Word.

The journey was so great that at its completion everyone, including the enemy, realized that God had been involved. He was the only One who could make this dream a reality, and the same is true of your project. Only God can lead you to a point of completion and success. When the work was completed in Jerusalem, the people signed a covenant stating that they would serve the Lord and no longer neglect the house of God.

As we look back over the work, we can see that Nehemiah truly understood the people of Jerusalem—their needs, their desires, and their failures. He remained patient in his commitment to the work, and the outcome of his faith brought glory to God.

As he promised, he returned to King Artaxerxes. However, at a later date, he returned to Jerusalem to review the completed project and to see how the city was doing. Nehemiah understood that there would be new problems that needed to be addressed. Once again, he reviewed the situation, prayed to understand the need, prepared a plan of action, assigned specific tasks to remedy the problem, and made sure that everyone understood the work he had assigned.

It is the same for us as it was for Nehemiah. The journey is never really over. Our world changes daily. New needs arise, and we, too, must be ready and willing to respond to God's call and to undertake the tasks given us at every turn in this life. I believe that it is possible to use Nehemiah as a guide and that God will reward our faith and efforts with success and victory.

The journey was so vast that at its completion everyone, including Nehemiah's enemies, realized that God was involved.

> *God needs more people like Nehemiah,*
> *His Kingdom needs more people like Nehemiah,*
> *And God's people need more people like Nehemiah—*
> *Someone who sees potential where others see problems,*
> *Someone who has a passion to help God's people,*
> *Someone who will pray before deciding,*
> *Someone who will plan before acting,*
> *Someone who will set the example,*
> *Someone who will celebrate,*
> *Someone who will inspire,*
> *Someone who will work,*
> *And someone who will return.*

NEHEMIAH'S JOURNEY *and* A GUIDE FOR YOURS

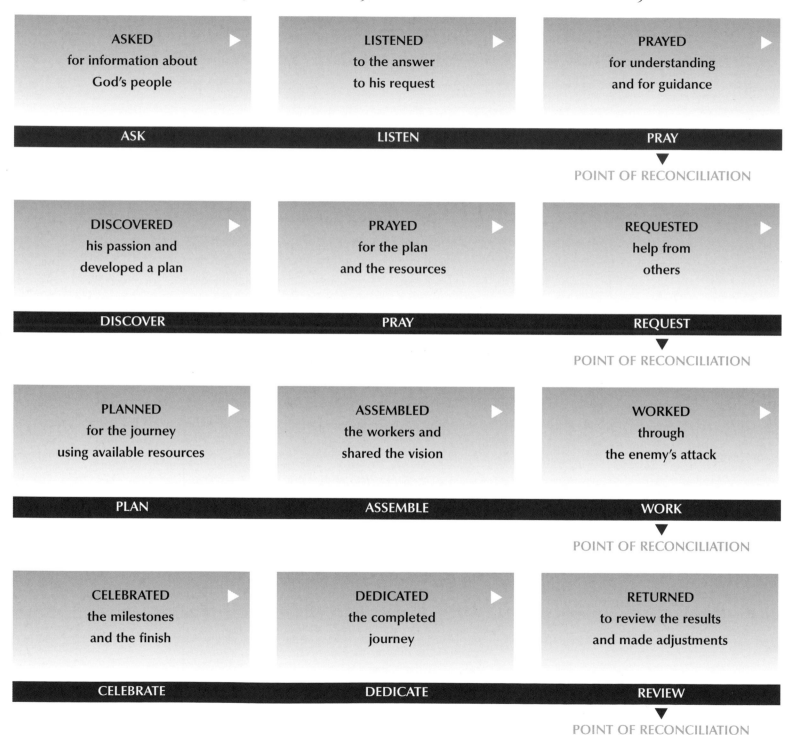

| **ASKED** ▶ | **LISTENED** ▶ | **PRAYED** ▶ |
| for information about God's people | to the answer to his request | for understanding and for guidance |

| ASK | LISTEN | PRAY |

▼ POINT OF RECONCILIATION

| **DISCOVERED** ▶ | **PRAYED** ▶ | **REQUESTED** ▶ |
| his passion and developed a plan | for the plan and the resources | help from others |

| DISCOVER | PRAY | REQUEST |

▼ POINT OF RECONCILIATION

| **PLANNED** ▶ | **ASSEMBLED** ▶ | **WORKED** ▶ |
| for the journey using available resources | the workers and shared the vision | through the enemy's attack |

| PLAN | ASSEMBLE | WORK |

▼ POINT OF RECONCILIATION

| **CELEBRATED** ▶ | **DEDICATED** ▶ | **RETURNED** |
| the milestones and the finish | the completed journey | to review the results and made adjustments |

| CELEBRATE | DEDICATE | REVIEW |

▼ POINT OF RECONCILIATION

YOUR JOURNEY

YOUR JOURNEY

THOSE WHO USE THIS GUIDEBOOK

Over the years, I have come to view the process of planning, designing, and constructing a new facility as a *journey*. It involves much more than moving from point A to point B. It is a journey whereby you and the members of your leadership team get to see your church project become a reality. As with all journeys, it will be made up of a series of complex, yet interrelated, steps and processes. You will find that gaining a firm understanding of where your church is in the process, and learning what decisions are required before proceeding on to the next step, are both essential to a successful journey.

The material in this book has been assembled to be used by members and potential members of church planning or building teams—those who are looking for a resource to help guide them through all of the actions and decisions that will be required to successfully complete their journey. It was compiled with the intent of helping people on these committees to avoid taking the wrong turns that other churches have taken.

Your church is about to launch one of the most exciting and rewarding efforts in its existence—truly, it is an opportunity of a lifetime. In order for you to make the most of this opportunity, this material has been designed to help you plan for the *entire* journey. It will provide the information your team needs in order to understand each step in the planning, designing, and building process. Long before any expectations are set within your congregation, you will discover that knowledge and understanding are essential to reaching the final destination.

Every effort has been made to keep you from getting bogged down or lost along the way. The goal of this book is to present material that provides clear, valuable insight into the process of designing and building a new church facility. It is written in such a way as to help you maintain a proper focus concerning the project that you are considering.

I'm sure you have heard stories about the terrible problems other church building teams have encountered, but your journey does not have to be like theirs. The following steps will help you avoid the detours and pitfalls that many

Your church is about to launch one of the most exciting and rewarding efforts in its existence— truly, it is an opportunity of a lifetime.

before you have experienced. The insights in this book have been gathered as helpful milestones for you to use in developing a critical path for a more successful journey.

With the right preparation and planning, this journey should be one of the greatest experiences in the life of your church. It will *not* be free of problems or difficult choices along the way. However, at the end, when the project is complete, and your new facility is full of people using it for its intended purpose, all that you have gone through will be worth the effort that has been invested.

No matter how well you plan and prepare, there will be times in the journey when you will need to keep your final destination firmly in mind. I have found that few other journeys in life help your prayer life more than being involved in building a portion of God's Kingdom here on earth.

There are several key questions that I always like to ask those who come seeking our assistance with the planning and construction of their new church facility. I begin by asking: "Is your church reactive or a proactive? Is there a plan in place for your future growth, or have you adopted a 'wait and react' position?" A church that waits and then reacts to growth usually finds that it has run out of space and can no longer effectively minister to the needs of its congregation.

I also ask if there is a methodical process in place for responding to ministry needs, or if the church allows the loudest voices to determine how it will respond to its current situation.

Many times, we become shortsighted in our view of the future. We can develop attitudes that hold us back and prevent us from becoming all that God has designed us to be. This can lead to stagnation and eventually hamper every ministry in the church.

Finally, I ask: "Do you believe that there is a better way for your church to grow and develop? Are your members content to provide for their current congregation only, or do they want to expand so that the 'unchurched' in your community can be reached?"

I admit that these are tough questions; it is necessary to ask and to answer them honestly. Each answer that is given determines how your church will prepare to face the future. Most importantly, the answers reveal whether or not the process explained in this book is right for you. I want to make it clear: this

You will find that gaining a firm understanding of where your church is in the process, and learning what decisions are required before proceeding on to the next step are both essential to every successful journey.

book was written for churches that want to be proactive—those that want to prepare for future growth and want to follow a methodical process that looks for and leads to the best solutions in the long-range planning for your church.

THE HELP YOU NEED

This material also was written for those who are *not* satisfied with their current status and for those who want to improve so that they can impact their community by providing room for the unchurched. If this describes your church, then this book could be the very tool you need to help your church set an itinerary along the right pathway of growth and expansion. During long months of planning and construction, it also will provide the information you need to stay the course, especially whenever difficulties arise. My personal goal is to help you finish the journey laid out before you.

I do want to say from the beginning that the material within this book was not written to establish a *set formula*. Instead, it is given to establish a process that your team will be able to follow and apply to the project you are considering. This process integrates all of the plans you will use on your journey. This is a "what to do" book more than a "how to do it" book.

There are entire books written on some of the steps in this book. My recommendation to you is to utilize the design team, construction team, and the consultants you hire to gather the detailed information required for your journey. I believe the topics addressed in this book can help clarify what detailed information you should request from these teams so you make informed decisions as you move from your dream to dedication.

As you read through the following chapters, I hope that you will also discover the best route for your church to take. Hopefully, it will be one that will prevent you from taking unnecessary detours and side trips as you move toward your final destination. However, there will be times when small exploratory searches should be encouraged, even if they appear to be detours. In the end, these too will be used to help you make informed decisions, while providing additional insight as you move forward to achieve your goals.

Many current planning guides provide a skeletal framework to keep the process on track and are just formulas that are very structured and inflexible. Others are more unstructured, and although very flexible, may not provide enough direction and guidance to keep your church focused or to give the help that is needed,

This book was written for churches that want to be proactive—those that want to prepare for future growth.

especially when you get off track. Therefore, it is the intent of this book to provide a methodical approach that is comprehensive, and while offering some structure, still allows for the inevitable and unplanned events that occur within the overall process. This flexible process will prove extremely valuable in solving the unique problems and difficulties that come with the development of any church project.

While this book *does not* offer a rigid formula to follow or the answers to *all* your questions, it will provide an overview and a methodical process that will lead you safely on a journey to discover a unique, strategic master plan for your church. After this plan begins to take shape, the material presented here will provide the resources that are needed for you to follow through. It also will give you the tools you need to ensure that your new church facility can be used to minister to your community and become all that God has called it to be.

FOLLOWING A CRITICAL PATH

The term *critical path* is a planning and construction term that is used to describe the logical sequence of critical decisions and actions required to keep a project on schedule and within budget. It describes the most direct and trouble free path on the journey—from the moment that your dream begins to take shape until its dedication. Without a clearly defined critical path, you may still get to your destination, but "wrong turns" and "miss-steps" often take the enjoyment out of the journey, turning your dream into a nightmare!

Most construction projects have a critical path schedule which is used to coordinate the entire construction process. This schedule is reviewed regularly, updated as needed, and used to make the decisions required by the construction team to keep the project on track. It is a tool used to put all of the critical decisions and actions in the proper sequence and in a format that allows the entire team to see clearly when something is out of order—so they can make the adjustments necessary to get the project back on schedule.

Correct guidance can help you scout ahead and uncover any roadblocks that will be encountered on the pathway.

Every successful journey requires four things: prayer, planning, preparation, and resources. Traveling into unfamiliar or uncharted territory requires even more planning and preparation. However, the right partnership will make the journey more enjoyable and reduce the risks associated with traveling in unfamiliar territory. The correct partners for such a journey are ones that have the necessary experience for a project like the one you are considering.

I also have found that the right preparation determines the right path for a

church to take. Correct guidance can help you scout ahead and uncover any roadblocks that will be encountered on the pathway.

Over the last 25 years, most of my professional life has been spent working with churches. I absolutely love what I have been called to do, and I could talk for hours about the planning, the design, and the construction of churches. However, I find most people just want the highlights, the executive summary, or the answer to a specific question, and that is the intent of this guidebook.

It was *not* written to be an encyclopedia or a detailed planning guide, but rather a tool to help your team find the correct path and then to give you insight into what may be lying ahead for you as you seek to help your church grow and make a difference in the lives it touches. I also have found over the years that there are no shortcuts to this process, and that what often seems like a shortcut usually turns out to be just another detour.

The right preparation determines the right path for a church to take.

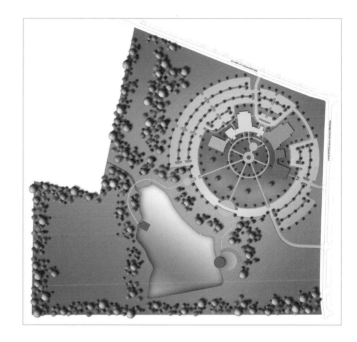

RIGHT PLANNING IS ESSENTIAL TO SUCCESS

I want to encourage you to take the time to plan ahead, get the correct team members in place, and gather and analyze the information that you will need to make informed decisions. When you do this, the process will be much more enjoyable for everyone. In order to complete this journey, you must be willing to travel the distance from the conception of your church's dream to its dedication.

There will be a time of strategic planning and a time of tactical planning to every step you take in this process. (Strategic planning seeks to answer the "what" questions. Tactical planning seeks to answer the "how" questions.) These are not isolated, independent steps that your church will be taking; you will need input from the entire partnership throughout this process. Select your partners well and they will serve you well. Because each of these steps is interrelated and complex, changing some of the variables or assumptions in one step will change the outcome of all of the succeeding steps.

Organizing a very complex set of often-independent decisions into a clearly marked set of steps, without having them become a simplistic set of formulas, is a very difficult task. Decisions that are made in one step of the process will affect the outcome of the following steps. However, at the time a decision is made, these outcomes are not always predictable or understandable, especially when your team is being asked to make decisions early in the process without the benefit of a clear path set before you.

The more clearly you are able to see your destination and understand the resources required to reach it, the better your decision making will be.

I have found that planning for this type of journey is very much like solving a complex mathematical formula where there are many unknowns. If you change one of the variables, you end up changing the outcome. However, if you fix several of the unknowns by making smart, well-informed assumptions, you can solve the other unknowns. And if the answer does not end up matching your resources, you always can go back and change a few of the assumptions until you get a solution that matches the journey your church has chosen. It is very easy to underestimate the future impact of changing what may seem like a small decision by your team. It takes experience to realize when a decision will steer your team off course, and it will take courage to speak up and ask for the team to reconsider their decisions when it appears that this has happened.

The steps outlined in this book will help you to look ahead, understand the processes involved in project, and see the impact every decision has on the journey you are undertaking. The more clearly you are able to see your destination and understand the resources required to reach it, the better your decision making will be, and the better the decision making process is, the more enjoyable the journey becomes.

In order to complete your journey, sooner or later you will complete each of the steps discussed in this guidebook. However, you may not need to complete them in the order that they are presented. Use these steps as a checklist to establish milestones to see where you are in the process, to confirm where you are going, and to determine what resources will be needed.

Sometimes, your team will get to a point where it becomes clear that you need to go back a few steps and "rethink" some of your earlier decisions before you can move forward. This is not necessarily bad, or a sign that your leadership team has made a mistake. This is a natural part of the process. Remember, it is best to remain flexible and open to change. When you make a decision, it is not always possible to know the outcome. Realize that the earlier you discover the need to rethink some of your decisions, the more resources you will be able to conserve and use for other steps.

ESSENTIAL STEPS IN THE PROCESS

Faulty or poor decision making early in the process is the surest way to find yourself being detoured and heading for a dead end. An important thing to remember is that if you take a wrong turn, there will be an opportunity for you to undo your decisions and redirect your project. However, this can be expensive and frustrating, and will ultimately delay the completion of your journey.

STEPS IN YOUR JOURNEY

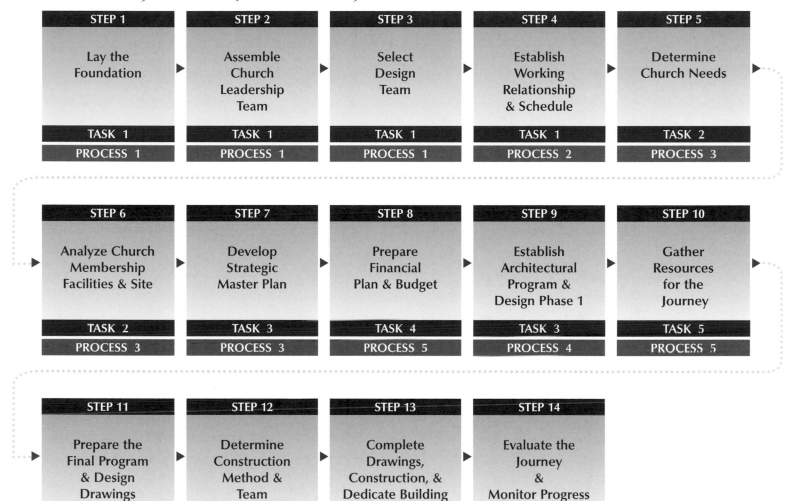

STEP 1	STEP 2	STEP 3	STEP 4	STEP 5
Lay the Foundation	Assemble Church Leadership Team	Select Design Team	Establish Working Relationship & Schedule	Determine Church Needs
TASK 1	TASK 1	TASK 1	TASK 1	TASK 2
PROCESS 1	PROCESS 1	PROCESS 1	PROCESS 2	PROCESS 3

STEP 6	STEP 7	STEP 8	STEP 9	STEP 10
Analyze Church Membership Facilities & Site	Develop Strategic Master Plan	Prepare Financial Plan & Budget	Establish Architectural Program & Design Phase 1	Gather Resources for the Journey
TASK 2	TASK 3	TASK 4	TASK 3	TASK 5
PROCESS 3	PROCESS 3	PROCESS 5	PROCESS 4	PROCESS 5

STEP 11	STEP 12	STEP 13	STEP 14
Prepare the Final Program & Design Drawings	Determine Construction Method & Team	Complete Drawings, Construction, & Dedicate Building	Evaluate the Journey & Monitor Progress
TASK 6	TASK 6	TASK 6	TASK 7
PROCESS 4	PROCESS 6	PROCESS 6	PROCESS 7

I believe that these steps and the process they outline will provide the opportunity for your team to see where you are in the journey and allow you to make sure all of the required decisions are in place before you get too far down your path. Informed decision making, early in the planning process, is your team's best insurance for controlling the process, the budget, and the outcome. The further you travel down the path, the less opportunity you have to make changes in the outcome of your journey.

THE SEVEN PROCESSES FOR YOUR JOURNEY

Process 1	Process 2	Process 3	Process 4	Process 5	Process 6	Process 7
Selection	Communication	Strategic Master Planning	Design	Funding	Construction	Review
1.1 Leadership Team	2.1 Information Inspiration	3.1 God's Call	4.1 Pre-design	5.1 Analyze Potential	6.1 Project Pricing	7.1 Record Results
1.2 Design Team	2.2 Team Communications	3.2 Church History	4.2 Schematic Design	5.2 Communicate Vision	6.2 Construction Schedule	7.2 Lessons Learned
1.3 Construction Team	2.3 Partnership Communications	3.3 Community Demographics	4.3 Initial Design Development	5.3 Capital Campaign	6.3 Project Permitting	7.3 Monitor Growth
	2.4 Congregation Communications	3.4 Site Capacity	4.4 Design Communication	5.4 Banking Relationships	6.4 Ground Breaking	7.4 Plan for Future Phases
		3.5 Worship Balance	4.5 Final Design Development	5.5 Construction Payments	6.5 Project Communications	
		3.6 Weekday Programs	4.6 Construction Documents	5.6 Final Payments	6.6 Construction Inspections	
		3.7 Resource Potential	4.7 Project Pricing	5.7 Campaign Follow-up	6.7 Building Dedication	
			4.8 Contract Administration			
			4.9 Project Closeout			

This is why a primary goal of this guide is to help you successfully reach your destination without having a major detour that stops you and delays the opportunity for growth of your church. As you begin to determine the destination, always keep in mind that this is a complex process. Plan ahead, gather the information you need, review the options, refine the assumptions, and make an informed decision before you move forward.

Success requires the coordination and management of a series of processes:

- Team selection
- Communication
- Strategic master planning
- Design
- Financing
- Construction
- Review

And it also requires the completion of several tasks:

- Pray, plan, prepare
- Find the current roadblocks to growth
- Find the method to remove roadblocks
- Determine funding capacity
- Determine funding priorities
- Complete the removal of roadblocks
- Evaluate and respond to growth

TASKS IN YOUR JOURNEY

Step 1, 2, 3, 4		Step 5, 6		Step 7, 9		Step 8, 10		Step 11		Step 12, 13		Step 14
Pray Plan Prepare	+	Find the Current Roadblocks to Growth	+	Find the Method to Remove Roadblocks	+	Determine Funding Capacity	+	Determine Funding Priorities	+	Remove the Roadblocks	+	Evaluate & Respond to Growth
Task 1		Task 2		Task 3		Task 4		Task 5		Task 6		Task 7

The challenge that faces many leadership teams is the proper integration of these various processes into one solid working plan—a strategic master plan with the common goal of leading your church from the initial dream to the dedication of your project.

God gave Noah the plan for the ark. He gave Moses a plan for the tabernacle, and to David, He gave the plan for the temple, which Solomon built. I strongly believe that He has a plan in mind for your church, too. To Nehemiah, He gave a vision of what the future could hold. But it was up to Nehemiah, just as it is for others who are called, to step forward and make a commitment to accept the challenge that was set before him. Nehemiah saw a need that was God-given. He was able to envision the walls around Jerusalem reconstructed and the city in a position for growth and development. However, he did not rush out, grab a few dozen workers, and begin to rebuild. Instead, he took time to pray for guidance, wisdom, courage, resources, and permission for the help that would be needed.

Only then did he review the situation and the problem at hand. He made plans to use the resources he had been given, enlisted help from fellow believers, ignored the taunts and challenges of those who wanted to stop him, and celebrated with everyone when the work was complete. I also want you to take note of the fact that after the walls of Jerusalem were rebuilt, Nehemiah returned to the project to review the finished work and to make any necessary changes. These are the same steps that you and your church will go through as you seek to be used by God to make a difference in the lives of the members of your congregation and in your community.

It is my sincere intention that this guide proves to be a useful tool to help you in this process. If you have any questions, please contact me at **thenextstep@cdhpartners.com**.

STEP ONE

Lay the Foundation

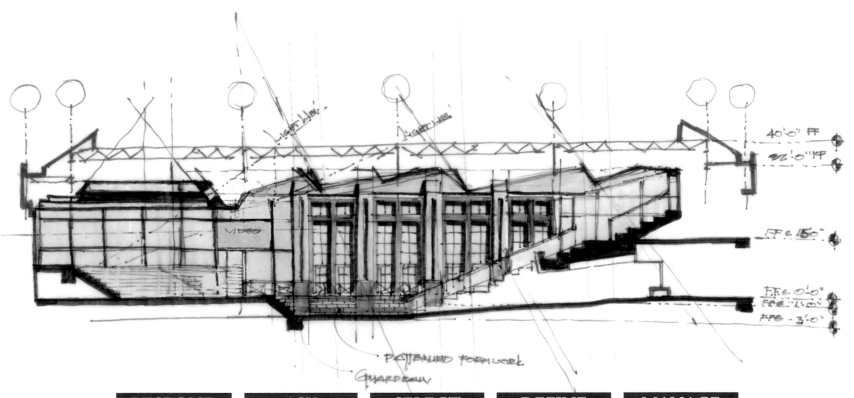

RESPOND	ASK	SELECT	DEFINE	MANAGE
Why make the journey?	*When should you begin?*	*Who takes the journey?*	*What is the journey?*	*How to make the journey?*

STEP ONE
Lay the Foundation

THE PROPER PREPARATION

The most important step you will take in your project is to take the time to lay a good foundation in order to ensure that you have the proper support. A good foundation is absolutely fundamental to any long-term success, and essential whether you are striving to reach a life goal or to build a new church facility. While preparing the information presented in this guidebook, I assumed that your church is continuously praying for wisdom and direction.

This information has been prepared for a healthy, vibrant, and growing church—a church that is intent on impacting its community. Otherwise, you would not be looking for the information that is offered in this book. Everything you do from this point on needs to be covered in prayer. In fact, prayer is an essential component of the foundation that you will be establishing. It is key to the success of your journey, and should become an integral part of each step your church plans to take. If the journey your church is planning is not covered in prayer, the information presented here will be of very little value.

The tasks, the processes, and the steps presented in this book were written for use by both small and large churches. The steps are the same. Smaller churches may need to outsource more of the analysis and some of the leadership required to guide the church through certain steps in order to complete all of the tasks. These consultants can conduct the analysis that is needed to provide essential information necessary for the leadership team to make an informed decision. Many large churches have in-house staff capabilities to complete this analysis.

However, churches of every size will profit from the strategic master planning process. Failure to spend the proper time and resources to prepare a master plan can be very costly and critical to the future of your church. This is why a church with limited property and limited prospects of securing additional property needs a good master plan for maximum utilization of its site. Also, a church that is growing rapidly needs the guidance of a master plan so that the required facilities can be designed in order to sustain its growth. Likewise, a church with

the *potential* for significant growth needs special assistance from the master plan so that its short-term facility development will mesh with its long-term growth requirements.

I want to make it clear that the size of your church does not matter, nor does the size of your dream. The same decisions still need to be made, and the same processes need to be managed. Therefore, before you move too far, I want to encourage you not to be afraid to hire whatever team members you need in order to receive excellent fact-finding information. Important issues do not change in relation to size, and every decision you make depends on the quality of the information you gather.

The steps outlined in this book apply to both new and established churches. Though, at times, the emphasis on the tasks may be different, the steps remain the same. A new church may spend more time on growth projections and site analysis, while an older church may spend more time reviewing the capacity and the usage of its existing facilities and site. This is why I believe that the leadership team for any church must gather good information in advance in order to make solid decisions—the kind that will successfully lead your church to its final destination. Speaking of this, you must have a final destination in mind before you ask your congregation to pack up and join you on this new venture.

The need for master planning is not limited to new congregations or to churches that are relocating. Churches in all stages of development need a master plan. This may be even more pronounced for older churches that have never engaged in this process.

The lack of a master plan may bring churches to a point where existing circulation routes are inadequate and confusing. Past failures to do long-range planning and master planning may have contributed to inefficient utilization of property. The leadership team may need help in deciding which properties adjacent to the church would be most beneficial for future growth and expansion. These and related problems can create an urgent need for a master plan. In most instances, a well-thought-out master plan can help solve these problems with solutions that never would have been envisioned without this methodical, open, and thought-provoking process.

It does not matter whether your church has many resources or a limited number. The processes outlined in this book apply to both of these situations. In

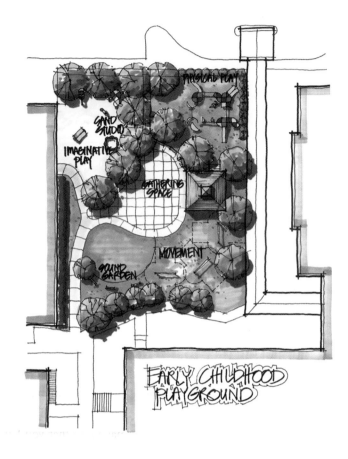

The size of your church does not matter, nor does the size of your dream. The same decisions still need to be made, and the same processes need to be managed.

many ways, a church with a limited amount of resources needs this information more than those that have an abundance of resources.

A church with fewer resources may have a much more difficult time recovering from a wrong turn than one that has more funds and assets. However, this does not mean that there needs to be a sense of "restriction" when seeking to reach a certain goal. It does mean, however, that there should be a good sense of stewardship and planning involved at each step along the way. The intent of every leadership team should be good stewardship of every resource—in physical, emotional, financial, and spiritual terms.

The issue is not how much your church has or even how much your church spends, but whether or not it has been a good steward of the resources that God has provided. This single issue, more than any other, is the reason the steps outlined in this guidebook need to be reviewed and understood before your church takes the next step in your journey. Remember, every church—regardless of age, size, or amount of resources—needs to think and plan before it begins to build.

Nehemiah took time to plan. He considered the cost from every aspect—physical, emotional, financial, and spiritual. Every project inspired by God has the potential to be tremendously encouraging to those involved. However, before you begin, make sure that you have considered all of the important issues. If you do, the journey and the achievement of your goal will be one of the most rewarding times in your church's history.

The issue is not how much your church has or even how much your church spends, but whether or not it has been a good steward of the resources that God has provided.

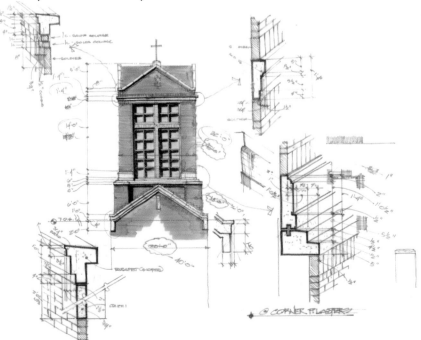

Why Should Your Church Make This Journey?

I have found that *growing* churches are usually the ones to answer God's call and remain committed to continue the journey. In other words, they want to keep growing so they can be all that they have been called to be.

Your church's mission statement should be a fundamental factor that influences the facilities you decide to build.

Your church's ability to provide additional resources to fund the future phases of your strategic master plan will be made possible by the growth that occurs after the completion of your current project. Always keep in mind the intention of your church's mission statement. It should be the fundamental factor that influences the facilities you decide to build. Your new building or buildings should be designed and constructed to enable you to move your church's mission forward. Likewise, your church should not have to restrict its mission due to a lack of space and facilities.

RESPOND TO

STEPS	Step 7	Step 8, 10, 11	Step 13	Step 4	Step 14	Step 14	Step 1, 2, 3, 4
Why make the journey? =	Answer God's Call +	Build Up Existing Congregation +	Provide for Future Growth +	Nurture New Members/ Programs +	Monitor Space/ Growth Needs +	Plan for Additional Growth +	Repeat Process/ Build the Next Phase
The Response	First Response	Second Response	Third Response	Fourth Response	Fifth Response	Sixth Response	Seventh Response

When Should You Begin This Journey?

Nehemiah found that the Lord was looking for someone to help rebuild the walls and to stand in the gap (a place of need) between Him and His people. Are you like Nehemiah? Are you ready to rise up and build for the glory of God?

When does your church need to start planning and preparing? The answer to this question is always the same: earlier than you think, and the sooner the better.

Often the journey takes longer than you think. Therefore, the time you

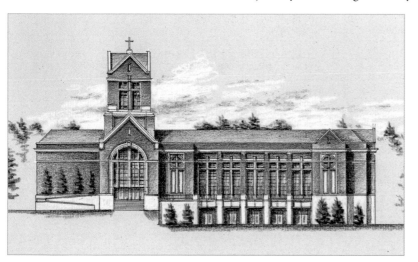

dedicate to planning before you act provides the very best opportunity to manage the overall cost. It always is better to start planning for a project long before you think you need to. It also is better to take your time, rather than to wait for a crisis to force you to begin planning in haste, and risk making decisions that you look back on later and realize were not the very best for your church.

In my experience, the time spent praying and planning is the very best investment you will make.

The time spent gathering all of the information and putting it into a useful format so that the necessary decisions can be made is usually much longer than planned. In my experience, the time spent praying and planning is the very best investment you will make and often the most overlooked. Ultimately, the success of your project will be determined in a large part by the quality of the preparation and planning that takes place before you begin the journey.

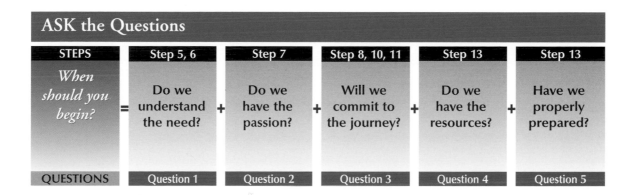

ASK the Questions					
STEPS	Step 5, 6	Step 7	Step 8, 10, 11	Step 13	Step 13
When should you begin? =	Do we understand the need? +	Do we have the passion? +	Will we commit to the journey? +	Do we have the resources? +	Have we properly prepared?
QUESTIONS	Question 1	Question 2	Question 3	Question 4	Question 5

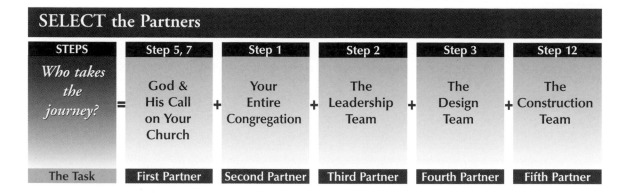

STEPS	Step 5, 7		Step 1		Step 2		Step 3		Step 12
Who takes the journey? =	God & His Call on Your Church	+	Your Entire Congregation	+	The Leadership Team	+	The Design Team	+	The Construction Team
The Task	First Partner		Second Partner		Third Partner		Fourth Partner		Fifth Partner

Who Will You Need to Take This Journey With You?

Who will help you find your way? I believe your best chance of success is to form a partnership—one that is assembled with the express intent of helping you plan and prepare for the entire project. Every partnership is a little different and much is dependent on the resources of your church. However, most of the successful ones are made up of the following: God (an awareness of His call on your church), your congregation, a leadership team of church members, a design team, and a construction team. This alliance should form a partnership committed to provide your church with all of the inspiration and information needed.

I believe that every successful venture or project is done in partnership with God. He knows where we are called to go, and is always available to counsel us with His wisdom. He provides the opportunities, and we respond by providing our time, our talent, and our treasure. If God is not in partnership with your church on this journey, then I believe that it will be impossible for you to have a successful journey. After all, He is the One who calls us into partnership. When we commit to give Him everything we have, He provides the needed increase and the blessings for a successful journey.

I have acted as a guide on many of these journeys. In this role, I am never the one to pick the destination. Instead, our design team makes a commitment to go on the journey with the church. The final destination only comes as a result of teamwork and commitment to do the best for your church. For this reason, every team member must be committed to constantly looking ahead and to being prepared to remove any obstacles that prevent the church from completing its journey.

We always need to remember that the unknown partners are the unchurched—those who may never attend church, especially if there is no room

If your church is growing, it is because it is doing many things right.

or parking available. The dedicated church member will come when it is crowded or inconvenient, but your church cannot grow and reach the unchurched without the proper ministries and corresponding facilities.

Remember, the entire partnership is built on an eternal foundation that was set in place long ago by our Master Builder. Our greatest call is to follow the example He has set before us. Some of us are called to plant, some to weed, and some to water. In every case, God provides the increase in all we plan to do and in all that we accomplish. While we water, work, weed, and wait, we must always remember to give the honor and praise to Him.

Tasks Required to Complete the Journey

What information do you need to move your church from its dream to its dedication? If you are growing and running out of space, you are experiencing a great problem. Nevertheless, it is one that still needs to be solved. If your church is growing, it is because it is doing many things right. However, if you fail to remove the inevitable roadblocks that will appear as a result of your growth, then sooner or later, you will be left to face another decision so that your growth does not stop. In order to complete your journey, your leadership team will need to accomplish seven varied but interrelated tasks.

- One — *Pray, plan and prepare* to ensure that you have *a solid foundation in place and that you have a firm understanding of the process* and direction you will be taking.

- Two — *Find the current roadblocks* that have slowed or stopped the growth of your church.

- Three — *Find the method to remove roadblocks* by providing the right plan and solutions so your church continues to grow.

- Four — *Determine funding capacity* and the amount of resources that your church can make available to fund the solutions you have uncovered.

- Five — *Determine funding priorities* and balance your available resources with the solutions you have discovered. This task is one of the more difficult ones on this journey. It requires prioritization. Therefore, take time to make a list of your solutions in their order of importance so your leadership team will be able to make a final decision on which solutions to fund.

The entire partnership must be committed to constantly looking ahead and to being prepared to remove any obstacles that may keep the church from completing a successful journey.

DEFINE the Tasks

STEPS *What is the journey?* The Tasks	Step 1, 2, 3, 4 Pray Plan Prepare Task 1	Step 5, 6 Find the Current Roadblocks to Growth Task 2	Step 7, 9 Find the Method to Remove Roadblocks Task 3	Step 8, 10 Determine Funding Capacity Task 4	Step 11 Determine Funding Priorities Task 5	Step 12, 13 Remove the Roadblocks Task 6	Step 14 Evaluate & Respond to Growth Task 7

- Six — *Complete the removal of roadblocks.* Hire, buy, rent, or design and build the solutions required to remove the roadblocks to your church's growth.

- Seven — *Evaluate and respond to growth.* Evaluate the results that occur when your church has removed these roadblocks. This task is accomplished by monitoring the growth in your church while looking ahead to envision any new roadblocks that may surface to impede its growth. If you complete the journey of providing the right ministries and facilities, your church will continue growing. Usually, there will come a point in time when you will hit another roadblock and will have to take the next step in order to provide additional space for further growth.

How Will Your Church Make This Journey?

How do you determine the destination and the right path for your church? The road to the construction of your new facility requires your church to select a leadership team and charge them with managing seven various processes.

The first is a selection process. This is used to select the leadership team, the design team, the construction team, and any additional special consultants. This process is fundamental in determining the quality and the success of the entire project. The people selected to work alongside you will set the tone and eventual outcome of all of the resources invested.

The second process is a communication process. This is used to establish communication with the various team members and with your congregation. Communication is critical to the overall outcome of your journey. All suggestions need to be honest and open. Any team member who is not willing to engage in this form of communication will hinder the process for the rest of the partnership.

The third process is a strategic master planning process. This will help your church determine what it needs to do to remove any roadblocks that are keeping you from growing. A strategic master plan becomes the working document that coordinates all of the other elements of your church's planning.

Your may already have a master plan for your facilities, your programs, your human resources, and your financial resources. Each of these planning documents may have goals and timetables, but only when they are brought together and coordinated into one overall planning document do you have a strategic master plan. Remember: if the current development plan does not provide the capability for your church to grow, you may not be able to fund the next phase of your strategic master plan.

The fourth process is the design process. This is when the design team selected by your leadership team translates your church's needs into a solution that can be communicated to your congregation and ultimately to your construction team. If properly managed, it will provide your church with the information needed to make strong and informative decisions—ones that will ultimately provide the right physical tools you need to meet your ministry goals.

The fifth process is the funding process. This determines the resources that will be available to meet the needs identified in your strategic master planning and design processes. This, more than any other, is the one that is most often left out

The people selected to work alongside you will set the tone and eventual outcome of all of the resources invested.

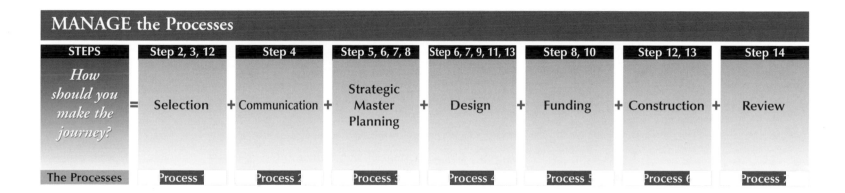

MANAGE the Processes							
STEPS	Step 2, 3, 12	Step 4	Step 5, 6, 7, 8	Step 6, 7, 9, 11, 13	Step 8, 10	Step 12, 13	Step 14
How should you make the journey? =	Selection +	Communication +	Strategic Master Planning +	Design +	Funding +	Construction +	Review
The Processes	Process 1	Process 2	Process 3	Process 4	Process 5	Process 6	Process 7

of the work of the leadership team. Yet, it will ultimately control the outcome of all of the remaining steps. Nothing detours your plans faster than a lack of resources. It is easy to set wrong expectations, but very difficult to undo. Therefore, be careful *not* to neglect the funding process, and don't wait until decisions have been made in other key areas, or you could find that you are out of sequence in your journey.

The sixth process is the construction process. This is where the design team translates its drawings into the completed project. It is the point where the church finally begins to see the fruits of all of your team's labor, and it is when the entire congregation really gets excited about the project. It also is when your church begins to envision the growth that will come as a result of providing adequate space to meet your ministry goals. From the viewpoint of the overall time line, the beginning of construction is usually about the halfway point of your journey.

The seventh process is the review process. This is the time your team takes to look back over the project and evaluate the journey that you have taken. The review is set up to ensure that your church records the process that it has just completed. It also is the point where you monitor and evaluate the growth that has occurred in your church now that the roadblocks have been removed. Finally, this step focuses on being proactive and looking for any future roadblocks, which are sure to appear as your church continues to grow.

LESSONS LEARNED

Many times, we don't know which way to turn. Extreme difficulties come, and we can't imagine how we will go on to fulfill God's plan for our lives. However He knows, and if we look closely and ask ourselves what in this life is truly of value, we will find that there is always a need that is waiting to be met. Effective ministry should be the goal of every church. Through praying, planning, and working together, we can position ourselves for an ever-increasing ministry, while demonstrating our sincere love for God.

Two things to consider—

- *Always continue to plan for the future of your church.* This can be done, along with setting a firm foundation for its growth, through the strategic master plan.

- *If you make uninformed decisions too early in the planning process, long-term growth can be critically curtailed.* Continue to review past decisions and make sure your team is building on a firm foundation. As an example of this, I usually take time to share a story a pastor shared with me years ago with the leadership teams:

Effective ministry should be the goal of every church.

There was a beautiful, old, large home located on a corner lot with wonderful grounds, large trees, and surrounded by a low brick wall. The odd thing was that there was a smaller modular home located on one corner of the property, which seemed so out of place. The pastor often wondered why it was sitting on the grounds of this fine old home. He soon found out that two sisters lived in the modular house, who were members of his congregation. When he got an opportunity, he asked them about the house and was told that a few years ago they began to hear noises and thought that some animal had gotten into the crawl space. So, they called an exterminator.

The exterminator went under the house and came back out in a big hurry. He told them that the bricks used in the foundation were beginning to crumble and that several had already fallen out! The house was in danger of collapse and he urged them not to go back into it. Therefore, the sisters were forced to move into the small modular home.

After a closer inspection, the pastor noticed that three of the walls looked fine but the fourth was falling down and had created a large hole in the side of the old house. The second floor supports had collapsed, and the heavy slate roof was beginning to slide off onto the ground. It became obvious that the weight of the roof was literally causing the house to destroy itself. The foundation could no longer support the weight of the roof and the walls. The old house grew so dangerous that it had to be destroyed.

The home's foundation had not been constructed adequately to support its weight. I am sure that if the original builders knew that the foundation was not going to support the house for years to come, they would have made it stronger. It is easy to place blame on them. However, I wonder how often we start to build without all of the needed information. Be sure that you make wise and informed decisions so that you can secure a firm foundation for the work that you are doing.

STEP TWO

Assemble the Church's Leadership Team

Job description for the church's leadership team

- Gather information for the analysis of all ministries—existing, and proposed

- Gather information for the analysis of the existing church buildings and property

- Interview and hire the design team

- Establish the required special teams

- Review the work of the special teams

- Plan times to celebrate throughout the journey

- Review and approve the program

- Review and approve the master plan

- Review and approve the phasing plan

- Review and approve the preliminary program and a budget

- Review and approve designs and cost estimates

- Coordinate the church finances at every step of the journey

- Keep the church staff informed of critical project information

- Keep the congregation informed of critical project information

- Gather information for a capital fund campaign

- Review and approve the final program and project budget

- Review and approve the design development drawings

- Decide on the method of construction

- Interview and hire the construction team

- Review and approve all construction documents

- Closely communicate with the finance team to review cash flow

- Apply for the building permits

- Plan the groundbreaking ceremony

- Start construction

- Meet with the design and construction team during construction

- Complete the project closeout

- Plan the dedication ceremony

- Return to evaluate the success of the journey

STEP TWO

Assemble the Church's Leadership Team

FROM DREAM TO DEDICATION

From the beginning, Nehemiah realized the magnitude of the job that was before him. He knew the task was great, but that God was greater than the scope of Jerusalem's ruin and destruction. He understood that the best way to face a challenge of any size is through prayer and proper planning. Even before he placed the first footstep on Jerusalem's soil, Nehemiah had given the project to God and was ready to follow His leading. He knew there would be many challenges for him to face—difficulties and trials. But he realized that he was doing something for a great purpose, and God would give him the strength and wisdom he needed to accomplish the task.

Do not be surprised if you have difficulty getting organized and started on your journey. Every successful church faces certain trials as it begins a new building project. Just as Nehemiah faced stiff opposition, you and your leadership may face the same. Without a doubt, there will be many who do not want your church to grow. However, I have found that the bigger the blessing God has in store for your church, the more difficulties you are likely to incur as you prepare and plan for the next step in your church's journey.

A journey that leads to a successful building program for your church does not just happen. When trials and crosswinds come, it takes a strong sense of dedication and steady commitment to hold firm to your course. A successful journey—one that leads from the moment you see your dream unfolding to the day of your building dedication—takes a tremendous amount of faith, good leadership, sound planning, and deliberate decision making.

In other words, a successful journey is the result of constant prayer, courage, and much hard work. Churches that have positive experiences with their building projects do so because they begin the process by counting the cost and by making significant investments in the journey—investments of their resources, particularly their time, talent, and treasure.

Then I said: "O LORD, God of heaven, the great and awesome God, who keeps his covenant of love with those who love him and obey his commands, let your ear be attentive and your eyes open to hear the prayer your servant is praying before you day and night."

—NEHEMIAH 1:5-6

I have found that often the bigger the blessing God has in store for your church, the more difficulties you are likely to incur as you begin to prepare and plan for the next step in your church's future.

During the beginning of this process, situations may come that threaten to drain these resources away. There is often a tendency for the project to become overwhelming. These are the times when your church must guard against the possibility of your proposed building program becoming the only item on your church's agenda—overshadowing and sidelining many other important church ministries.

The best way to keep this journey in perspective and to keep it from overwhelming other church activities is to establish some basic guidelines and milestones to follow. Churches who invest the time to adequately plan ahead, who develop a plan that provides a clear path to follow, and who keep a strong sense of the church's mission before the congregation, significantly increase their potential of completing the journey successfully.

THOSE WHO WILL LEAD YOU

The church's leadership team also must be willing and capable of guiding other committees within the church as they develop plans for the future of the church. Plans that are based on surveys, studies, and analysis should help to establish a clear path for your church to follow. In order to succeed, these leaders will need to create and maintain an atmosphere of confidence and expectation within the congregation. The leadership team should be expected to help communicate and explain the church's vision, along with generating hope, excitement, and energy—all of which are required to bring this challenging journey to a successful conclusion.

There are many *ineffective* models used to create these teams. Many churches choose to establish a long-range planning committee to initiate the building-planning process. Other churches may choose to start with a feasibility team and later elect a building team to complete the assignment. During the planning-design-construction period, some churches decide to establish several specialty teams that function independently. However, any of these multiple team organizations may result in a duplication of responsibilities. Also, due to transitions in the project, there can be omissions in the work of the various teams, resulting in a lack of continuity. For example: with several separate teams working on planning, one team may incorrectly assume that another committee has already dealt with a certain issue.

Often a team that follows up the work of a previous team may not support the recommendations of the preceding team. A system of multiple teams functioning independently also can lead to confusion. One team may think a final decision has been made in a certain area without realizing that all the data has not been collected. These early, uninformed decisions can end up inadvertently blocking a decision made by other teams.

An example of this would be that the finance team could vote to set the building budget before the church growth and program team decides what building needs and project budget to recommend to the leadership team. It is not that these teams did anything incorrectly, it is just that the overall team process was not properly designed to connect all of the decisions from each team into one strategic master plan.

Over many years of watching churches make their journeys, I feel that the most effective and trouble-free team seems to be one that establishes an overall planning-design-construction steering committee or leadership team. This leadership team then guides the church on the entire journey. Each member of this team also become the head of the separate specialty teams assigned to specific areas of the journey, expanding this to more than just a building committee. In this guidebook, this group of leaders is referred to as "the leadership team."

Over many years of watching churches make their journeys, I feel that the most effective and trouble-free team seems to be one that establishes an overall planning-design-construction steering committee or leadership team.

THE FIRST CRITICAL STEP

The intent of this team organization is not to minimize the input or limit the work of other teams but to make sure that everyone knows who is responsible for what task and which process. One team needs to have the responsibility to make the decisions required to keep the church focused on the journey. Team members need to understand what approvals are necessary and who will make them as the project moves forward. Those involved in this journey with you also need to know who is providing the support and the information needed to make informed decisions. Finally, they must be kept informed of the decisions being made.

Without a clear understanding of who makes the decisions, who has authority to approve the decisions, who provides support, and who needs to be kept informed, the leadership team will never really know where it stands and how to proceed through the various steps of the project. Before the leadership team gets too far down the path, take time to outline the responsibilities for each of the major decisions. This will help you avoid taking major detours—ones that could lead you to make a decision without the proper approval from the church governing body or even from the entire congregation.

The selection of the team organization and its members represents the *first critical step* in your journey. Some churches choose to call this team the long-range planning committee, the building committee, the leadership team, the project steering committee, or the dream team. Whatever you choose to call it, this is your church's leadership team, and it should be treated like a microcosm of the church—with each team member passionate about a different ministry within your church.

There are many ministries in your church, and they all need to have an advocate somewhere on your leadership team. This will ensure that the leadership team gets input from each ministry area before it is time to share the decisions that they have made with the church.

Assembling the correct team to represent your church in planning and managing your journey is one of the most fundamental and critical tasks undertaken. Therefore, this step needs to be treated with special care.

Few other leadership roles in the church have the potential to produce such far-reaching and long-term benefits as the planning, design, and construction of new church facilities. Buildings that are well planned, well designed, and well constructed will become effective ministry tools for many generations.

As we all know, a building that has been inadequately planned, poorly designed, or improperly constructed can restrict the ministries and burden the church for just as many generations. A journey that leads to the successful completion of your building program will help strengthen and enrich the fellowship and commitment of the entire congregation. When successful, these journeys will help the entire church focus its energies and resources on God's work, while forming more effective ministry within the church.

BUILDING FOR EFFECTIVE MINISTRY

The leaders selected to serve on the leadership team and to lead your building program need to be models of integrity in each interaction with other team members and with the congregation. They need to be discreet in the way they assemble the analysis and establish the program for the needs of a new building. These leaders also need be very careful when trying to establish the priority for potential future buildings based on the capacity of the existing buildings and site.

The overall perception in the congregation may be that the present space is not yet completely filled. Although widely held, this may be the very area with

Your church's leadership team should be treated like a microcosm of the church— with each team member passionate about a different area of your church's ministry.

the greatest need for expansion. Often church members realize the specific need in one area of the church's ministry, but will be completely unaware of significant needs in areas used by other members. The leadership team needs to understand and deal with these perceptions in order to help the entire congregation understand that the goal of the journey is to provide a balance between each of the church's ministries, to remove the current roadblocks, and to provide space for the church to grow.

A very important qualification for the leadership of this team is that each member have a consistent involvement and support in the life and work of your church. The best leadership team members have a record of long-term commitment and faithful support to the total church program. It is also tremendously important that they share the church's vision.

Sometimes uninvolved or new members may be asked to serve on this committee with the hope of this role leading them to a more active involvement in the church. However, this has the potential to create real problems because they may not be spiritually mature enough to handle the complex issues that the leadership team will inevitably face. They also may not have enough experience in the total life of the church to make the informed decisions required to lead the church on this type of difficult journey. This is not a leadership role for new or uninvolved church members, unless there are some extraordinary circumstances.

Another common mistake made in selecting leadership team members is assuming that technical or vocational skills are a primary qualification for an individual to serve on the leadership team. Churches often assume that people in a profession with financial or building experience are automatically qualified for this leadership team. Church members, if they possess these special qualifications, can be very valuable committee members. However, if their only qualifications are in technical or vocational areas, they should not be placed on the leadership team. They may actually be more help serving on a special team or involved in other ways at strategic points in the journey.

An experienced accountant or banker who is only casually associated with the church cannot be expected to provide the kind of visionary, financial leadership required to complete your journey. In fact, he could be a real liability in the planning process if he does not completely understand the vision and ministry of the church.

A very important qualification for the leadership of this team is a consistent involvement and support in the life and work of your church.

difficult to keep on task, and take a much longer time to develop a working consensus.

Adding special committees or special teams assembled to work on specific tasks has proven to be a great opportunity to involve more of the church membership on this journey, without creating the problems associated with an unmanageable leadership team. The right leadership team and the right team leader are an essential, and often misunderstood, foundation to a successful journey. Therefore, take the time and effort required to pick the right leadership team along with the right team leader, and your church will be a long way down the path to a successful journey. Make a wrong turn here and the rest of the journey will become more difficult for everyone.

Since the leadership team is given the major responsibility of overseeing this journey and of making sure the journey is a success, it needs to be organized to match the anticipated journey. You can always add additional special teams if the need arises.

For a larger or more complex project, several special teams may be assembled to assist the leadership team on specific portions of the journey.

For a small or simple project, one team may be able to guide all the planning, design, and construction with the help of the church staff. For a larger or more complex project, several special teams may be assembled to assist the leadership team on specific portions of the journey. It works best when a member of the leadership team serves as the team leader of each of the special teams.

He or she will be expected to lead the special team and to present the special team's work back to the leadership team. The leadership team needs to be made up of church leaders who represent and have the confidence of the entire congregation. Men and women should come together to work as a team—one that is organized to match the journey your church is seeking to take.

Leading a journey of this significance is a huge responsibility. It will affect the growth potential of every one of your church ministries—present and future. As always, it is imperative that every church resource be invested wisely. Neither the pastor nor the team leader can solely take on this responsibility. It is important to establish a functional leadership team organized to distribute the responsibility to more than just one individual.

Use the team structure wisely by delegating specific tasks to the leadership team and to the other specialty teams. Prepare a preliminary master schedule outlining the steps and the milestones of your journey and use this schedule to plan the timing of the various decisions required to complete the journey. This journey will be less overwhelming and more successful for everyone if each step is outlined in advance, the responsibilities for each task assigned, and the resources required for each step understood and funded in advance.

Nehemiah understood that the task he was undertaking would require thoughtful planning and the input of those who knew the city of Jerusalem best. He was willing to make a commitment on his own, but he knew he could not make the journey of rebuilding the city walls without prayer, help from others, and the wisdom of God.

Balancing the vision, the resources, and the schedules for your journey will be much more difficult than you can imagine. Like Nehemiah, you will need the help that is offered by others, the wisdom that only God can provide, and a right perspective from time spent in prayer. Even when you have these in place, the pathway you follow will not always be easy, but it will ultimately lead you to your desired destination.

ORGANIZATIONAL EXAMPLES

The following organizational models are based on project size and complexity. These are guidelines to help your church organize your teams in preparation for the journey of a lifetime.

The *leadership team* is responsible for providing the overall leadership and guidance required throughout the journey. This includes analyzing and processing the surveys along with the data collected, master planning, and program development. This also is the team that approves the design and construction of the project. This leadership team should receive reports and recommendations from all of the special teams, refine and balance the special teams' work, and develop the final recommendations that are presented to the church.

The intent of this team structure is to provide an open and reliable forum where every building-related issue affecting the church can be reviewed and revised for final approval. Under no circumstances should a special team go directly to the church with its recommendations.

It is possible to make several well-intended decisions, often spread out over time, without fully realizing their combined impact on the outcome.

The only practical way to manage and monitor this journey effectively and successfully is to centralize the overall decision-making process. If all the recommendations are routed through the leadership team, then they will have the controls in place that are required to maintain the balance throughout the entire journey. Without this control, a strong special team could to go to the church early in your journey and gain approval for a proposal that would be completely out of sequence with the other goals and proposals developed as you proceed in your journey.

If this system is working properly, your leadership team will undoubtedly receive some great and visionary recommendations. These suggestions cannot possibly be implemented within the context of the resources and priorities of this journey. The responsibility of the leadership team is to review and evaluate all of the recommendations and then to prioritize and compile a strategic master plan for the church to review and approve. The proposed strategic master plan should be challenging and visionary, but it also must be practical and accompanied by a plan to provide all of the resources required to complete the journey.

As your leadership team continues to develop the plans, you will need to organize a few additional special teams. These special teams should be organized like the leadership team, with a team leader who should also be a member of the leadership team, and four to six other members with specific special interests or talents. Try to establish only the special teams that apply to your project and make sure that their tasks and schedules are well defined before they begin their work. The following is a list of the special teams used on most projects:

The responsibility of the leadership team is to review and evaluate all of the recommendations and then to prioritize and compile a strategic master plan for the church to review and approve.

• *Church programs/ministries* — studies the programs and ministries of the church and recommends actions in response to the church growth special team's findings and related program needs. This team accumulates adequate data on growth possibilities and projections, and recommends appropriate strategies.

• *Property, grounds, landscaping* — evaluates existing property and deals with issues related to acquiring additional property.

• *Building design* — works with the architect in the process of developing complete construction plans and specifications for the new facility.

• *Furnishings, finishes, and equipment* — inventories and evaluates existing furnishings. This team also determines what new furnishings are needed, orders these, and sees to their placement prior to the occupancy date.

The only practical way to manage and monitor this journey effectively and successfully is to centralize the overall decision-making process.

- *Finance and fund raising* — develops arrangements for capital fund-raising, interim and long-term financing, and financial packaging for the entire project.

- *Promotion/publicity* — keeps the building program before the congregation and the community, often plans the celebration from groundbreaking to dedication.

- *Construction* — works with the design team and contractor team during the time of construction and is involved in the final inspection and acceptance of the building.

Leadership Team for a Large Project

The leadership team for a large or complex project should include the following:

- Chair of leadership team
- Chair of property team
- Chair of furnishings team
- Chair of promotion team
- Chair of church program team
- Chair of building design team
- Chair of finance team
- Chair of construction team

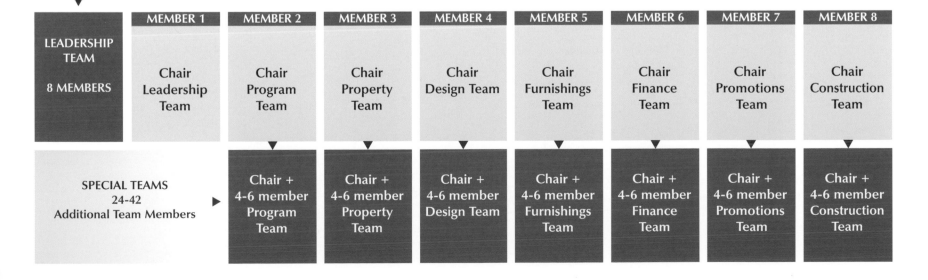

CHURCH GOVERNING BODY		MEMBER 1	MEMBER 2	MEMBER 3	MEMBER 4	MEMBER 5	MEMBER 6	MEMBER 7	MEMBER 8
LEADERSHIP TEAM **8 MEMBERS**		Chair Leadership Team	Chair Program Team	Chair Property Team	Chair Design Team	Chair Furnishings Team	Chair Finance Team	Chair Promotions Team	Chair Construction Team
SPECIAL TEAMS 24-42 Additional Team Members			Chair + 4-6 member Program Team	Chair + 4-6 member Property Team	Chair + 4-6 member Design Team	Chair + 4-6 member Furnishings Team	Chair + 4-6 member Finance Team	Chair + 4-6 member Promotions Team	Chair + 4-6 member Construction Team

Team Organization for a Small Project

Each of the special areas of responsibility for a large project are important to every successful journey. However, a small or simple project does not require the same organizational structure or number of team members that a large, complex project requires. In most situations, your church can combine several special teams. The following combinations are proven to work well:

- Chair of leadership team
- Chair of program and promotion team
- Chair of property and construction team
- Chair of design and furnishings team
- Chair of finance team

Combining these areas of responsibility does not reduce the thoroughness of the planning and evaluation required for the journey. Each team member should have a good understanding of the goals for his team and be committed to producing the work required for the church to have a successful journey.

To help ensure a successful journey, the leadership team and its special teams should be provided with a period of orientation and training. The entire leadership team will need an orientation session before it forms any special teams, and the special teams will need training before they are organized into workgroups. If your church is to complete this journey without too many detours, each and every team member must have a complete understanding of the overall expectations, the timetable, and the procedures for making reports and recommendations.

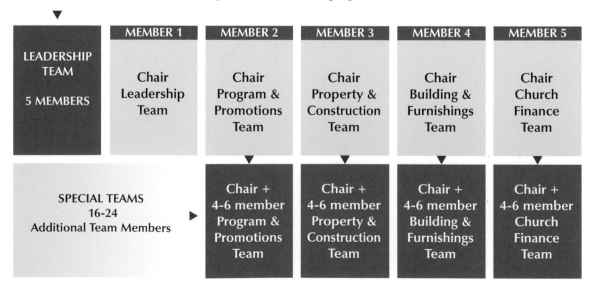

CHURCH GOVERNING BODY	MEMBER 1	MEMBER 2	MEMBER 3	MEMBER 4	MEMBER 5
LEADERSHIP TEAM **5 MEMBERS**	Chair Leadership Team	Chair Program & Promotions Team	Chair Property & Construction Team	Chair Building & Furnishings Team	Chair Church Finance Team
SPECIAL TEAMS **16-24** **Additional Team Members**		Chair + 4-6 member Program & Promotions Team	Chair + 4-6 member Property & Construction Team	Chair + 4-6 member Building & Furnishings Team	Chair + 4-6 member Church Finance Team

Giving each team this information at the beginning of the journey will help keep the entire process on track and will reduce any misunderstandings regarding procedures. The training sessions should be designed to stress teamwork and to establish a level of trust and cooperation for everyone involved in setting the course of this journey. Each special team must feel that the leadership team will fairly and objectively hear its recommendations, and that they will be kept informed of the decisions made by the team which is charged with the responsibility of providing a comprehensive focus to the entire journey.

LESSONS LEARNED

At the first meeting of a new leadership team, one team member stated that he thought the church should build a new sanctuary. The entire leadership team discussed it, and voted unanimously to build the new facility. After all, everyone knew that was what the church really needed.

Then one of the other team members said that he thought the best place for the new sanctuary was in the exact location of the existing one. This site was the most visible portion of their property. The leadership team discussed this for quite a while, and after several alternatives were suggested, they voted unanimously to build the new sanctuary in the exact location of the existing one.

Shortly after this vote, another team member made the comment that the existing sanctuary should continue to be used until the new one was completed, since they did not have another space where they could gather for worship. Once again, they all evaluated this suggestion and finally agreed that this would serve the congregation very well. Again, the vote was unanimous. They would leave the existing sanctuary in place until the new one was completed.

Independently, the leadership team had three good ideas and independently, they made three good decisions. Each one was properly discussed and votes were cast. However, even with the most careful planning and preparation, it would be impossible to carry out these decisions since one facility had to be removed before the new one could be built. This type of planning would never lead to a successful journey.

I know as you read this illustration the conclusion seemed obvious. The initial decision-making process was flawed. However, you would be amazed at how many churches begin building programs this same way. It is possible to make several well-intended decisions, often spread out over time, without fully realizing their combined impact on the outcome.

As you begin your journey, be very careful not to set expectations that are beyond your reach. As one client told me, "Be careful not to promise more than you can produce and always plan to produce more than you promise." Wait until you gather all the information and complete the planning before you allow any expectations to be set and communicated to your congregation.

STEP THREE

Select the Design Team

THE DESIGN PROCESS

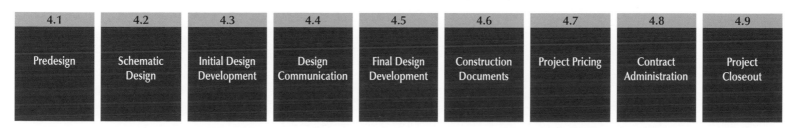

4.1	4.2	4.3	4.4	4.5	4.6	4.7	4.8	4.9
Predesign	Schematic Design	Initial Design Development	Design Communication	Final Design Development	Construction Documents	Project Pricing	Contract Administration	Project Closeout

STEP THREE
Select the Design Team

Nehemiah had a fixed focus. The goal was set before him, but he knew better than to jump into the project without the proper team members and without the proper plan in place. He took time to survey the scope of the project. He considered the need, the purpose, and the direction he would take. He did this quietly and without drawing attention to himself and the fact that Jerusalem's walls were about to be rebuilt. He wasn't anxious or boastful; he was discerning and wise. All of us can learn a tremendous lesson from Nehemiah. His journey is an excellent example for you to follow as you begin the design phase of your project.

What Does the Design Team Do?

The design of church projects has become much more complicated over the last several years, and the benchmarks for the expectations of successful projects continue to rise. These changes have been like a breath of fresh air to most new church projects. However, they also have made the process of designing and building a worship facility much more complex. In order to have a successful journey, you will need the input of specialists—though in the beginning, you will need only a few. As your journey proceeds, you will need to add others who will prevent you from taking wrong turns.

The term *design team* is used here to encompass all of the design professionals required to provide you with the information you need to make the informed decisions required to successfully complete your journey. Often, at the beginning of the journey, it is impossible to know exactly which type of professional expertise you will need. So choose a design team, and especially a design team leader, with experience in the type of project you expect to undertake.

Your *design team leader* should be qualified to assemble the exact design team that your project requires. He or she is usually an architect whose role includes leading the entire design team to complete the analysis, designs, drawings, and construction services required for your project.

Choose a design team, and especially a design team leader, with experience in the type of project you expect to undertake.

I went to Jerusalem, and after staying there three days I set out during the night with a few men. I had not told anyone what my God had put in my heart to do for Jerusalem.

—Nehemiah 2:11-12

- Begin your search for this person by looking for an architect or architectural firm that has the specialized experience and understanding of church design.

- Be sure to choose a team leader whom you believe will understand your church's ministries and has the experience to provide the leadership required for the planning, design, and construction of your project.

Even before the project begins, you want to make sure that you have plenty of time set aside to talk with the proposed design team leader. This team probably will be made up of professionals who specialize in church master planning, architecture, interior design, construction management, civil engineering, electrical engineering, mechanical and plumbing engineering, and structural engineering. You may also need to contact experts in acoustical and audio design, lighting design, construction estimating, financial planning, graphic design, kitchen planning, and video and television production.

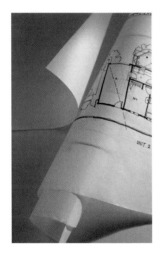

Be sure that the culture of the design team matches the culture of your leadership team.

- Keep in mind that you need a leader who will be your partner, advocate, and guide throughout the entire journey. This person should be able to offer wise counsel as you make choices for the critical path that lies ahead of you and your church.

- Look for a leader who is committed to assembling the right team for your journey—one who knows when to include other team members in order to ensure that your expectations for high quality results are met.

- The person that heads up your design team needs to be experienced in leading others and must ensure that the proper team is assembled at the right time for each part of the journey.

When certain specialists are required to provide the information needed to take the next step, the design team leader should have the experience to know and bring them on board as needed to keep the project on the right path and to keep your leadership team out of trouble. Not all design teams are the same. Some are service-oriented and normally work well with teams, while others are much more design-oriented and tend to be more difficult for your leadership team to work with. Both types of firms have much to offer. Just be sure that the culture of the design team matches the culture of your leadership team, and that the design team's expertise matches the journey you are planning to take.

How Does the Design Team Work?

It is important to make a distinction between the design team's basic services and other additional services and indirect costs that your church may incur. Under most owner-architect agreements, the basic services are listed in six major project phases:

- Pre-design phase
- Schematic design phase
- Design development phase
- Construction documents phase
- Bidding or negotiating phase
- Construction contract administration phase

Most design teams base their fees on the basic services relative to these phases, including all the services required to design the basic building and develop the surrounding site. This includes structural, mechanical, plumbing, electrical, and, usually, civil design.

These all come under the umbrella of basic architectural services. Unless specified in advance as part of your formal agreement, the basic services do not include interior design services, landscape design services, acoustical design, specialized equipment layout, or pre-design services such as existing facilities surveys, detailed site utilization studies, environmental studies, or zoning processing. These services ordinarily fall under the heading of additional services as outlined in the standard agreements.

Before any work is authorized, the leadership team and the design team should have a clear under-standing about which are basic services and which are additional services.

Before any work is authorized, the leadership team and the design team should have a clear understanding of which are basic services and which are additional services. Through mutual agreement, design services can be customized under the owner-architect agreements to include all of the services require to complete your project. Most leadership teams will need to include the work required to communicate the strategic master plan to the church members for approval, and will probably need to make sure that the work to provide the information required for the capital fund drive is included in the anticipated scope of the project.

THE VARIOUS PHASES OF YOUR JOURNEY

Pre-design Phase

This is the phase of the journey where you gather all of the information required to make the informed decisions that will form the foundation of your master plan. Information on the existing church, site conditions, and programs is gathered and reviewed to provide a basis for the rest of the planning process. The development of the preliminary master plan usually falls under this phase. This plan helps to focus the leadership team on the decisions regarding the priorities for development. Once established, the process can move forward with the schematic design phase

Schematic Design Phase

This phase involves a preliminary evaluation and balancing of the project budget, the program, the expectations for quality, the cost, and the preliminary building designs. These variables combine to create a critical balance in every construction project.

4 THE DESIGN PROCESS

	4.1 PRE-DESIGN	4.2 SCHEMATIC DESIGN	4.3 INITIAL DESIGN DEVELOPMENT	4.4 DESIGN COMMUNICATION
FOCUS ▶	Gather	Define	Solve	Communicate
APPROVAL ▶	Leadership Team & Staff	Leadership Team	Congregational Review	Congregational Approval
ACTIVITY ▶	Gather site information Gather historical data Review growth projections Review master plan options	Organize project information Establish expectations Define the problem Select direction	Test assumptions Refine expectations Refine problem definition Refine direction	Share decisions Communicate expectations Present problem solutions Communicate direction
METHODS ▶	Program information Conduct church analysis Conduct site capacity study Review similar projects	Explore site options Explore building options Explore exterior elevations Explore exterior finishes Explore interior design Explore interior finishes Explore engineering options Explore building systems Establish equipment list	Refine site solutions Refine building solutions Refine exterior elevations Define exterior finishes Define interior finishes Refine interior finishes Refine engineering options Refine building systems Refine equipment lists	Present site solution Present building solution Present exterior design Present building design Present interior design Present interior finishes Present engineering solutions Present building systems Present equipment list
GOALS ▶	Review program options Review budget considerations Review schedule options	Establish program Establish budget Establish schedule	Refine program Refine budget Refine schedule	Present program solution Present budget information Present schedule

The first three of these variables can be controlled in design. At the time of construction, the current construction market will determine the actual construction cost, which is impossible to predict years in advance. However, the design team should be able to help you establish a range based on market history. Just remember, construction costs are difficult to predict and you will want to update them at each step of your journey.

The leadership team will be required to establish and set priorities among these variables along with an acceptable range for each one. This is the one of the most difficult tasks required of the leadership team. Only after an assumption has been established for each variable can the design team provide alternative approaches to the design and construction of the project.

Based on the preferred design approach, the mutually agreed upon project program, and the budget, the design team can then prepare drawings and other documentation illustrating the preliminary design. The preliminary designs should be accompanied by a statement of probable construction costs and should be reviewed thoroughly and approved by the committee. The completion of this phase of work is usually the point where your team has the information required

4.5 FINAL DESIGN DEVELOPMENT	4.6 CONSTRUCTION DOCUMENTS	4.7 PROJECT PRICING	4.8 CONTRACT ADMINISTRATION	4.9 PROJECT CLOSEOUT
Solve	Implement	Coordinate	Construct	Evaluate
Leadership Team Approval	Leadership Team Approval	Congregation Approval	Team Approval	Team Approval
Test assumptions	Complete drawings	Coordinate with construction team	Approve schedule of values	Prepare final punch list
Refine expectation	Coordinate consultants	Provide supplemental pricing information	Approve construction schedule	Set retainage to cover punch list
Refine problem definition	Coordinate drawings	Review pricing options	Approve shop drawings	Coordinate owner training
Refine direction	Complete specifications	Coordinate final pricing & drawings	Review requests for information	Issue certificate of substantial completion
			Coordinate weekly updates	Approve final closeout manuals
Refine site solution	Finalize detailed site solution	Price site solution		
Refine building solution	Finalize detailed design solution	Price design solution		
Refine exterior elevations	Finalize exterior details	Price exterior details		
Refine exterior finishes	Finalize exterior finish selection	Price exterior finish selection		
Refine interior design	Finalize interior design details	Price interior design details		
Refine interior finishes	Finalize interior finish selection	Price interior finish selection		
Refine engineering options	Coordinate engineering	Price engineering solutions		
Refine building systems	Finalize building systems	Price building systems		
Refine equipment list	Finalize equipment selection	Price equipment selection		
Reconcile program	Finalize program	Establish final project scope	Conduct monthly review meetings	Approve final pay request
Reconcile budget	Finalize budget	Establish contract amount	Approve applications for payment	Set dedication
Reconcile schedule	Finalize schedule	Establish completion date	Review construction quality	Review the entire process

to make a presentation to your congregation and begin preparing for a capital fund campaign.

Initial Design Development

As we have spent time working on the design of churches, we have found it becoming more beneficial to divide the normal design development phase into three separate tasks. The goal of the first task is to develop the architectural design to a point that it can be shared with the leadership team and ultimately with the congregation. The intent of this portion of the design development is to communicate the architectural vision to your church without spending any more of its resources than is absolutely necessary.

Once this is completed, your team should have enough information to share the architectural design with the congregation. Only after the congregation has approved this vision, should you spend the additional resources required to complete the design development drawings. There is no need to invest the resources required to define the structural, HVAC and AV systems until the congregation has approved the architectural design and gathered the funds necessary to construct the project. Once the actual funding process is completed, it is not uncommon to redesign portions of the project. Therefore, your team needs to preserve the resources required to begin design of the systems until the funding is well established.

Design Communication

The goal of this process is to have the design team prepare the drawings, renderings, printed materials, models or videos required to communicate the design with the congregation. This does not require detailed design of the building systems. However, it does require that the exterior design and the interior design be completed enough to explain the design intent and to make sure that your committee has properly set the expectations that will be met by the completion of the construction.

Final Design Development

Based on approval of the initial design development and the project budget, the design team can then proceed to prepare more detailed design development documents. These documents will thoroughly describe the scope, size, quality, and character of the proposed construction project. This includes prelim-

The preliminary designs should be accompanied by a statement of probable construction cost and should be reviewed thoroughly and approved by the committee.

inary information related to the structural, mechanical, and electrical systems, special construction required for special acoustical lighting or video requirements, along with designation of probable construction materials and other architectural elements necessary to provide a more detailed construction cost statement. These drawings are often used as a pricing set and given to the construction team to verify construction cost before the church sets the final project budget.

Construction Documents Phase

Following approval of the design development documents and the project budget, the design team will prepare the contract documents, consisting of the constructions drawings and specifications which set forth in detail the construction requirements of the entire project. These drawings describe the location and quantity of each building component, while the specifications establish the quality and execution of the construction work.

As a part of the basic services related to this phase, the design team should assist the church in the preparation of the paperwork necessary for bidding or negotiating the final construction cost.

Omitting either of these portions of the construction documents could leave the church open to unpleasant surprises as the work progresses. As a part of the basic services related to this phase, the design team should assist the church in the preparation of the paperwork necessary for bidding or negotiating the final construction costs. They also should assist in preparing the construction contract and submitting it for the necessary government approvals and permits.

A thorough and complete understanding of the design is necessary for any meaningful evaluation. The design team should be able to do this in layman's terms, in the clearest possible manner. They also need to be willing to take whatever time is needed to answer all of your team's questions and make any clarifications necessary to satisfy all leadership team members.

Graphic illustrations are often used to assist in these presentations. Ideally the design team, the leadership team, and the construction team will work together to achieve the optimum balance between the program, the design, the schedule, and the construction cost.

Project Pricing Phase

During this phase of the project, the design team will assist the leadership team in obtaining bids or negotiated proposals from the construction team. They also will help to set the final cost of construction and assist in preparing

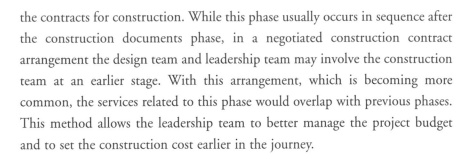

the contracts for construction. While this phase usually occurs in sequence after the construction documents phase, in a negotiated construction contract arrangement the design team and leadership team may involve the construction team at an earlier stage. With this arrangement, which is becoming more common, the services related to this phase would overlap with previous phases. This method allows the leadership team to better manage the project budget and to set the construction cost earlier in the journey.

Contract Administration Phase

In the construction phase, the design team becomes the church's advocate. They interpret the construction documents and provide additional information when required for the construction process. During this phase of the project, the design team also works to guard the church against defects and deficiencies. This task is important, but many leadership teams misunderstand the actual responsibilities of this team in this phase. The design team does not supervise construction or have the responsibility for construction means, techniques, sequences, procedures, or construction schedule. This responsibility belongs to the construction team.

The design team is a valuable resource, but it cannot be expected to make a complete and accurate assessment of the entire construction process without significant communication and evaluation from the leadership team.

The design team does visit the site at appropriate intervals, evaluates the progress of the work, and renders impartial interpretations of the contract documents. Under the contract documents, this team has the authority to reject work that does not conform to the stated agreement. Additionally, it authorizes payment requests made by the contractor, while making sure that they reflect the amount of work actually performed. In case of the contractor's default on the project, this will help protect the church from financial loss. In many cases, the lending institution for the construction project requires this type of certification for their protection.

Without a doubt, the design team is a valuable resource, but it cannot be expected to make a complete and accurate assessment of the entire construction process without significant communication and evaluation from the leadership team. This is the main reason project phases are built into the process, along with regularly scheduled progress reviews. During these reviews, the leadership and design teams review and then move on through the process together in a partnership.

Project Closeout

Once the construction of your project is completed and ready to be commissioned, the design team will prepare a punch list itemizing all of the items that need to be repaired or replaced in order to comply with the contract documents. Once this list is compiled, the design team will set an amount of money to cover this work and hold these funds until all of the items have been completed.

At this time, the contractor also will set up the training sessions that may be required for the operation of the mechanical, sound, video, and lighting systems. If possible, videotape these training sessions so that volunteers or additional workers will have the opportunity to view these sessions at a later date.

Once the governing authorities have issued a certificate of occupancy, the design team will issue a formal certificate of substantial completion. This certificate establishes the beginning date of the warranties issued by the contractor and manufacturers. The contractor should be required to place all of the closeout documents into binders. Then the design team will review these documents to make sure the required papers are included. Once the design team verifies these, they will send the documents to the church. All documents of this nature need to be stored in a safe place. They contain telephone numbers and information the church will need concerning warranties and maintenance. As technology becomes more available, contractors are beginning to provide this type of information on a CD rather than in binders.

The right design team will help enable your leadership team to keep your dream from turning into a nightmare.

Fees

The design team's fees generally cover only the professional services provided. They do not cover expenses for travel, mileage, long-distance phone calls, photocopying, and reproduction of project-related documents, presentation-quality renderings, and finished models.

At the beginning of the working relationship, the leadership team should clarify each of these items with the design team and make necessary adjustments to the agreement. Your leadership team may wish to include renderings, models, or video animation as a part of the basic service, or obtain a fixed cost to provide these as an additional service.

If your leadership team is having a problem comparing design fees, you may want to ask each firm under consideration to provide a fee for the same defined scope of services. Although your team may not engage the firm on the exact scope outlined in your request, it will give you an opportunity to compare fees from different firms for the same scope of work.

Selecting the Design Team

As you begin to think about future expansion, start building a list of potential design teams. Find out who has previous experience in designing churches. Ask your congregation for names and get recommendations from other churches that have completed similar journeys.

Every church has limited funds and wants to ensure the best and most efficient use of every available resource dedicated to the journey. If possible, look for a design team who has worked on several projects similar to the one you are planning and understands the importance of being a good steward with each and every decision that your leadership team must make. The right design team with the proper experience in working with churches will help enable your leadership team to keep the expectations, program, budget, and schedule in balance and help keep your dream from turning into a nightmare.

Request for Qualifications — "The RFQ"

Contact each firm on your list in writing. Describe the anticipated scope of your project and the proposed timeline, and ask if the firm is interested and able to work with your church on this project. If they are interested, request that they submit material outlining the firm's qualifications and experience. When possible, outline the specific information you need to review their qualifications, including the expected range of professional fees.

Reviewing for Information

The materials you receive from each interested firm should include a letter of interest, brochures or portfolios including general information about the firm, fact sheets, photos of past work, references from past projects, and biographical materials about key personnel.

Begin this phase of the search by looking beyond the style of the submitted material to determine which firms have the right experience and capabilities for your project. Also, be aware that the material sent to you represents the firm and their image to their clients. A firm that takes time to prepare a well-thought-out

A firm that takes time to prepare a well-thought-out and complete information package will be more likely to handle their communication with your team and church in the same professional manner.

and complete information package will be more likely to handle their communication with your team and church in the same professional manner.

Check to see if the individual the firm selected to work with you signed the letter of interest, or if someone in their marketing department signed it? Notice whether or not someone from the firm follows up with you to make sure that you received the materials you requested. A firm that is interested in working with you will want to know if you have any additional questions.

If there is no follow up, this may mean that they are too busy for your project. Remember, the way a firm responds to your request will tell you a lot about how they will handle all of their communication and interaction with your leadership team.

It is a common practice to ask the firm for references from past clients. These references are invaluable. Be sure to check up on several of these and try to determine how the firm interacted with other clients. Did they listen? Were they responsive? Did they follow up on their commitments? Did they provide creative solutions? Were they flexible in looking at several design options?

By this point in the search, you need to narrow your list to the best three or four firms that seem like the right match and are a fit for your team and your church. Any of these final firms will probably have the ability to act as your design team.

Your next job will be to narrow this field down to the one firm that you believe can make your dream of a new church facility a reality. Ask each of the remaining three or four firms to meet with your leadership team for an interview, making sure that each firm understands that they are responsible for all of the costs associated with the interview. If a firm is traveling from another town and expects to be compensated for their travel expenses, make sure that there are no misunderstandings before they agree to come.

The Interview

The interview process is the next crucial step in your journey because it gives your leadership team the best opportunity to meet the individual who will be acting as your design team leader for the remainder of your journey. During the interview you need to check to see if his or her personality is a good match for your team.

A firm that is interested in working with you will want to know if you have any additional questions.

- *Are you comfortable with this firm and their representative?* Remember, you and your team will be working closely with this firm for an extended period of time; in most instances the completion of your journey will take several years.

- *How well do you think the representative will listen to your team?* The entire leadership team needs to have confidence that the selected design team will be compatible. You also want to make sure that the design team will listen and will be responsive to your specific project requirements.

The Interview Process

The interview is usually scheduled to take place at your church or a site of your choosing, perhaps the conference room of one of the leadership team members. If the interview is held at your church, it will allow the design team to become familiar with your existing facilities, and will allow you to set up all the interviews on the same day.

- Do your best to limit the number of interviews to the three or four design firms that you feel offer the best possibility of a match. Do not interview a firm that does not appear qualified based on the information that they have submitted to you. It is a waste of your time and a waste of the firm's time.

- Allow an hour to an hour and a half for an interview. Most interviews last about one hour and 20 minutes. Instruct each design team in advance that they have 20 to 30 minutes for their presentation, and an equal amount of time set aside for questions from the leadership team. It is beneficial to everyone involved if some of your team's questions are prepared in advance. If possible, consider supplying the list of specific questions to each design team a week in advance, especially if there are specific questions about fees or detailed services that will require prior preparation.

- Make sure there is enough time allotted to answer all of your questions without your feeling rushed. Assign one of your team members to be the designated timekeeper. His responsibility should be to let everyone know when the design team should complete their presentation, and to let all of your team members know when it is time to end the interview.

- You should allow 15 to 20 minutes between interviews for each firm to set up their presentation. Even with the best of intentions, it is difficult to keep everyone on track and on schedule, so allow this extra time between each interview. Make every effort to make sure that every one of your team members gets his or her questions answered.

Deciding What the Design Representative Knows

The design team should show you examples of their past work and describe how their experience and expertise will help you on your journey. They should also explain how they will interact with your team and what expectations they may have of the leadership team. Pay attention to the way the design firm presents its experience.

- Are they confident?
- Do they look you in the eye and answer your questions?
- Do they seem like team players?

A very important question to answer is whether or not you think you can sit across a table from this group of professionals for the next several months and work out all the details required to ensure your church has a successful journey.

Asking the Right Questions

During the interview, the leadership team should ask questions, some of which include the following:

- How busy is the firm?

- Do they have the capacity to take on your project? Insist on meeting the person who will actually be the design team leader on this journey.

- What is the firm's design philosophy?

- What percentage of the firm's work is spent in church design?

- How long has the firm been doing church design?

- Does the firm have in-house engineering, or do they subcontract that work out?

- What kind of track record do they have with the special consultants required for your project?

Talk about your budget and find out the range of fees that the architect would anticipate for your project. During the course of the presentation, if there is something you don't understand, ask for clarification. If you feel intimidated or if the design team doesn't explain things in a way that you can understand, then this team may not be the right match for your team or your church.

Pay attention to the way the design firm presents their experience.

Resist the temptation to rush through the interview process. There is always a tendency to hurry this process along and pick someone in order to get started. This is a critical milestone in the successful completion of your journey. Therefore, allow adequate time to make sure that you have selected the right design team to guide you. After the interview process, if you are still unsure of the best choice, ask the firms still under consideration to take you to one or two of their completed project sites. Seeing the work that they have completed will help you make a final selection.

Final Selection

Ultimately, you should choose the firm that you trust, has the experience you need, and appears to be the right match for your church and your leadership team. It is important that everyone on your team agrees with this decision. If there is someone who disagrees with the choice of the design team, try everything possible to get a unanimous vote. This journey will be difficult enough without one of your team members waiting for an opportunity to find fault.

You should choose the firm you trust, has the experience you need, and appears to be the right match for your church and your leadership team. It is important that everyone on your team agrees with this decision.

Unlike buying a pre-manufactured item like a car or an appliance, you cannot see the final product and test it out until the end of the journey. The design team you commission will provide a professional service—not a pre-manufactured product. The right team will be the one who can provide you with the judgment, experience, creativity, technical expertise, and communication skills that fit your needs, budget, schedule, and dreams.

Don't select a design team just because they appear to have the lowest fee. You need to do enough research to know what services they are going to include within their proposed fee.

One design team with a low initial fee may charge extra for some services that another design team includes in their basic fee. However, sometimes a low fee indicates that the design team needs more work, and they may in fact be the best choice. Fees should be one of the criteria used to select a design team, but should not be used as the only basis for selection.

Solid qualifications, experience, and interest in your project should be the prime criteria for your selection. The professional fee paid to the design team will be a small portion of the total project cost, and the correct selection at this point in your journey could save you more than the entire fee paid to your design team. Likewise, the wrong choice at this point could prove to be one of the most expensive decisions your leadership team will ever make.

Each design team will establish its own approach for working with your church and leadership team. Look carefully to find the design team and leader that matches your team's values and attitudes. It also is important to find a design team that understands your style of worship, has designed other churches, and has worked with other leadership teams. However, it is equally important to find someone who will listen, respond to your requests, and seek to become an integral team member. Honesty is a key concern.

Whenever possible, select a design team leader who is actively working on several church projects. He or she will be better able to understand the needs of your church, share lessons learned from other church projects, help you make informed decisions earlier on in the process, and help your leadership team stay on the right path. Make sure that the individual you select will be truthful and steer you along the right path, especially when he thinks you may be taking a wrong turn.

Whenever possible, select a design team leader who is actively working on several church projects.

Method of Payment for Professional Fees

Design firms charge for their professional services in many different ways, and this can be very confusing. There are no industry standards or set fees for particular types of projects or professional services. Professional design fees are established in a number of ways and are dependent upon the project size and type as well as the extent and nature of the services required by the owner.

During the early portions of the project, when you are trying to analyze the program and timing, it is best to establish the project size and budget. I believe that the fees are best contracted on an hourly rate or as a fixed fee. Once the project scope and budget have been clearly identified, you can establish a contract for professional fees based on a fixed fee or a percentage of the construction cost.

It is difficult for a professional design team to give you a total fee for their services until the entire scope of the work on your project has been clearly defined and understood. With most church projects, this usually requires some pre-design and master planning work.

Before the final project scope can be established, the design team will need to spend time working with your leadership team analyzing existing conditions and needs, as well as reviewing several options for the solution to your problem. At

If you have made the correct choice in selecting a design team, you will be comfortable in working out a method of payment that is fair to both parties.

this point, it is most economical to work on an hourly basis with some predetermined guaranteed maximum amount. This will allow your leadership team to analyze and explore the basic problems, review several solutions, and begin to establish the project budget before you enter into a contract for the major portion of the design team's work. Before you make the selection final, sit down with the selected design team and discuss the way they would prefer to establish the fee on your project. Most firms will work with your church to establish a combination of the methods mentioned above.

The basis for the fee, the amount, and the payment schedule are issues for you and the design team to work out before you enter into a contract. If you have made the correct choice in selecting a design team, you will be comfortable in working out a method of payment that is fair to both parties. This is the first chance for both teams to establish a working relationship and your first opportunity to see if the partnership will be a promising one.

Leadership teams that are experienced in working with design teams recognize that adequate compensation for the work being done is a basic requirement. This is the way you can be assured that the type and level of services given will fulfill your expectations.

As soon as you have settled contract issues, contact the other design teams by telephone or letter. Tell them that you appreciated the time and interest they had in your project; however, you have selected another design team. Do not be caught off guard or surprised if they ask for you to share with them the reason they were not selected and how they could improve their response in the future. This is how many good firms continue to learn and improve. Remember that they have spent a lot of effort and resources to prepare for their interview with your leadership team.

Get It in Writing

Once a clear statement of project requirements is established and all the contractual arrangements are made with the design team, the project can proceed through the designated phases without unexpected surprises. Now that your design team has a leadership team to work with, you can determine the methods of payment, and put into writing the terms of your agreement, the scope of work, the services expected, and compensation plan.

Once a clear statement of project requirements is established and all the contractual arrangements are made with the design team, the project can proceed through the designated phases without unexpected surprises.

This written agreement can take many forms. Most design teams will generate the first draft and prepare the final version for your signature. A letter of agreement is often the best way to begin a project, once the preliminary scope of services has been identified.

The American Institute of Architects (AIA) and the Design/Build Institute of America (DBIA) have both developed a variety of standard contract forms that are used industry wide. These contracts present a consensus among organizations representing owners, lawyers, contractors, engineers, and architects. They are "coordinated" to fit together to form a family of agreements, which will be important when you establish the construction contract. No matter which option is taken, the agreement should be formalized in a contract. Even though everyone intends to have a good experience, no handshake is firm enough to reach all the understandings about the roles and obligations of the church and the design team.

LESSONS LEARNED

Whoever you chose to work as your design team should understand your traditions and worship style, the way technology is impacting today's churches, and the critical importance of balance between parking, worship, and support spaces. A poor selection will make your journey seem much more perilous and ultimately less successful. The best guide for your leadership team and your church will be a design team leader who is involved in working with many churches and who truly understands that your church wants to sustain the ministries needed to maintain vibrant growth.

Selecting the design team and design team leader is another of those critical decisions you will make. This leader will help you select the rest of the team that will take the journey with you. As the church's leadership team begins to analyze and plan for the expansion of your church facilities, you should try to select the design team as early as possible. This will allow you to take full advantage of their experience. It also will place them in a position where they can begin to help you plan for a successful journey. This includes determining what roadblocks are preventing the church from growing. The leadership on the design team must completely understand the analysis, the programming, and the pre-design process that every church must go through before the actual design can begin, or they will run the risk of beginning to design a building before the real needs have been determined.

Sometimes, in very large or complex projects, a program or construction manager is hired to act as representative of your leadership team. This is a person who provides professional assistance in assembling the design and construction teams. Most program or construction managers come from the real estate, architectural, or construction professions. These firms act as an owner's representative and can help assemble the data needed for the master plan and help select the design and construction teams. They usually base their fee on a percent of the construction cost and are hired by churches that do not have anyone in the church with adequate time or experience to manage the process.

EXAMPLES

Interview Questions for the Design Team Representative

PRE-INTERVIEW *Set date, invite architect, and schedule time.*
Provide the architect with following the information prior to the interview:
- Site information
- Preliminary sketches of project if any are available
- General building budget information
- Building program information and requirements

INTERVIEW *Prepare questions for the architectural firm.*
1. Give us a brief overview of the firm.
   - What are your qualifications and experience?
   - Have you done other church projects? Describe them.
   - What is the range of project sizes and costs with which your firm usually works?
   - May we have a list of previous clients with projects similar to ours?

2. Describe the services of your firm as they relate to each phase of the architectural and construction process for our project.

3. Tell us about your firm's associates and technical specialists.
   - Who in the firm would be primarily responsible for our project?
   - What other personnel in the firm would be assigned to our project?
   - Would an interview with any of these people be beneficial?
   - Do you have in-house engineering or do you use consulting firms?
   - Are there other specialists who would be needed on our projects?

4. Describe briefly the interrelated roles of the church, architect, and contractor.

- Based on your perception of our project, how would you propose to work with us?
- Why do you feel you are the architect/firm who meets the needs of our church on this project?

Contracts and Fees

- What type owner-architect agreement would you propose? Do you have a copy for review?

Fees:

- How do you base your fee?
- When is it due?
- If it is based on a percentage, will you guarantee a maximum fee based on the scope of the project?
- What specifically is included in your basic fee? (mechanical, electrical, plumbing, fire protection, structural, acoustical, interior design, landscape design, color elevations, models, etc.)
- What is not included that we may need?
- What do you think it will cost?
- Does you firm carry errors and omissions insurance? Describe benefits of this
  coverage.

Timing

- What is your estimate of the time required for each phase of the architectural and construction process?
- Estimate the total time required for the project.

Cost Containment

- What is the firm's record for designing within budget?
- What factors will affect the balance between economy and quality?
- Who is responsible for value engineering to bring the project within budget?
- How would you propose client and architect work together to control costs of the project?

Construction Phase

- What would your role be during the construction phase?
- How often do you visit the construction site?
- Do you have a preferred construction method?
- What are some options for contraction team selection?

DURING THE INTERVIEW

- Listen for the architect's sensitivity to the church's needs and desires. How would he deal with unrealistic expectations by the committee? Does he reveal a healthy regard for work done by previous committees?
- Does the architect listen and seem to understand the committee?
- Does he give evidence of being a good communicator?
- Are suggestions and alternate approaches offered?
- Does he seem familiar with local codes and building issues?

STEP FOUR

Establish the Working Relationships and a Working Schedule

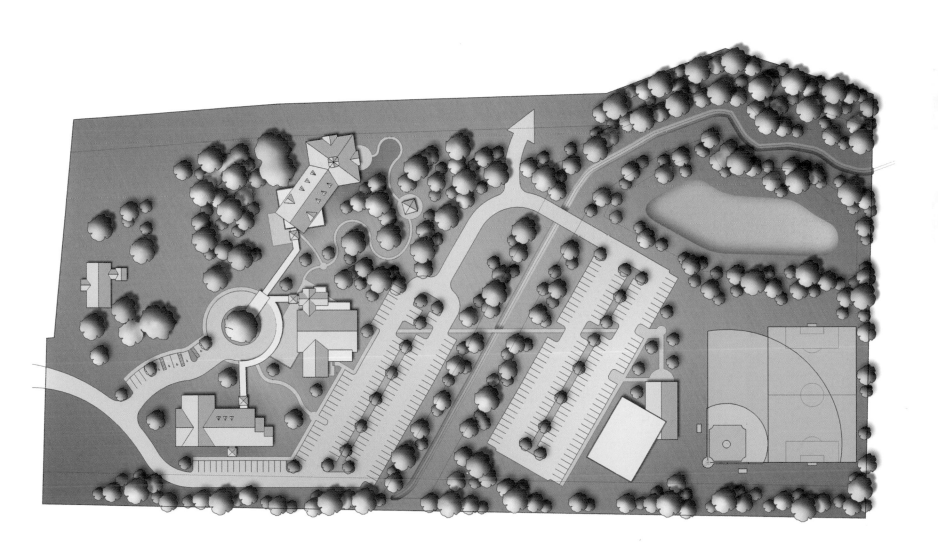

STEP FOUR

Establish the Working Relationships and a Working Schedule

WORKING RELATIONSHIPS

Have you ever started a project only to discover that it was too much for you to do on your own? No one had to explain the depth and the scope of the project that was facing Nehemiah. The moment he heard the news of the destruction of the walls surrounding the city of Jerusalem, he knew that it would take a team of people to rebuild what had been destroyed. His heart was grieved over what Jerusalem's enemies had done, and also because he could not conceive how he would fit into the scheme of the reconstruction. However, God had a plan.

In the Old Testament, a city's walls were its only form of protection from enemy attack. If the city was not protected, it could not flourish. The people would lose heart and leave, but Nehemiah refused to let this happen. Yet, he could not do the work alone. He needed experts on the job—men and women who would work alongside him, never thinking of sounding the horn of retreat. While Nehemiah's focus was set on reconstruction, your focus probably is one of expansion and growth. Jerusalem did grow and expand, but it all began with a strong sense of teamwork, dedication, and mutual commitment.

Establishing working relationships between each team in your partnership should be the next step in your journey. Your church, the church's leadership team, the design team, and ultimately the construction team, must all work

together in a partnership throughout the planning process, the design process, the financing process, and the construction process. To produce the very best results, each team should be involved and contribute throughout their portion of the journey. The following areas are the most important ones to be established early in the working relationships, and the most important to monitor and maintain throughout your journey.

Then I said to the nobles, the officials and the rest of the people, "The work is extensive and spread out, and we are widely separated from each other along the wall. Wherever you hear the sound of the trumpet, join us there. Our God will fight for us!"

—NEHEMIAH 4:19-20

Communications

Clear, open, honest, and regular communication is the key to every great partnership. In order to ensure a great partnership, members needs to know what is expected from their team at every point along the journey, and they need to know the expectations of each team.

Although honest, open communication is essential for a successful journey, this can be hard to achieve. Everyone in the entire partnership must be dedicated to being completely honest. This is easy to say, but it can be difficult to do. There always is the tendency for the team to develop a way of thinking where its members become intimidated and do not speak out or question the assumptions or direction that the group seems to be taking.

Some of our best journeys came as a result of one person on a church's leadership team who had the courage to speak up and question our proposals. Even though he thought that his opinion was in the minority and would get little support, his questions were asked and people considered what was being said. Several other team members, who had also been afraid to speak up, were able to express the same concerns, and we responded with a better solution to the problem. It happened all because someone had the courage to speak up.

Every team's input and approval are critical each step of the way. Each team should establish a communication process with the common goal of eliminating surprises and keeping the dialogue open and honest among all of the team members. The design team you select also should be open and honest with you, and they should be able to expect the same of your leadership team. If you have questions, ask. If you are not sure of the findings, question. That is the real work of the church's leadership team: to review, question, approve, and, of course, to communicate.

Some of our best journeys came as a result of one person on a church's leadership team who had the courage to speak up and question our proposals.

Always keep in mind that this is your church's journey. You have been given the responsibility to represent your congregation, and you must speak up and let your true feelings be known, even if it is not comfortable.

You and your leadership team are a vital part of the entire process, and it is essential that you participate openly, honestly, and actively. The design team will need your help during every step of this journey, providing information, reviews, and approvals.

A good design team will depend on you for feedback at each meeting. The design team can help to set the direction, but they too would be lost without your input. The design team's success in this partnership should be gauged one review and one approval at a time. By taking frequent compass readings and adjusting the direction, the design team should continually keep track of the overall direction of the partnership and the progress being made towards your final destination.

The design team should not be hired as the experts who already know who you are and where your church is going. Instead, they are there to help you reach your destination. Speak up, be an active team member, challenge conclusions and results that you do not understand, and make sure that the chosen destination is correct before you spend time and resources determining the best way to get there.

By taking frequent compass readings and adjusting the direction, the design team should continually keep track of the overall direction of the partnership and the progress being made towards your final destination.

The primary goal of all of the research and the presentations should be to provide you with the necessary information required to make an informed decision. The design team's responsibility to provide you with information is important even if their ideas are not popular with the entire leadership team. Remember, if you cannot have open, honest discussions in the leadership team meetings, it will be difficult to make sure you choose the correct path for your journey. The design team should be willing to lead you on whatever journey you choose.

In my opinion, one of the worst things that can happen at a ground breaking is for a member of the congregation to turn to someone on the leadership team and say, "We should have thought about building over there." Or, "We really should be providing for this ministry need" and for the leadership team to know immediately that the member was right. Take the time to gather the required analysis and review all options before you decide to make an important decision.

Beware of team members with hidden agendas and make sure that each team member completely understands his role in this journey.

People with interests in architecture, interiors, or construction are valuable team members. However, it becomes very unproductive for a team member to use this opportunity to seek to control the process in order to fulfill a lifelong interest. Beware of team members with hidden agendas and make sure that each team member completely understands their role in this journey.

There is a big difference between influencing a decision, helping make an informed decision, and in exerting unreasonable influence and being dictatorial. Strive to be a positive team member.

A Positive Team Member

- Follows direction.
- Shares the responsibility of success.
- Is biased toward action.
- Is always part of the answer.
- Always has a program.
- Says, "Let me do it for you."
- Sees an answer for every problem.
- Says, "It may be difficult, but it's possible."

A Negative Team Member

- Is off on his own journey.
- Wants all of the credit for the success.
- Looks for someone else to do the work.
- Is always part of the problem.
- Always has an excuse.
- Says, "It is not my job."
- Sees a problem with every answer.
- Says, "It may be possible, but it is too difficult."

EXAMPLES

The following examples are guidelines to be used for the purpose of establishing a preliminary working schedule. Try to review each step with the special team responsible for completing the work outlined, and work with the special team to get them to commit to a specific time frame. As other special teams get organized and involved, they can provide your leadership team with more accurate time estimates for their work.

Examples of a Preliminary Working Schedule

ITEM	TASK	DURATION
Item 1	Lay the foundation for the journey	
Item 2	Pray for wisdom, guidance, and courage	
Item 3	Determine the needs of your church	30–45 days
Item 4	Assemble the leadership team	30–60 days
Item 5	Assemble the design team	30–60 days
Item 6	Establish the working relationships	14 days
Item 7	Prepare a master schedule	14 days
Item 8	Analyze the dream, the potential, and the program	30–60 days
Item 9	Analyze the capacity of your existing facility	30–60 days
Item 10	Analyze the capacity of your site	30 days
Item 11	Develop the master plan	30–60 days
Item 12	Prepare a financial plan	30–60 days
Item 13	Prepare the project budget	30 days
Item 14	Determine the project scope	30 days
Item 15	Prepare the preliminary building design	60–90 days
Item 16	Initiate the capital fund drive	30 days for presentation drawings 60 days for video animation 45–60 days for capital fund drive
Item 17	Prepare the detailed building program and project budget	30 days
Item 18	Prepare the design development drawings	60–90 days
Item 19	Determine the method of construction	14–30 days
Item 20	Assemble the construction team	30 days
Item 21	Establish the final construction cost	30 days
Item 22	Complete the construction drawings	45–60 days
Item 23	Secure the construction permits	30–90 days (in some jurisdictions this may take longer)
Item 24	Begin construction	14 days
Item 25	Monitor the construction process	10–12 months for smaller projects 12–18 months for larger or more complex projects
Item 26	Construction close out	14 days
Item 27	Building dedication	1 day
Item 28	Review the master plan	After 6 months, review your master plan assumptions. After 12 months, review your church's growth and determine when you need to begin planning for the next journey.
Item 29	Prepare for the next journey	

MASTER MEETING SCHEDULE – EXAMPLE

DEVELOP SCHEDULE

MEETING 1
Date: TBD
Subject Matter:
- Review draft one, functional and space program.

MEETING 2
Date: TBD
Subject Matter:
- Review draft two, functional and space program.
- Discussion of project development budget.

MEETING 3
Date: TBD
Subject Matter:
- Review final draft, functional and space program.
- Discussion of project development budget.

MEETING 4
Date: TBD
Subject Matter:
- Review draft one, master and phase one site development plan.
- Review draft one, schematic master and phase one building floor plans.
- Finalize project development budget.

MEETING 5
Date: TBD
Subject Matter:
- Review draft two, master and phase one site development plan.
- Review draft two, schematic master and phase one building floor plans.

MEETING 6, 7 AND 8
Date: TBD
Subject Matter:
- Focus group meetings (Selected ministerial and lay leaders invited to provide design input into their specific area of service)
  - Worship
  - Bible study
  - Administration
  - Recreation
  - Music
  - Weekday early childhood education
  - Fellowship
  - Building and grounds

MEETING 9
Date: TBD
Subject Matter:
- Review draft two, master and phase one site development plan.
- Review draft two, schematic master and phase one building floor plans.
- Finalize project development budget.

MEETING 10
Date: TBD
Subject Matter:
- Town Hall meeting (Congregation invited to view preliminary plans and give input)

MEETING 11
Date: TBD
Subject Matter:
- Review final draft, master and phase one site development plans.
- Review final draft, master and phase one preliminary building floor plans.
- Review final draft, exterior building design.
- Review final draft, project development cost estimate.

MEETING 12 AND 13
Date: TBD
- Subject matter: church leadership and congregational presentations.

STEP FIVE

Determine the Needs of Your Church

THE PROGRESSION OF A SUCCESSFUL JOURNEY

MISSION	MINISTRIES	STRATEGIES	FACILITIES	RESOURCES
The **RESPONSE** to God's call on your church	The **PLAN** to respond to your mission	The **GOALS** to reach your ministry plan	The **PHYSICAL TOOLS** required to meet your strategies	The **RESOURCES** to provide programs and facilities

STEP FIVE

Determine the Needs of Your Church

We know now that when Nehemiah asked for information concerning the city of Jerusalem, he was told that the walls were in ruins and that the gates had been burned. Sadly, many other people had this same information, but they did nothing to remedy the problem. However, when Nehemiah heard the news, he took a different path. Not only did he mourn over what he had heard, he spent time before the Lord in prayer and asked Him to provide an opportunity for him to do something about the situation in Jerusalem.

Like Nehemiah, many today know about the plight of God's people. There are many who long to know God and to have a place to worship Him. Some choose to leave the problems of our culture for others to solve, but there are those who step forward to help. Like Nehemiah, when they do, they find that God has opened a door of opportunity and equipped them to do mighty things—including building a place of worship for God's people.

A JOURNEY WORTH MAKING

The only journey worth making in this life is the one that comes from our passion to help God's people. Without a doubt, He has a plan for every church. But only when the call of God creates a passion within the hearts of His people to do something about the problem, do we need to prepare to take a journey. Many of our unsuccessful journeys fail because they were undertaken without the God-given passion needed to sustain us throughout the long process that takes us from the beginning of a dream to the dedication of the project. The complex journey you are about to take through planning, designing, and building a new facility makes even more sense as you realize that there is a greater goal and purpose to be achieved than just construction.

No amount of planning and preparation can overcome the frustrations that arise from trying to solve the wrong problems. Equally, there is no end to the futility that comes from seeking to solve the right problem at the wrong time. Therefore, before anything is set in motion, make sure that your passion is for people and not buildings or things, that God is truly calling you to begin a

"The wall of Jerusalem is broken down, and its gates have been burned with fire."
—NEHEMIAH 1:3

The only journey worth making in this life is the one that comes from our passion to help God's people.

building program at this point in time, and that you are willing to go the course and complete the journey.

When the passion is from God and you realize that He has set the timing for your project, nothing will stop your church from completing the course that has been laid out for it. However, even then, you will face problems along the journey and you will need to plan ahead in order to avoid detours that have the potential to slow down your progress.

Unsuccessful building projects will constrict your church's potential and hinder it for generations to come. However, a truly successful building project will help your congregation grow stronger in its faith, which ultimately will affect your ministry for the glory of God.

THE TOOLS YOU WILL NEED

Along the way, the kind of tools and the amount of resources you will need depend on the journey you are preparing to take. Knowing your destination before you complete assembling the required tools and resources is the only way to ensure a successful journey. However, most churches do not conduct building programs or construct buildings often enough to know what this process entails. They have little or no past experience. Therefore, as members of the leadership team, you need to be open to learning from the experiences of other churches.

The strategic master planning issues coordinate your church's mission, ministries, strategies, facilities, and resources. These are five separate and too often unconnected elements of your church's mission that must be coordinated in your strategic master plan. When these are not properly connected, your journey can be detoured before you even get started.

The only way you can limit your risk and improve the probability of a successful journey is to set up a process that links these five elements under the oversight of one team. All too often, the teams working on the design of the new building spend valuable resources on designs that cannot be properly funded. Expectations for church design continue to increase, and as they become more complex, it becomes more important to have someone or a team to coordinate the plan you will follow. This is why I have found that developing a strategic master planning process works best. This one process connects all areas into one comprehensive planning process.

Take a look at the chart below. Each point is interrelated to the others and underscores the fact that this entire effort will be a planning process requiring your leadership team to balance each component of the strategic master plan. The strategic answers to these questions provide the *what* and *why* component of the strategic master plan. The tactical answers to these questions answer the *how* and *when* components to the strategic master plan. The strategic questions must be answered so that you know that you are doing the right thing. The tactical questions must be answered in order for you to know whether or not your church will be able to keep its ministry goals on track.

Your mission and the vision of your church must be first—all the other elements of the process will fall into place once these are in place. Remember, you are trying to bring unbelievers into the church. Real church growth comes from the unchurched. Therefore, you must make things convenient for them. They will become church members through your outreach programs. You must decide to be either a high-quality small congregation or a large regional congregation—to remain in the middle is very difficult. Either way, you must provide quality. The church must be visible—visitors come to churches that they have seen and that they remember, and because someone invites them to come.

WHY A STRATEGIC MASTER PLAN?

You will be using your existing resources to fund this journey, and you will be planning on using your future resources to build each additional phase of your plan. The growth you experience after this phase of the journey phase is complete will supply the resources required to fund the future phases of your master plan development. Your strategic master plan should help you predict when you will reach roadblocks in the growth of your church. It also should help you to be pro-active for the future by setting the right plans in place in order to remove these roadblocks before they completely stop your advancement.

THE PROGRESSION OF A SUCCESSFUL JOURNEY

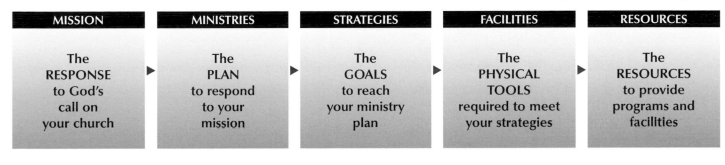

MISSION	MINISTRIES	STRATEGIES	FACILITIES	RESOURCES
The **RESPONSE** to God's call on your church	The **PLAN** to respond to your mission	The **GOALS** to reach your ministry plan	The **PHYSICAL TOOLS** required to meet your strategies	The **RESOURCES** to provide programs and facilities

Whatever the cost in time or in money, the development of a strategic master plan is good stewardship.

Developing a balance in your church's ministry also means that your team will need to develop a plan to meet the requirements to support each area of your church's ministry plan. The purpose of the strategic master plan is to develop a phased development plan that is in balance with your ministry needs and can be supported with your funding resources. Whenever any one of these elements is out of balance you will be continually fighting the successful completion of your plan. The development of a strategic master plan requires the gathering of accurate information from several sources within your church, an accurate analysis of this information, and the assembly of this information. All of this merges into one comprehensive planning document, your strategic master plan.

As you begin this process, it is often the financial elements that are the most difficult to coordinate, analyze, and incorporate into the early planning required to produce a valid strategic master plan. The most common shortcoming of the pre-design planning process is in the area of finance. As you begin, it is difficult to know what resources are going to be available for your project, let alone future expansion.

Most church members like to view themselves as men and women of faith. Many are not comfortable talking about the resources of their churches. However, that does not change the reality that you will need to properly invest your church's resources so that you will be able to make this journey. Additional resources will be required in order for you complete the plan that God has for you—so that you can grow into your fullest potential as a church.

Whatever the cost in time or in money, the development of a strategic master plan is good stewardship. This plan should include—as well as represent—who you are, what you want to do, where you are going to do it, and how you are going to get there. It should be considered a working document—an itinerary and a road map.

However, do not let this plan become a millstone that keeps your church from adapting to changes and new opportunities. Set real goals, monitor your progress, and adapt your goals as you gain new or more accurate information. The strategic master plan needs to include the mission and ministry statements of your church, along with the historical data of your church. It also should contain projections of your future growth, your site capacity study, your existing facility capacity study, and your funding resources. Each of these elements must be compiled, analyzed, and coordinated into one planning document to form a true strategic master plan.

HAVE THE CORRECT UNDERSTANDING

One of the very the first things that needs to be understood is the mission of your church. From this comes the development of your ministries and from your ministries come the development of your facilities. You will find that all facility needs must be balanced with your resources. This is why you must *think before you begin to design, and plan before you start to build.* Healthy churches consistently seek to provide a balanced scope of ministry between worship, fellowship, children, youth, adults, and parking.

At the completion of each phase of your development, the overriding goal should be to provide the balanced facilities required to allow your church to bring in new members, disciple them, and send them out to bring in additional new members. Churches need to provide people with a place to connect with others and with God. It needs to be a place where people can measure themselves and the lives they are leading. The truth is that most of us lead busy lives, and we all also need a place of rest, reflection, and peace.

Your church should plan your journey in small well-defined steps—steps that are planned around the goal of minimizing your church's risk and investment of resources.

With these thoughts in mind, the leadership team should strive to gather as much information as possible about the journey that lies ahead and to complete it with the smallest possible investment of resources. I believe that your church should plan your journey in small, well-defined steps—steps that are planned around the goal of minimizing your church's risk and investment of resources until you have a program, a design, a budget, and a schedule in place that is supported by your congregation. Only after your leadership team has completed these steps are you ready to move ahead and commit the rest of the resources required to complete the design documents and make the preparations needed to begin construction.

The financial resources you spend to complete a strategic master plan will be a very small portion of the total cost of your journey. It takes far fewer people to conduct this planning process than it does to prepare the contract drawings or to construct the building. Taking the time required to plan well is the most cost effective and valuable time spent on this journey. You have more potential to control the project budget and to invest your resources wisely during this strategic master planning process than at any other time on your journey.

The only way you can limit your risk and improve the probability of a successful journey is to set up a process that links these five elements under the oversight of one team.

DISCOVER THE IMPORTANT NEEDS OF YOUR CHURCH

In order to discover the needs of your church, you must take time to ask questions and be willing to listen for answers before you begin to form any assumptions or make any commitments about a proposed solution. Everyone in the congregation has a partial understanding of the overall needs of the church.

The pastor and worship leader see the view from the chancel on Sunday morning. The nursery workers have another view of Sunday—one that is from behind the door of the nursery. The youth workers view Sunday from their perspective, and the adult leaders see the view from their classrooms. The young family who cannot easily find a parking space views the church from another vantage point, and the first time visitor sees yet another view of the church.

Listen to each ministry area and remember that it is natural for the people representing these areas to focus on the problems that directly affect their areas. Only after listening and understanding each of your church's ministries and their needs can you begin to form a picture of the overall potential of your church. It is exciting and enjoyable to listen and to gather information, but a little later in the journey, you will need to prioritize these needs and suggestions so that you can develop a plan that matches the resources of your church with the ministry goals of your church. So listen and analyze, but also be careful not to make any immediate promises or create any expectations that you may not be able to fulfill on this journey.

It is not uncommon for churches to undertake this first step in the journey with one set of the primary needs at the forefront. However, they quickly discover that there are other crucial roadblocks and needs to be dealt with before ministry growth can take place. All ministry needs must be understood, and a plan must be developed to address these in an overall master plan. However, the order of importance and the timing required to meet all of the needs may change as you learn more about the ministries of your church and as you begin to adapt to new information as it becomes available to you.

When interviewing your church's staff members, you will be collecting information to understand three separate issues:

- First, what is working well in the individual areas of ministry and why.

- Second, what is *not* working well, and what is preventing these areas from growing? Is there a need for more space, a wider range of ministry programs, or are there scheduling problems?

• The third issue that needs to be addressed involves the future of the church's ministry. What are the long-range goals? Where do church leaders want the ministry to be in five years, and what resources will they need in order to reach their goals?

Once this information has been gathered, you can begin to determine the overall scope of the changes that will need to be made. Your team then can define and prioritize each step as you develop a strategic master plan for the church.

It is exciting and enjoyable to listen and to gather information, but a little later in the journey, you will need to prioritize these needs.

Another opportunity that should not be missed on a journey like this is to develop the maturity of your church's congregation in the area of personal relationships. A project like the one you are considering invariably introduces a number of potentially divisive issues—decisions such as whether or not to buy additional property, what type of facility to construct, how to finance the project, what the building should look like, or if the church should relocate to a new site. These issues bring challenges for maturity and spiritual growth.

Certainly, the congregation will be involved in the study, debate, deliberation, prayer, and determination of most major decisions. Capable leaders know how to keep everyone's focus on issues—not individuals. Mature people will recognize that not everyone will agree on every decision. This journey will provide many opportunities for the church to deliberate, make decisions in faith, accept the outcome, and move forward. When handled properly, each of these opportunities will also be a chance for the church to grow closer and stronger.

Left unmanaged, a building program will take on a life of its own, consuming everything in its path. If not kept in check, it has the potential to consume all of a church's time, resources, and concern—often keeping other church ministries from receiving the very resources they need in order to grow. If these ministries become sidetracked and are not properly managed, the spirit and vitality of the church will suffer. The church's leadership team needs to continually monitor this and keep the building program from consuming resources to the detriment of the development of other ministries. Never let the congregation forget that these ministries are at the heart of your church's purpose and the very reason for your journey.

IS YOUR MISSION WELL-DEFINED?

In order to answer this question, you will need to take the time to

• Analyze your church's potential.

• Define your dream.

• Determine the current roadblocks that are keeping your church from growing. Is it lack of staff, lack of programs, lack of resources, or lack of the proper facilities?

• Establish the building program for your journey.

This is a time to make sure that you have a well-defined mission for your church. It is also a time when every ministry area in the church needs to be reviewed. What works? What needs to be changed? What does each ministry need in order to provide for future growth? This is the best time to decide about any program changes that might need to be introduced. Gather information from each area of your church's ministry, from the staff, and from the congregation. Some churches have had good success with conducting special focus groups. Workshops or focus groups conducted with the church leadership can be held to establish the goals and the wish lists that respond to each ministry of the church.

The only way you can limit your risk and improve the probability of a successful journey is to set up a process that links these five elements under the oversight of one team.

The leadership team also might want to survey the congregation to determine the concerns and the expectations of the members and to determine the potential for a particular ministry. Where possible, the design team should assist you in these surveys in order to ensure that all of the required questions have been asked and that you get accurate and honest responses.

Have one open meeting for each area of the church's ministry and invite anyone in the church who is interested in that particular area of ministry to attend. This will allow everyone in the congregation to become a part of the process and will eventually help them to become involved in obtaining the financial resources required to go from dream to dedication.

The more involvement and the more input you get before establishing your destination, the more likely you will have a successful journey. This type of process will uncover many more opportunities for growth than can be funded. However, it also will allow your leadership team the opportunity of selecting the very best option for your church's future.

ADOPTING THE RIGHT STRATEGY

Every church needs to take the time to adopt a strategy for growth before deciding what to build next. Once this strategy has been formulated, the church leadership team can properly prioritize the building requirements that will help implement this strategy. Keeping this as the central focus during the planning process will help the leadership team decide which of the ministries most need the new space.

The critical focus should never be on what kind of building the leaders want, but on which ministries and what type of space will be most effective in meeting the church's growth strategy. If the space dedicated to serving a particular age group is running at capacity and you cannot find a way to reassign other space to meet its needs, then new space may need to be built to allow this ministry room to grow. However, you must still decide if this need is critical to church growth.

In a sanctuary or worship center, the commonly used guideline states that when the average attendance is running at 80 percent of the capacity, the building has reached its saturation point, and that it will look and feel full. At that point, unless the church adds another service or additional seating, it will probably lose the momentum of its growth. A church that only occasionally has an attendance of 80 percent capacity is not running at full capacity.

The point of the guideline is that when the average attendance is consistently at 80 percent of the capacity, then the church is at the point of saturation in the worship service. In order for the church to achieve that average, attendance will often run well above the 80 percent mark. The rule does not mean that the church stops growing as soon as attendance reaches 80 percent of the capacity. Indeed, many churches reach 95 to 105 percent capacity and still continue to grow. They go to multiple services, find additional space for people, and continue to do the things that generate growth.

There seems to be a mystery concerning the actual seating capacity of a sanctuary or worship center. Most current fire codes or building codes dictate that we must calculate the seating based on 18 inches of pew length per person. By code, 1,500 feet of pews would provide a seat count of 1,000 people. According to the codes, this is the seating capacity of the facility, and we would be required to use this number to calculate the size and number of the exit stairs, corridors, and doors.

The critical focus should never be on what kind of building the leaders want, but on which ministries and what type of space will be most effective in meeting the church's growth strategy.

Now, the actual comfortable seating width is closer to 21 inches per seats. So in reality, the same 1,500 linear feet of pews really only comfortably accommodates 857 people, a 14 percent decrease in the stated capacity derived from the code requirements. However, the architectural drawings would be required to state that the capacity of the space is 1,000 people. This is why it is seldom possible to seat the total number of people posted as the capacity of a worship center. I often hear pastors say, "I was told the worship center was going to hold 1,000 people, but we can only get 825 comfortably seated when it is full."

Be sure that you understand the terms being used by the design team and be sure to keep asking questions until you are confident of the decisions you are being asked to make. High attendance days, like Christmas or Easter, are good indicators of the size your regular attendance could be in a few years, especially if your church could provide the balanced facilities required to adequately handle this attendance on a regular basis.

Set a goal to communicate often with your congregation. Keep them informed of your progress, and ask for their input when you are looking for direction.

Never tell your congregation that the church cannot grow until you get a new building. A church that wants to grow will make the commitment to continue to do those things that produce growth. Its leaders will continue to find creative ways to grow, even when all of the space is being used at capacity. However, at the same time, a church running at capacity must be planning to adequately provide for this growth, or it will eventually hit the saturation point and begin to loose momentum.

Also, set a goal to communicate often with your congregation. Keep them informed of your progress, and ask for their input when you are looking for direction. This will help your membership know that they are an important part of the entire process.

LESSONS LEARNED

Prayer works! I often tell people that if you do not believe in miracles, come and work with me for a while. It is so easy for each of us to miss opportunities to see God at work right in front of us each day. When we take time to pray and trust God, we will see the miraculous take place.

I believe that prayer must be a part of each step of your journey.

• Pray, asking for direction and wisdom as you make the decisions necessary for the church to complete its journey.

- Pray for the entire team and for the work they are doing to help you on your journey.

- During the design process, pray for the entire design team. The work they are doing will set the foundation upon which the rest of the project will be built, and their experience will produce the direction and drawings required to translate your vision into a building.

- During the construction process, pray for the safety of everyone working on the project. Every construction worker is a team member, and your journey could not be completed without his or her efforts. Unfortunately, all too often they are the forgotten team members, though they are the very ones who need a word of prayer the most. Challenge every member of the church to make prayer the foundation for the entire journey.

- Take time to celebrate the process and what God is doing! Do not wait until the end of the journey to rejoice over the progress that you are making. There are many steps along the way where your church should stop and be joyful over the journey. This is what Nehemiah instructed the people to do. They had worked hard and sacrificed, and needed a break in the action long enough to rejoice and praise God for His faithfulness.

Once your church has a comprehensive knowledge of the community, the team will find itself in a better position to devise an informed response to meet the ministry goals of your church.

You should plan to celebrate at different stages of your journey—when you complete your master plan and your fund-raising efforts, when you begin construction, and when you top out your new building's structure. Challenge the leadership team to come up with times of celebration and add them to the master schedule. Then plan ahead and involve the entire congregation in the celebration.

Is important to remember that this will be a long journey, and it only makes sense to have some fun along the way. Celebrations like the ones I have mentioned, encourage your congregation's continued support. Members are not as involved as the leadership team, and need points of connection built into the process so that they can remain excited and encouraged.

Truthfully, they will only really hear what is going on when you communicate with them. If you do not take the time to communicate, someone else will, and this is not the best way for news of the journey to travel. It takes longer to undo misinformation and uninformed communication than to schedule regular times for sharing the information you gather on your journey.

FOCUS GROUP DESIGN SESSION
DISCUSSION TOPICS

CHURCH OFFICES

1. Program space requirements
2. Adjacencies of offices and work stations
3. Satellite vs. centralized office suites
4. Central vs. decentralized records and files
5. Counseling accommodations
6. Work room needs
7. Supply/ Storage needs
8. Records storage, membership and financial
9. Staff accommodations for breaks and meetings
10. Reuse vs. replacement of office furnishings
11. Data and communications

WORSHIP FACILITIES

1. Overview of campus development plan
2. Overview of master building development plans
3. Program space requirements
4. Style of worship
5. Chancel furnishings
6. Use of facility for weddings
7. Communion
8. Choir and instruments
9. Acoustical considerations
10. Special lighting considerations
11. Video overflow

NURSERY/ PRESCHOOL/ CHILDREN EDUCATION

1. Room size/ occupancy
2. Room layout and design
3. Room furnishings, equipment and cabinetry
4. Room finishes (floor and wall coverings)
5. Plumbing requirements
6. Resource/ supply room needs
7. Tackboard/ markerboard needs
8. Access control and security
9. Large assembly space

YOUTH EDUCATION AND FELLOWSHIP

1. Classroom size/ occupancy
2. Room furnishings
3. Room finishes (floor and wall coverings)
4. Assembly/ fellowship area design criteria
5. Snack kitchen design criteria
6. Resource/ storage needs
7. Tackboard/ markerboard needs
8. Large assembly requirement

ADULT EDUCATION

1. Classroom size/ occupancy
2. Room furnishings
3. Room finishes (floor and wall coverings)
4. Resource/ storage needs
5. Tackboard/ markerboard needs

SENIOR ADULTS

1. Program requirements
2. Special space requirements
3. Frequency of use
4. Relationship to adult education

MUSIC FACILITIES

1. Overview of campus development plan.
2. Overview of master building development plans.
3. Program space requirements.

STEP SIX

Analyze Your Membership, Your Facility, and Your Site

Nehemiah knew that before he began the reconstruction of Jerusalem's walls, he had to take time to survey the area. However, Nehemiah did more than conduct a survey, he envisioned what the walls would look like once they were back in place. The walls that he planned to build would not be just like the old ones—they would be even better and offer even more protection from enemy threat. We can imagine that his plans for construction did not stop with walls and gates. He envisioned the city of Jerusalem once again as a hub of commercial activity. He may have had his heart set on rebuilding, but he knew that once the walls were reconstructed, the city would grow and people would come to worship within its gates.

This is why it is important to analyze and evaluate your existing church facilities, their present use, and your site in order to help define the problems that are keeping you from growing. Should you build or should you move? These are important questions to consider. Why are you building in the first place? How many people do you need to build for, and how can you make the best use of your existing facilities? How can you keep your ministry program areas in balance? Should you build in phases. How much will each phase cost? How should you devise a master plan for your site? These are all questions that need to be answered before you take this next step.

By night I went out . . . examining the walls of Jerusalem, which had been broken down, and its gates, which had been destroyed by fire. Then I moved on toward the Fountain Gate and the King's Pool, but there was not enough room for my mount to get through; so I went up the valley by night, examining the wall.

—Nehemiah 2:13-15

FOUR BASIC AREAS OF FOCUS

There are four basic areas of focus for a church master plan: spiritual, human, financial, and physical. Each of these areas within your church should be analyzed and reviewed. A thorough understanding of each one will contribute to the church reaching its mission. Therefore, it is wise to ensure that the pre-design time is used to gather information that will be helpful to every aspect of your journey. Collect data on the goals for your existing and future ministry, worship attendance, education attendance, administrative staff, fellowship, and music ministry.

God offers His gracious gift of salvation to each one of us. Always make sure that at the core of your mission is a God-driven desire to provide for all of His people. Each church must discover its own unique way to express its mission. The purpose of your journey of expansion is to provide buildings that are planned and constructed to meet the needs of your growing congregation.

Since most churches have their primary base of operations in one particular community, your leadership team should gather some basic information about the community you are trying to serve. The church needs to understand the economic, social, health, educational, moral, and religious conditions in the community.

You also need to gather additional knowledge about commercial, residential, and recreational developments planned for the community. Once your church has a comprehensive knowledge of the community, the team will find itself in a better position to devise an informed response to meet the ministry goals of your church.

Therefore, your church should spend a little time early in the planning process to learn about the people in your area:

The goal is to make sure that your leadership team has a complete understanding of your membership and the attendance ratios of each ministry program in your church.

- Is the population growing, stable, or decreasing, and at what rate?

- What is the trend in age-group population?

- How many people in the area are not going to church?

- Is church growth keeping up with the population growth in the area?

- What do people perceive to be the greatest church ministry need in their area?

- What types of programs or ministries are most appealing to the people in your area?

Whenever your congregation becomes involved in the issues relating to church planning and building needs, they will need to have some comprehensive and current information about themselves. This is one of the primary areas where many otherwise good leadership teams make serious mistakes. They assume that their congregation fully understands themselves as a church, and that the entire congregation is in touch with the dream and mission of their church.

Many congregations do not have a well-focused, clearly-defined understanding of their church. Many church members are probably not aware of the church's history and heritage. Others may only really understand some of the many special ministries supported by their church. Once again, this is the time to review this aspect of your church, to make an honest evaluation of the current status, and to clearly communicate your findings. Use this portion of the journey as a time to help the congregation review and clarify some internal issues, such as:

Who are we as a church?

What is our primary mission?

Why do we need to grow?

How are we going to achieve our mission?

TAKE A CLOSE LOOK AT YOUR MEMBERSHIP

Begin to analyze your membership by compiling your last five years of attendance in your worship and in your Christian education program. Group them by age. The usual breakdown includes nursery, preschool, middle school, high school, and adults. If you have a large college age class, it can be a separate category in your breakdown. Then gather your worship attendance according to each worship time. Select the single largest worship attendance, and get a ratio of the Christian education attendance to the corresponding worship attendance.

It is possible to have a space problem in the nursery during the worship service and not to have a problem during the Christian education time.

Once you have completed this breakdown, determine the numbers in each age group as a percent of the total number in your Christian education program. For example, if your 9:45 worship service is your largest, then compare that service to the 11:00 Christian education program. Also be sure to look at the attendance numbers in the nursery and preschool program during the 9:45 service. Remember that nursery and preschool age children will use this space up to two hours while services are held in the worship center. Therefore, it is possible to have a space problem in the nursery during the worship service and not to have a problem during the Christian education time.

The ratios of Christian education to worship will be a reflection of the demographics of your membership and of your ministry programs. The goal is to make sure that your leadership team has a complete understanding of your membership and the attendance ratios of each ministry program in your church. Look for the ratios of growth in each area; compare them and see if there is a pattern. Did each group grow by the same percent? Is one sector clearly growing faster than the others? Did you start a new ministry or hire a new staff member, or is the demographic of your community changing?

The same analysis needs to be done for the weekday ministries. Look at the

Parking is often the limiting factor in the growth of a church and must always be considered as your team plans for growth.

type of activities that your fellowship is involved with: day school, Bible studies, weddings, and funerals. Ask if there is a weekday ministry that needs additional space.

This analysis should include the administration area, the music area, storage, and kitchen area. Often during this analysis, it is possible to identify changes to your ministry programs that will help your church continue growing without the addition of any more space. As with every other step in this journey, think about the information you are gathering, question any results that do not seem consistent with your understanding of your church, and look for creative ways to solve the problems you identify. The more efficient your church is with the space you have, the more effective you can be with your ministries and the more you can continue to grow and impact your community.

Using standard square footage allocations, you can compile a program based on these standards and determine how much space your church will need to adequately provide for the current attendance. This program is based on the net square footage required for each ministry. To arrive at a total overall area, you will need to add an additional 40 to 45 percent to these numbers to account for the corridors, restrooms, and associated service space.

During this analysis, have someone count the cars in your parking lots and compare this number to the number in worship. If you have 1000 people on site in the 9:45 worship service and 500 cars in the parking lot, your ratio is one car for every two people. This ratio is also dependent on the demographic of your membership. It usually stays fairly consistent as you grow unless you add an additional worship or education opportunity. Add the parking ratio to the numbers you are tracking as your church grows. Additional parking will always be a factor as you grow in worship attendance—parking is often the limiting factor in the growth of a church and must always be considered as your team plans for growth.

GATHER ACCURATE FACTS ABOUT YOUR CHURCH CAMPUS

Gather information on your current facilities. Compile an accurate drawing of your existing facilities—you may need your design team to help you with this. Once you have this drawing, label each room that is used on Sunday mornings. Some rooms may be used twice and this should be noted by adding the proper labels. Next, add up all of the space being used by each of the age groups identified in your membership analysis. Be sure to include the space dedicated to your worship service.

Then add up all the space used for administration, fellowship, music, and any other dedicated use. If you add up all of the space being used for ministry and subtract it from the total square footage in your facility, you will get the ratio of *net useable* area to *total* area, or as is commonly said among designers— the *net-to-gross ratio.*

Be sure to give each age group and ministry a different color. Then, color code your existing facility by use. Look for patterns. Are the groups organized efficiently? Is it easy to find each area of ministry? Does it appear that your church is using its existing space efficiently and effectively?

Once you have completed this analysis, compare the actual area that your church uses for each ministry with the recommended area you calculated in the membership analysis. Look for groups that vary by more than 10 percent from the recommended areas. Can the leadership team explain the variance? Is there a special program that requires more space than average? Or is there space that is not being used efficiently and that can be reallocated to help another ministry continue growing?

When the totals of both actual and recommended square footages are added up and compared, your team will begin to have an understanding of your existing membership and facilities and what needs to be added in order to get your facilities back in balance. This information does not tell you where or how to add the additional space—only that you need additional space to meet the needs of your existing membership.

After your team has an understanding and agrees on where you church needs to add space in order to meet the needs of the existing membership, your team can easily project the needs of your church, especially if your goal is to continue to grow. The leadership team can make a projection of the growth over a period of time, and by increasing the worship attendance and leaving all of the other ratios the same, can see quickly how much total area would need to be added to keep your facility in balance with the worship attendance. If your leadership team feels that the demographics of the church will change, you can adjust any of the ratios and again quickly see what these changes mean to the growth of your church.

After your team takes the time required to completely understand your

existing membership and the use of your existing facilities, then you can easily change the rate of growth, the ratios of worship to Christian education, or the ratio of the age groups within the Christian education program in order to generate varied scenarios of growth options for your church. Each of these scenarios will generate the associated additional space and parking requirements so that you can begin to balance the growth projections for your church with the capacity of your site.

What Is Your Site Capacity?

If the church does not have a current property survey, now is the time to hire a land surveyor to identify your property boundaries, zoning conditions, building locations, utilities, parking areas, and topographical information. This is the time to uncover any problems with the existing site. The earlier these problems are uncovered, the easier they will be to solve. A few dollars spent to uncover a potential problem now will save thousands of dollars in the construction process.

Evaluating the adequacy of the existing church property to find out if it has the capability to accommodate the expansion potential defined in your preliminary program is the next step in the journey. The design team should be able to assist you by providing preliminary site capacity studies that indicate the amount of land required for your church to build all of your proposed facilities.

If the studies indicate that the existing property is inadequate and additional land is required, this study will identify the total amount of additional land needed to meet your church's proposed program requirements. If one of the options is to move off site, these studies will also provide you with the information required to identify the development potential for any new piece of property under review.

Your site must be adequate to meet the long-term development goals set by your church. How much property does a church need? Usually, a church needs to plan on developing one useable acre for every 100 to 120 people in worship. Note that this rule of thumb is based on useable land and not land within setbacks or in unusable areas.

Also, this planning number does not allow for large recreational fields. If your church is planning to develop a large recreational ministry, you will need to add approximately three acres for each recreational field. However, recreational fields

Usually, a church needs to plan on developing one useable acre for every 100 to 120 people in worship.

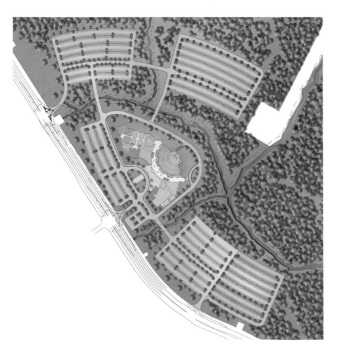

often can be built in the setbacks or otherwise unsuitable lowlands. This guideline also assumes that the site does not have an extreme length-to-width ratio, no extreme angles, no severe setback requirements, no limiting easements, no wetlands, and no steeply restrictive slopes.

This guideline also allows for what is generally regarded as an average church program. Churches that want to develop specialized ministries or weekday schools will need to provide more property for development. With an average program, a church that wants to grow to 1200 in worship attendance will need approximately 10 to 12 useable acres. That size site will provide for a balanced program of adequate parking, worship space, education space, support space, and green space.

Actually, this guideline is only to be used as a general planning principle. It cannot be arbitrarily applied to every situation, without the risk of your getting into trouble later on in your journey. As soon as you begin reviewing property for future development, you will want to take a much wiser approach by examining each site carefully in the light of the following questions:

- Are there restrictive factors on this site such as large setbacks, easements, topography, wetlands, or an odd shape of the property?

- Are there restrictive local codes that should be evaluated such as land coverage allocation, buffer requirements, water retention, or environmental impact?

- Will the church want to provide special ministries such as recreation facilities or a weekday school?

- What is the zoning classification, and can it be changed?

- Are their adequate site utilities?

- What plan will be followed in the development of the facilities—campus or multilevel building plan?

In order to make an informed decision about the suitability of any new property being considered for development by your church, your leadership team will need to evaluate seriously each potential site by dealing with all these issues. It takes a sizable investment of your resources to make a comprehensive evaluation of a potential site, but this cost is minimal in comparison to the potential risk of finding a major problem during the development of the site.

Churches that want to develop specialized ministries or weekday schools will need to provide more property for development.

Most current site zoning requirements will also have building and parking setbacks, landscape buffers, and new landscaping requirements.

Leadership teams often ask about the minimum size for a church site. The answer is always the same: if possible, always buy more than you think your church will ever need. The most frustrating problem for an established, growing church is to run out of land and find that it has no possibility of purchasing any additional property. Many churches are facing the difficult task of relocation because they have outgrown their current property, and did not have a growth strategy and a strategic master plan in place during their previous development.

These site capacity studies need to be quick, preliminary studies, undertaken with the goal of providing your leadership team with the information required to make informed decisions without your spending any more resources than necessary. If one of the options looks promising, you can ask for a more careful study to develop that one option. At this level of study you are not trying to get a detailed final design, but instead a quick study to determine the best use and capacity of the property under consideration. These studies usually begin with your gathering information about the site. Whether it is an existing site or a new site, much of this preliminary work is the same.

Be sure to check the current site zoning, and ask if there are any restrictions affecting the site's use as a church. If so, what are the requirements and possibilities to allow you to use the property? Are there possible opponents to the church using the property? Check to see if an acceleration and deceleration lane for traffic is required. Also check to see if any other requirements, such as additional right of way or sidewalks, will be required when the property is developed. Most current site zoning requirements will also have building and parking setbacks, landscape buffers, and new landscaping requirements.

The requirements for water quality and site run off continue to become more and more restrictive and must be researched as part of this study. This is also the time to verify all of the site utilities, the capacities, and the cost to make any required improvements in order to develop the site to meet your program requirements.

- Be sure to ask if there is a sanitary sewer available to the site. If so, does it have the capacity to handle the proposed development? If not, how close is the nearest sewer line?

- Will you have to install a pump to get to the line? If the sewer connection is not possible, a soils engineer will need to test the site to be sure the soils will support a septic system.

• On what side of the road will the underground utilities be located?

• What size is the nearest waterline, and will it serve the property?

• Is the nearest fire hydrant within the required distance to any location of the proposed development? If not, a new fire line will have to be run into the property at the expense of the church

• Does the site have exposed rock, or are there any unsuitable soils on the site? Removal of rock or unsuitable soil is an expensive undertaking.

It is always advisable to have subsurface borings made before the development or purchase of any property, to determine the type of soil and its bearing capacity. Also, consider road noise from major highways or nearby railroad tracks.

All of these interrelated site issues will affect the capacity of the site under study, as well as the cost to develop the site to accommodate the program under consideration by your church. Again, the goal at this stage is to uncover the problems early and to develop a strategy to solve them before you invest a lot of your resources on detailed site development studies.

Most of these are typical property development costs that may be required by the local authorities. They are not usually open for negotiations, and it will be the church's responsibility to fund them as part of the overall project cost. The site development costs are the hardest to estimate, the most difficult to control, and the hardest to value engineer once the final design is underway. Every dollar spent on site development costs comes from your overall project budget and reduces the resources available to fund the facilities needed to allow the church to grow.

If your church decides to begin looking for a new site, there are many considerations that must be examined to determine the true value of the land to the church. For example, your church may have the opportunity to purchase 35 acres for a cost of $55,000 per acre. This may appear to be a good deal when compared to the price of other sites under review. However, you may find after the site capacity study is completed that several acres will be lost to site setbacks, road expansion requirements, utility easements, and wetlands and flood plain areas. These problems might result in only 15 acres of land suitable for development.

The site capacity study will quickly determine if the land under consideration is actually more expensive per useable acre than other sites under consideration. In

The site development costs are the hardest to estimate, the most difficult to control, and the hardest to value engineer once the final design is underway.

Become aware of the community's growth by checking with your chamber of commerce and planning department for growth statistics.

your comparisons, determine the actual price of the usable acreage on each site under review. Take the total acreage and subtract the area required for setbacks, easements, road improvements, flood plains, and any other restrictions to the site. The acreage remaining for development is the actual usable area. Use this area to determine the actual cost per usable acre by dividing the total purchase price into the usable acreage.

Consider the following questions: Is the proposed site above or below the street? Whenever possible, the church should try to sit above the street, in order to be visible by the community and to ensure proper site drainage. The property should contribute to establishing a strong visual presence for the church. Does the proposed site have any gently sloping areas? The parking for the church will require a large, relatively flat area. If the grades on the site are too steep, then a large amount of site work must be planned to accommodate the development. Does the shape of the site hinder the usable acreage? Irregularly-shaped sites and ones that are too narrow will reduce the usable area at a greater rate than square or rectangular sites.

Once again, take your time and research every aspect of the potential site before you commit to its development. Is the surrounding area residential development? Does the area match your own church demographics, and is the site located near the geographic center of the congregation? Become aware of the community's growth by checking with your chamber of commerce and planning department for growth statistics. The entrance to the property should be apparent from the major traffic way. Does the speed and density of traffic at the entrance allow for access and egress? Will the local traffic authorities permit you to have an entrance where you have determined it needs to be? Is fire protection available for this location? Have an attorney check for a clear title to the property.

The site selection process is an extremely important part of the master site planning process for your church. To plan development on an undesirable location because the land seemed inexpensive or because it appeared to be a good buy could prove to be a very costly decision as your church continues to grow. The selection of property for development by a church should be done intelligently and purpose-fully, based upon the stated long-term goals of the church. The final decision should be made only after a thorough site capacity study is completed and your entire church understands the true cost of development.

Any growth that your church experiences must be supported by adequate capacity in the following areas: parking spaces, nurseries, children's rooms, and youth and adult space. You will also need to provide adequate space for fellowship and administration needs. A critical shortage in any of these areas can create a roadblock to your growth. The answer to these issues may not be the construction of new facilities, but if you are going to continue to grow, a way must be found to accommodate these requirements. Your leadership team must analyze your existing facility to get a clear overall picture of your current conditions before you can devise a plan to remove the roadblocks and continue growing.

One of the greatest opportunities for cost control in any construction project is realized during this step. By reviewing your existing ratios of worship attendance, education attendance, fellowship attendance, and parking, and by reviewing how the existing buildings are used, the design team will begin to get a feeling for your church. These findings can be projected into the future, and the design team can present several growth variations for your team to review.

This process will allow the entire leadership team to make an informed decision concerning the correct path for your journey. Once this is complete, the leadership team can begin to review building options that will solve the problems defined during this programming analysis. The preliminary program and the completed site analysis can then be combined into a preliminary master plan. At this point, the discussions should also include preliminary talks about the financial resources and staffing requirements that the completed master plan will require.

If you build a facility that is balanced in terms of parking, worship, and support facilities to be used for one hour, you can reuse this facility as many hours as you want. You just need to provide adequate parking, additional circulation, and a gathering space to provide for the multiple services. Your master plan should be based on the maximum worship attendance at one service, including the educational programs planned for the same time as the worship service. The ultimate worship capacity of your facility is then based upon the number of services you are able to provide. Your site capacity will be impacted by the other uses you propose for the site. Are you planning to provide a licensed day care, recreation facilities, a private school, an assisted living center, a retreat or conference center, or any special community use facilities? If you ever intend to provide for any of these uses you must set aside a portion of your site during the master planning process.

The completion of this step will enable the leadership team and the congregation to receive the most accurate information and insight into the needs and capabilities of the church, with a minimum expenditure of time and money. Without properly completing this step, your church would not have the

Any growth that your church experiences must be supported by adequate capacity in the following areas: parking spaces, nurseries, children's rooms, and youth and adult space.

information required to make an informed decision required to meet the needs of your congregation. A decision made without complete and accurate information could well be one of the most expensive decisions ever made by your congregation.

Your leadership team, armed with this analysis of your membership, your facilities, and your site, will be able to properly focus on making the informed decisions required to allow your church to move ahead. Keeping the entire congregation informed of this process each step of the way is vital to a successful journey. Delivering several reports back to the congregation is recommended.

Take time to report on the work in process and ask for feedback. Just a half-page handout asking for input will give your leadership team a good compass check to make sure that the entire team is on the correct course. Ask for the best aspect of the plan, if they see anything they think could be improved, if they would support this plan, and for comments.

Review these feedback sheets, tabulate the results, compile the comments, and share them with your membership. This is a good method of developing a consensus within the membership. Sharing the results of the feedback gives the entire congregation a feeling of how the reaction to the plan relates to the rest of the church membership.

LESSONS LEARNED

You realize you need more space, and everyone who comes to your church knows it. But what kind of space do you need? Can your existing space be better utilized, or do you need to add to your present facility? Do you have the land required to expand, or will you need to relocate or start a mission church? These questions need to be asked and clearly answered during the needs analysis portion of the master plan study.

A decision made without complete and accurate information could well be one of the most expensive decisions ever made by your congregation.

Your design team should help you complete a facility and a site capacity study as a part of the master planning process. These need to be completed before the church proceeds with any detailed plans or fund raising involving the membership at large. Having an unbiased, outside source help to conduct these studies allows for a better understanding of your church's needs.

Once the church gets beyond the individual emotions and feelings of the leadership team, the facts become clearer. A facility capacity study and a site capacity study will help the church clearly understand where it is now and what it will take to meet their needs over the next several years. This step needs to be completed to ensure that what the church does today will not prohibit the growth it plans for the future.

Studies like those mentioned above should include possible locations of additions and the internal relationships of functions within the church. Proper planning now will allow your church to grow and to minimize future disruptions as you continue to grow. The facility and site capacity study will help the church determine the building and site requirements necessary to meet the church's ministry goals. If possible, build for "future needs" so that you are not overcrowded the day you move in to your new facility. Remember that the total time for the planning, design, and construction of a new building will take the better part of two years. Therefore, make sure that you plan ahead, and in doing so, plan for your future.

Site Capacity Study

As you begin these site studies, ask the design team to study two extremes: the most economical and safe solution, and a radical solution that searches for the optimal solution regardless of cost. By studying both extremes, you can look for options without constraints and without setting expectations that cannot be met. The best solution to your site capacity study is often found somewhere in between these two extremes.

No longer can a church develop its existing property or buy a new site to develop without giving serious consideration to the impact its development will have on neighbors and the environment. No longer is a church development automatically considered to be a positive addition to some communities. You need to communicate with the neighbors and explain your expansion plans early in the process. Do not underestimate the power of a well-organized neighborhood association. Even under the best of circumstances, these can often be difficult negotiations. Start discussions early, be prepared for resistance, listen to concerns, and, most of all, be flexible.

Space and Dimension Recommendations

A *rule of thumb* is useful only in making approximations early in the planning process and should not be used in every case. Understanding the variables affecting their values is essential in their application to specific situations. Rules of thumb are used primarily for estimation of property, building space, and other needs during the master planning process. As a prerequisite to the actual programming and planning, they must be used prior to each phase of construction.

How to Structure Your Site Planning

- Worship center, educational space, fellowship space, administration space, and parking: allow one acre per every 100-125 members planned for in the worship center.

- Recreation building and/or outdoors recreation: allow for 2-3 additional acres per field.

Worship Center Space Allocation

- Capacity up to 500: 15 square feet per person
- 500(plus) capacity: 13 square feet per person with balconies included

Educational Building Space Allocation

- Adults: 15 square feet per person
- High School: 20 square feet per person
- Middle School: 25 square feet per person
- Elementary: 30 square feet per person
- Preschool: 35 square feet per person
- Nursery: 35 square feet per person
- Special Needs: 60 square feet per person

First unit buildings, multiple use: 35-45 square feet per person

Small churches with standard programs: 45 square feet per person

Large churches with extensive programs: 55 square feet per person

Recreation Building

- Gymnasium with small restrooms/dressing rooms and junior high-size court (42 feet x 74 feet): average 7000 square feet.
- Gymnasium with activity rooms, multipurpose rooms, secondary fellowship function, kitchen, restrooms, dressing rooms, exercise rooms, running track, senior high-size court (50 feet x 84 feet): average 15,000 square feet.

Parking

- Minimum parking requirement: one space for every 2.5 seats in worship
- Average parking requirement: one space for every 2.0 seats in worship
- Requirements for dual sessions: one space for every 1.7 seats in worship

These averages assume an efficient layout, with parking on both sides of drives and minimal islands for trees.

- 110-125 spaces per acre when developed for parking only
- Standard parking space ground coverage per space:

    90 degree: 279 square feet (two-way drive)

    45 degree: 290 square feet (one-way drive)

- Average parking space dimensions:

    Standard: 9 feet by 18 feet

    Compact: 8.5 feet by 16 feet

    Handicapped: 14 feet by 18 feet for single space

Worship Center Planning

Pulpit platform

- Front to back depth: 8-10 feet minimum—larger buildings may require 12-15 feet
- Height:

    Average of 2 feet with less than 12 rows of congregational seating

    Average of 3 feet for up to 18 rows of congregational seating

- Distance from the platform to the front pew:

    7-9 feet recommended

    10-12 feet recommended for large worship facilities

Choir Area

- Choir capacity: normally 10-12 percent of congregational capacity until the worship capacity reaches 2,000. Above this size the choir usually remains in the 200-member range.

- Choir rows: 3 feet minimum depth, back and front rows

- Seating: Movable chairs allowing 24 inches width per person

- Floor covering: hard surface such as hardwood or vinyl. Carpet is not recommended under piano or in choir area.

- Surfaces: Acoustically reflective floor, walls, and ceiling surfaces recommended

Orchestra Area
- Small orchestra or band (5-10 instrumentalists) allow 15 square feet for each
- Large orchestra or band (15-30 instrumentalists) allow15 square feet for each

Congregational Seating
Local building codes and the National Life Safety Code adopted by the locality should be consulted for additional minimum requirements.
- Row spacing:
    36 inches or more recommended
    48 inches minimum if last row against a wall
- Pew lengths and seating:
    Average space per person, 21 actual inches width (code 18 inches width)
    13 or 14 persons maximum on each row
    - Row length: 21 feet 6 inches to 23 feet 4 inches

Aisle Widths
Center or main aisle: 4 feet minimum; 5 feet or more recommended
Side aisles: 2 feet 8 inches minimum; some codes require more

Vestibule/Lobby/Narthex
- Worship center entry lobby:
    1-3 square feet per seat in worship center
    Gathering space between education and worship: approximately 20 percent of the worship center area

Balcony
- Capacity:
    Usually less than 40 percent of main floor seating
- Riser depth:
    3 feet 6 inches for first row
    3 feet 2 inches for the back row
    3 feet for other rows
- Aisles: 4 feet minimum across balcony

- Other aisles: Same as aisle width on main floor
- Stairwells: minimum of 2 to outside exits

Chapel
- Seating capacity at 15 square feet per person
- Bridal dressing room: minimum 12 feet by 12 feet recommended

Administrative
- Pastor's study: 250 square feet recommended
- Staff offices: 150 square feet recommended
- Other office space: offices for support staff, workroom(s), reception area, storage, restrooms, lounge, conference rooms, break room, and kitchenette

Music
- Rehearsal room: Capacity at least 10 percent more than worship center
- Choir area: 20 square feet per person
- Robe rooms: 6 square feet per person
- Music library: 2 square feet per choir member
- Orchestral rehearsal room: 25 square feet per person
- Individual practice rooms: 12 square feet per person
- Voice and piano practice rooms: 8 feet by 10 feet minimum

Fellowship Hall
- Dining capacity: approximately 40-60 percent of worship capacity
- Space required for table seating:
    Minimum of 13 square feet per person recommended
    Fifteen square feet per person with round tables
    Allow additional space for stage
- Institutional kitchen: approximately 25 percent size of dining area
- Basketball court:
    Clear ceiling height: 20 feet minimum, 25 feet desirable
    Side and end lanes: 3 feet minimum, 10 feet preferred
- Senior high-size court: 50 feet by 84 feet
    Room size: 70 feet by 104 feet preferred (7,280 square feet) plus
    3 feet for each additional row of spectator seating
- Junior high-size court: 42 feet by 74 feet
    Room size: 62 feet by 94 feet preferred (5,828 square feet) plus
    3 feet for each additional row of spectator seating

- Game rooms: average of 20 feet by 30 feet
- Group meeting rooms: 15 square feet per person
- Storage: a direct access room with double wide doors for roll-in table/chair carts
- Separate storage space for recreational equipment, craft supplies, kitchen pantry, janitorial supplies, and equipment
- Additional rooms or space: snacks/vending, crafts, exercise, control, and office

Mechanical and Electrical Equipment Rooms, Corridors, Restrooms
- Space requirements:
    Allow additional 40-45 percent of net program area

Provisions for the Handicapped
- Extra wide parking spaces: 10 feet space plus 4 foot clearance for wheelchair access
- Slope of walks not more than 1 foot in 20 feet
- Slope of ramps not more than 1 inch in 12 inches
- Clearances: 36 inches minimum door width, 5-foot minimum hallway width
- Restroom dimensions to allow a 5-foot turning radius
- Hand rail at ramps and grab bars in toilets
- Wheelchair spaces in the worship center
- Elevators

SAMPLE QUESTIONNAIRE
For Existing Church Data

A. SITE DATA —

1. Approximate site acreage: _____ acres
The following data will be required for proper site evaluation and planning. Please indicate which data, if any is available.

2. Boundary survey
   ❑ Yes ❑ No

3. Topographical survey
   ❑ Yes ❑ No

4. Geotechnical subsurface report
   ❑ Yes ❑ No

B. EXISTING FACILITIES —

5. Existing Sanctuary seating capacity: _____ seats
Is sanctuary a multi-purpose room?
   ❑ Yes ❑ No
If yes, then list multipurpose functions:

_____

_____

_____

6. Existing fellowship hall seating capacity:
   _____ performance seating arrangement
   _____ table seating arrangement

7. Existing music rehearsal seating capacity:
   _____ seats

8. Existing education capacities:
   _____ Preschool
   _____ Children
   _____ Youth
   _____ Adult

9. Existing parking spaces
   _____ spaces

C. CURRENT MINISTRIES —

10. Current congregational membership:
   _____ members

11. Current worship attendance:

	Time	Attendance	Style*
Sun AM	_____	_____	_____
Sun AM	_____	_____	_____
Sun AM	_____	_____	_____
Other	_____	_____	_____
Other	_____	_____	_____

* T- Traditional; C- Contemporary; B- Blended

12. Is a separate children's church provided on Sunday mornings?

	Time	Attendance	Age
Service	_____	_____	_____
Service	_____	_____	_____
Service	_____	_____	_____

13. Special worship services (if applicable):

	Type	Attendance	Day/Time
Service	_____	_____	_____
Service	_____	_____	_____
Service	_____	_____	_____

14. Current education attendance:

	Session 1 Attendance	Session 2 Attendance
Time	_____	_____
Preschool (0-5 years)	_____	_____
Children (Grades 1-5)	_____	_____
Youth	_____	_____
Adults	_____	_____

15. Attendance records:
A. Average worship total

	Attendance – Largest	All Services
5 years ago	_____	_____
4 years ago	_____	_____
3 years ago	_____	_____
2 years ago	_____	_____
1 year ago	_____	_____
current	_____	_____

B. Average education

	Attendance – Largest	Total
5 years ago	_____	_____
4 years ago	_____	_____
3 years ago	_____	_____
2 years ago	_____	_____
1 year ago	_____	_____
current	_____	_____

16. Current church ministries—activities and frequency of programs, services or activities (not including Sunday worship or education):

Activity	Interval
_____	_____
_____	_____
_____	_____
_____	_____
_____	_____

17. Current music programs:
A. Adult music membership

	Session 1 Attendance	Session 2 Attendance
Time	_____	_____
Male	_____	_____
Female	_____	_____

QUESTIONNAIRE *(Continued)*

B. List other music programs:

Program	Attendance
Praise team	_____
Band	_____
Orchestra	_____
Children's choir	_____
Youth choir	_____

18. Current library/media program

A. Library

❏ Yes ❏ No

B. If yes, approximate number of volumes

_____

19. Current outdoor recreation programs:

_____

_____

_____

_____

20. Current indoor recreation programs:

_____

_____

_____

_____

21. Current full-time and part-time ministerial staff, including support staff (5 years future):

Staff position	Full-time	Part-time
Pastor	❏	❏
Associate pastor	❏	❏
Music minister	❏	❏
Youth minister	❏	❏
Children's minister	❏	❏
Business administrator	❏	❏
Singles minister	❏	❏
Preschool director	❏	❏
_____	❏	❏
_____	❏	❏
_____	❏	❏
_____	❏	❏
_____	❏	❏
_____	❏	❏
_____	❏	❏

22. Current weekday childcare/education programs (future):

Pre-kindergarten	❏ Yes	❏ No
Kindergarten	❏ Yes	❏ No
Preschool(Ages 2-3)	❏ Yes	❏ No
Licensed daycare	❏ Yes	❏ No
Elementary school (Grades ____ - ____)	❏ Yes	❏ No
Middle school (Grades ____ - ____)	❏ Yes	❏ No
High school (Grades ____ - ____)	❏ Yes	❏ No
Mother's morning out	❏ Yes	❏ No

A. List any other accreditation requirements:

_____

_____

_____

_____

23. Current non-english speaking ministries:

_____

_____

_____

_____

24. Current benevolence ministries:

_____

_____

_____

_____

D. FUTURE MINISTRY CRITERIA —

25. Based upon demographic data and objectives of the church with respect to outreach programs, what growth projections are considered reasonable:

	5 Years Out	10 Years Out	15 Years Out
Church Membership	_____	_____	_____
Worship Attendance	_____	_____	_____
Education Attendance	_____	_____	_____
Preschool Attendance	_____	_____	_____
Children's Attendance	_____	_____	_____
Youth Attendance	_____	_____	_____
Adult Attendance	_____	_____	_____

26. Based upon demographic data, available land area, church philosophy with regard to starting mission churches, and basic goals of staff, state ideal maximum congregational membership:

_____ members

27. If growth potential is desirably unlimited, is additional property available?

❏ Yes ❏ No

QUESTIONNAIRE *(Continued)*

28. Future library/media center growth:

	5 years out	10 years out	15 years out
Collection Growth	_____	_____	_____
Weekly Operation Hours	_____	_____	_____

29. Future music ministry programs:

	5 years out	10 years out	15 years out
Praise team	❏	❏	❏
Band	❏	❏	❏
Adult choir	❏	❏	❏
Orchestra	❏	❏	❏
Youth choir	❏	❏	❏
Handbells	❏	❏	❏
_____	❏	❏	❏
_____	❏	❏	❏
_____	❏	❏	❏

30. Should provisions for drama be incorporated into design of activity spaces?

Space	❏ Yes	❏ No
Sanctuary	❏ Yes	❏ No
Fellowship hall	❏ Yes	❏ No
Children's church	❏ Yes	❏ No
Youth	❏ Yes	❏ No
_____	❏ Yes	❏ No
_____	❏ Yes	❏ No
_____	❏ Yes	❏ No

31. Future fellowship activities (fellowship hall and kitchen):

A.

	5 Years Out	10 Years Out	15 Years Out
Banquet Seating Capacity	_____	_____	_____

B. Is it acceptable to utilize fellowship hall space for adult education space by utilizing a system of moving partitions to subdivide space?

❏ Yes   ❏ No

C. List activities other than large meal time gatherings that the fellowship hall will be utilized for:

_____

_____

_____

_____

32. Would a small chapel (150-350 seats) be desirable when sanctuary seating capacity reaches 1,000 seats or more?

❏ Yes   ❏ No

33. If counseling services are provided, would they be provided within the church office suite or at a remote location?

_____

_____

_____

_____

34. Future recreation and leisure activities:

	5 years out	10 years out	15 years out
Softball	❏	❏	❏
Soccer	❏	❏	❏
Football	❏	❏	❏
Playgrounds	❏	❏	❏
Basketball	❏	❏	❏
Volleyball	❏	❏	❏
Aerobics	❏	❏	❏

Arts & crafts	❏	❏	❏
Game room	❏	❏	❏
_____	❏	❏	❏
_____	❏	❏	❏
_____	❏	❏	❏

35. Future special activities requiring building usage:

	5 years out	10 years out	15 years out
Scouts	❏	❏	❏
Lock-ins	❏	❏	❏
Youth rallies	❏	❏	❏
Day camp	❏	❏	❏
VBS	❏	❏	❏
Conferences	❏	❏	❏
Concerts	❏	❏	❏
_____	❏	❏	❏
_____	❏	❏	❏

36. Can multipurpose space be used for any of the following combinations?

Worship/education	❏ Yes	❏ No
Education/fellowship	❏ Yes	❏ No
Sunday school/school Classrooms	❏ Yes	❏ No
Recreation/fellowship	❏ Yes	❏ No
Recreation/worship	❏ Yes	❏ No

Comments: _____

_____

_____

37. Sanctuary seating preferred layout:
Conventional

Rectangular nave	❏ Yes	❏ No
Fan-shaped nave	❏ Yes	❏ No
Balcony	❏ Yes	❏ No
Terraced	❏ Yes	❏ No

QUESTIONNAIRE *(Continued)*

38. Is a radio ministry anticipated in the future?

    ❑ Yes   ❑ No

39. Is a television ministry anticipated in the future?

    ❑ Yes   ❑ No

40. Frequency of communion services:

    _____

    _____

    _____

    _____

41. Frequency of baptismal services:

    _____

    _____

    _____

    _____

42. Preferred architectural style:

Strongly traditional	❑ Yes	❑ No
Moderately Traditional	❑ Yes	❑ No
Rustic	❑ Yes	❑ No
Contemporary	❑ Yes	❑ No
Modern	❑ Yes	❑ No
Postmodern	❑ Yes	❑ No

43. Will sentimental attachment to any existing structure preclude its eventual replacement?

    ❑ Yes   ❑ No

44. Regardless of sanctuary seating capacities, will double session worship services be implemented for congregational convenience?

    ❑ Yes   ❑ No

45. Is it desirable to provide assembly space for any of the following departments?

Children	❑ Yes	❑ No
Youth	❑ Yes	❑ No
Adult	❑ Yes	❑ No

E. Financial Resources —

46. Church membership social/economic class breakdown:

Church membership	Percentage
Upper class	_____
Upper middle class	_____
Middle class	_____
Lower middle class	_____

47. Projected annual operating budget:

5 years ago	_____
Last year	_____
Current	_____
5 years out	_____
10 years out	_____
15 years out	_____

48. Current church debt (Operations and salaries):

    _____

    Terms: _____

    _____

    _____

    _____

49. Is the church to carry any short-term debt or long-term debt:

    _____

    _____

    _____

    _____

    _____

    _____

    _____

CHRISTIAN EDUCATION WORKSHEET
For Existing Church Data

PRESCHOOL DIVISION

Organization		No. of Rooms	Current		Attend % of Enroll	5 Years Ago		Last Year		5 Years Out		10 Years Out	
	Ages		Enroll	Attend		Enroll	Attend	Enroll	Attend	Enroll	Attend	Enroll	Attend
Sunday School	0-1												
	1												
	2												
	3												
	4												
	5												
TOTAL													

CHILDREN'S DIVISION

Organization		No. of Rooms	Current		Attend % of Enroll	5 Years Ago		Last Year		5 Years Out		10 Years Out	
	Grades		Enroll	Attend		Enroll	Attend	Enroll	Attend	Enroll	Attend	Enroll	Attend
Sunday School	1												
	2												
	3												
	4												
	5												
TOTAL													

YOUTH DIVISION

Organization		No. of Rooms	Current		Attend % of Enroll	5 Years Ago		Last Year		5 Years Out		10 Years Out	
	Grades		Enroll	Attend		Enroll	Attend	Enroll	Attend	Enroll	Attend	Enroll	Attend
Sunday School	6												
	7												
	8												
	9												
	10												
	11												
	12												
TOTAL													

ADULT DIVISION

Organization		No. of Rooms	Current		Attend % of Enroll	5 Years Ago		Last Year		5 Years Out		10 Years Out	
	Class		Enroll	Attend		Enroll	Attend	Enroll	Attend	Enroll	Attend	Enroll	Attend
Sunday School	1												
	2												
	3												
	4												
	5												
TOTAL													

ATTENDANCE PROJECTION STUDY

Worship Time 9:15 a.m.

	Existing	Phase 1	Phase 2	Phase 3
Worship Center Seating	650	1,350	2,800	4,500
Worship Attendance	**578**	**1,200**	**2,489**	**4,000**
Percent of Capacity	89%			
% Increase	108%	107%	61%	
% Education vs Worship	143%			
Total Christian Education	**827**	**1,716**	**3,559**	**5,720**
Senior Adults	20%	350	712	1,144
Adult Sunday School	22%	375	783	1,258
Singles	7%	125	259	417
College	3%	50	104	167
High School	8%	96	285	458
Middle School	8%	120	285	458
Elementary School	20%	400	712	1,144
Preschool	6%	100	207	333
Nursery	6%	100	207	333
People on Campus per Hour	**1,405**	**2,916**	**6,048**	**9,720**

Worship Time 11:00 a.m.

	Existing	Phase 1	Phase 2	Phase 3
Worship Center Seating	650	1,350	2,800	4,500
Worship Attendance	**625**	**1,298**	**2,692**	**4,327**
Percent of Capacity	96%			
% Increase	108%	107%	61%	
% Education vs Worship	95%			
Total Christian Education	**594**	**1,233**	**2,558**	**4,111**
Senior Adults	0%	0	0	0
Adult Sunday School	35%	432	895	1,439
Singles	0%	0	0	0
College	0%	0	0	0
High School	10%	123	256	411
Middle School	10%	123	256	411
Elementary School	21%	259	537	863
Preschool	12%	148	307	493
Nursery	12%	148	307	493
People on Campus per Hour	**1,219**	**2,531**	**5,250**	**8,438**

EXISTING SPACE ALLOCATION COMPARISON

1650 SEAT SANCTUARY FUNCTION	SPACE ALLOCATION	PEOPLE	S.F.	(A) REQUIRED	(B) ACTUAL	(B-A)VARIANCE
Sanctuary	Seating	1,452	11	15,972	14,350	-1,622 sf
Chancel	12% of Seating	198	12	2,376	1,200	-1,176 sf
Narthex	25% of Seating	413	13	5,363	5,300	-63 sf
Sub Total Seating		**1,650**		**23,711**	**20,850**	**-2,861**
Chapel	Seating	315	11	3,465	0	3,465 sf
Chancel	10% of Seating	35	12	420	0	-420 sf
Narthex	20% of Seating	70	13	910	0	-910 sf
Sub Total Chapel		**350**		**4,795**	**0**	**-4,795 sf**
Sunday School Attendance at	100%					
Senior Adults	20.0% of total	330	15	4,950	4,000	-950
Adults	23.0% of total	380	15	5,693	6,500	808 sf
Singles	8.0%	132	15	1,980	1,250	-730
College	3.0%	50	15	743	1,000	258
High School	8.0% of total	132	20	2,640	2,500	-140 sf
Middle School	8.0% of total	132	20	2,640	2,500	-140 sf
Elementary School	20.0% of total	330	25	8,250	9,200	950 sf
Preschool	6.0% of total	99	30	2,970	3,300	330 sf
Nursery	6.0% of total	99	35	3,465	3,800	335 sf
Sub Total Sunday School	**102%**	**1,650**		**33,330**	**34,050**	**720**
Recreation / FLC				22,200	22,000	-200 sf
Fellowship Hall	60.0% of Sanctuary Seating	990	13	12,870	12,000	-870 sf
Administration	3.0% of Sanctuary Seating	50	225	11,138	10,500	-638 sf
Media Center / Bookstore	2.0% of Sanctuary Seating	33	25	825	390	-435 sf
Music Rehearsal Suite	10.0% of Sanctuary Seating	165	40	6,600	4,200	-2,400 sf
Storage	15.0% of Sunday School			5,000	6,000	1,001 sf
Kitchen	25.0% of Fellowship Hall			3,218	3,700	483 sf
Sub Total Support				**61,850**	**58,790**	**-3,060 sf**
Total Net Area				123,685	113,690	-9,995 sf
Circulation / RR / Mech. / Misc.	45% of Net Area			55,658	70,000	14,342 sf
Total Campus Area				**179,343**	**183,690**	**4,347 sf**
Property	1 acre per 115 people			14.35	14.34	-0.01 acres
Parking	1 car per 1.7 Seat			971	928	-43 spaces

FUTURE SPACE ALLOCATION COMPARISON

2800 SEAT SANCTUARY FUNCTION	SPACE ALLOCATION	PEOPLE	S.F.	(A) REQUIRED	(B) ACTUAL	(B-A)VARIANCE
Sanctuary	Seating	2,520	11	27,720	14,350	13,370 sf
Chancel	10% of Seating	280	12	3,360	1,200	-2,160 sf
Narthex	25% of Seating	700	13	9,100	5,300	-3,800 sf
Sub Total Seating		**2,800**		**40,180**	**20,850**	-19,330
Chapel	Seating	315	11	3,465	0	-3,465 sf
Chancel	10% of Seating	35	12	420	0	-420 sf
Narthex	20% of Seating	70	13	910	0	-910 sf
Sub Total Chapel		**350**		**4,795**	**0**	-4,795 sf
Sunday School Attendance at	120%					
Senior Adults	20.0% of total	672	15	10,080	4,000	-6,080
Adults	23.0% of total	773	15	11,592	6,500	-5,092 sf
Singles	8.0%	269	15	4,032	1,250	-2,782
College	3.0%	101	15	1,512	1,000	-512
High School	8.0% of total	269	20	5,376	2,500	-2,876 sf
Middle School	8.0% of total	269	20	5,376	2,500	-2,876 sf
Elementary School	20.0% of total	672	25	16,800	9,200	-7,600 sf
Preschool	6.0% of total	202	30	6,048	3,300	-2,748 sf
Nursery	6.0% of total	202	35	7,056	3,800	-3,256 sf
Sub Total Sunday School	**102%**	**3,360**		**67,872**	**34,050**	-33,822
Recreation / FLC				22,200	22,000	-200 sf
Fellowship Hall	60.0% of Sanctuary Seating	1,680	13	21,840	12,000	-9,840 sf
Administration	3.0% of Sanctuary Seating	84	225	18,900	10,500	-8,400 sf
Media Center / Bookstore	2.0% of Sanctuary Seating	56	25	1,400	390	-1,010 sf
Music Rehearsal Suite	10.0% of Sanctuary Seating	280	40	11,200	4,200	-7,000 sf
Storage	15.0% of Sunday School			10,181	6,000	-4,181 sf
Kitchen	25.0% of Fellowship Hall			5,460	3,700	-1,760 sf
Sub Total Support				**91,181**	**58,790**	-32,391 sf
Total Net Area				204,028	113,690	-90,338 sf
Circulation / RR / Mech. / Misc.	45% of Net Area			91,813	70,000	-21,813 sf
Total Campus Area				**295,840**	**183,690**	-112,150 sf
Property	1 acre per 115 people			24.35	14.34	-10.01 acres
Parking	1 car per 1.5 Seat			1,867	1,300	-567 spaces

STEP SEVEN

Develop Your Strategic Master Plan

PHASED STRATEGIC MASTER PLAN

▼

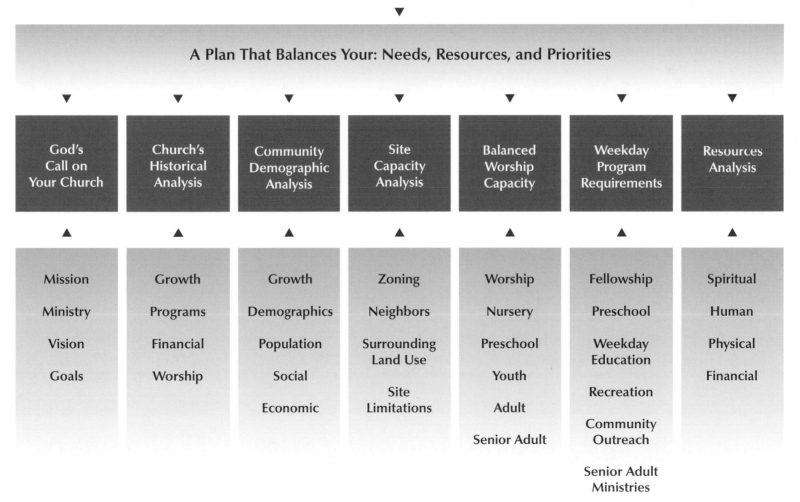

A Plan That Balances Your: Needs, Resources, and Priorities

God's Call on Your Church	Church's Historical Analysis	Community Demographic Analysis	Site Capacity Analysis	Balanced Worship Capacity	Weekday Program Requirements	Resources Analysis
Mission	Growth	Growth	Zoning	Worship	Fellowship	Spiritual
Ministry	Programs	Demographics	Neighbors	Nursery	Preschool	Human
Vision	Financial	Population	Surrounding Land Use	Preschool	Weekday Education	Physical
Goals	Worship	Social	Site Limitations	Youth	Recreation	Financial
		Economic		Adult	Community Outreach	
				Senior Adult	Senior Adult Ministries	

STEP SEVEN

Develop a Strategic Master Plan

Focus, clarity, and determination are among the greatest gifts that we can receive from the Lord, especially when we are entering a building program of any kind. When Nehemiah sensed that the intensity of the work on the walls had grown to a point of being overwhelming, he challenged the people to *remember* the Lord. You may wonder why this would be important. As with any process, the journey from start to finish can become long and involved. Over time, a project that began with celebration and feelings of bravery and excitement can become a long, drawn out task that has to travel through many phases—some of which will be difficult and stressful. There will be those in your group who may tire, while others will stay strong and focused on the completion of the project.

Nehemiah understood the meaning of having a fixed focus. He set the eyes of his heart and mind on the finished task and not on the distractions along the way. He knew that if he *remembered* the Lord in all that he did, he would be given the strength he needed to face the challenges as they came and to complete the work.

However, he did not keep this truth to himself. He encouraged others to do the same and to fight for their families and friends. As you do for your church, Nehemiah had a vision for the future—one that he knew was from the Lord. Sometimes, the fear of the future and the risk that is required to complete a project like the one Nehemiah and the people of Israel had undertaken, can seem overwhelming. Be sure that when you take a step of faith and begin to trust the Lord for a new avenue of ministry through the expansion of your church campus, there will be opposition. Yet, this will fade as you go forward and trust God to work out every detail to your advantage—no matter how great or small.

SET THE RIGHT COURSE EARLY

I have written this to say that any journey like the one you are about to take will have many twists and turns. However, developing and then following a well-thought-out road map will help you to remain steady throughout the entire process. This is what a strategic master plan is for your church—a road map and

After I looked things over, I stood up and said to the nobles, the officials and the rest of the people, "Don't be afraid of them. Remember the Lord, who is great and awesome, and fight for your brothers, your sons and your daughters, your wives and your homes."
—NEHEMIAH 4:14

When you take a step of faith and begin to trust the Lord for a new avenue of ministry through the expansion of your church campus, there will be opposition.

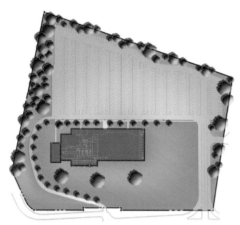

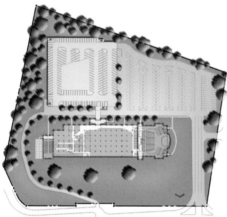

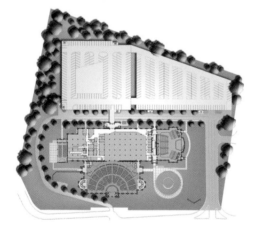

Planning for a new construction project is part jigsaw puzzle, part mathematical formula, and part art.

the most crucial part to your journey. Developing a strategic master plan is part science and part art. It takes an unusual group of individuals to gather the information needed, to analyze it, and then to determine the best solution for your church to take as it considers its future and how to expand its ministry. Many people are good at gathering and organizing information. Some are great at analyzing information, and others are talented in the creative aspects of planning the destination of a journey.

It is rare to find one individual who is really talented and skilled at every part of this process. For this reason, these complex journeys are most successful when they are the result of a partnership of teams—each bringing a unique set of skills and experiences into play so that the right solution for your church will be found. The key to making this process work is uniting all information in a well-organized format so that it can be easily explained to your congregation.

The most successful strategic master planning involves the true collaboration of the leadership team and a professional design team, whose special training and experience gives them the expertise required to undertake the master planning process for a church. The correct design team will bring talent and insight to this planning process, save you from taking many detours, and help bring an impartial view to your master planning process. In most cases, they have spent years working with other churches developing master plans that satisfy a broad spectrum of needs, programs, properties, and challenges. This experience and the time spent listening to the various needs of churches, big and small, will assist you as you develop your own master plan and prepare to build.

Usually, most of us like easy formulas, sure things, low risk strategies, and clear steps to follow that will ensure our success. By now, you probably have realized that this book does not offer an easy, step-by-step formula. Honestly, the journey you are undertaking will be complex and risky at times. As events over which you have little control unfold, you will find yourself seeking a process to discover the proper path to follow.

Planning for a new construction project is part jigsaw puzzle, part mathematical formula, and part art. The only way to solve the formula is to fix the value of a few unknowns and then to solve the problem. I mentioned this earlier, but it bears restating: if you do not like the solution to that equation, then you can change some of the assumptions you made and solve the problem once again.,

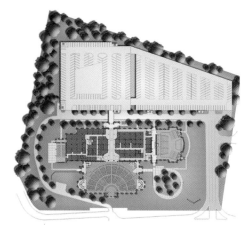

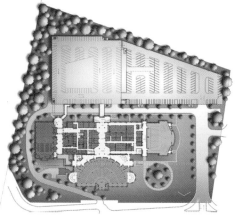

A strategic master site plan balances your history, vision, physical facilities, site capacity, and resources.

Continue changing the fixed values until you arrive at a solution that works for your church. This should add a great deal of peace of mind as you move forward with your project.

In actuality, the leadership team has two congregations to consider during the strategic master planning process: your existing congregation and your future congregation. There are also two conclusions to draw on from the establishment of your strategic master plan: one provides only for your existing members. The other provides space for growth and for new members.

When you are projecting the future growth of your church, you need to be honest about all of your projections. If you are projecting your yearly growth to increase over the next few years, you need to have a plan in place to support this projection—especially since your growth rate will probably not increase without a corresponding change, either through additional staff, programs, worship services, or facilities. Be sure to set realistic growth goals to match your strategic master plan. The assumptions you make about your growth will impact your ability to fund the future phases of your strategic master plan. An incorrect assumption of your growth will impact the resources available for the continued development.

The time of strategic master planning for a church is a time when every program and ministry in your church becomes unfrozen. It is a time when every ministry, every option, and every opportunity has its place in your discussions concerning the future of your church.

Developing a strategic master plan involves combining your church's mission with the comprehensive analysis of your membership and programs, along with future ministry plans, the capacity of existing buildings, and the capacity of your property. This strategic master plan also deals with the development of the church's dream and the translation of this dream into a plan that addresses the space and property required.

Over the years, we have found that unless there are some extraordinary circumstances, it is difficult for an existing congregation to build a new worship facility that is more than 2.5 to 3 times larger that their existing sanctuary. The final project budget is almost always directly proportional to the operating budget, making it very difficult to build more than 2.5 to 3 times more seating than is available at the beginning of the journey. Therefore, make sure you set goals that are realistic even at this phase of the process. Otherwise you may create a detour that will add several unexpected months to your working schedule.

A strategic master plan is needed in order match your future goals and dreams with resources that are available today. It is a plan that balances your mission, history, vision, physical facilities, site capacity, and resources. You do this by implementing a phased development program based on the strategic master plan that you are developing. The time you spend listening to your congregation and working with your design team drawing up this plan will be critical to your outcome.

From these congregational "wish lists," the design team can begin to develop the phased site development plan, preliminary floor plans, and preliminary exterior sketches that depict the characteristics of the new facility being designed to meet your needs. When refined and completed, these studies and sketches will become the basis of your phased master plan and also will provide the basic materials you will need. They also will be very useful in the capital fund campaign by providing visual images of your proposed development for your congregation.

The strategic master plan has the ability to bring into focus all of the complex issues that touch the mission and work of your church.

This process will help the leadership team evaluate and prioritize both the program and the ministry needs. When it is done properly, the strategic master plan has the ability to bring into focus all of the complex issues that touch the mission and work of your church, the potential for the development and utilization of your property, the design and construction of church buildings, and the required development of facilities to match the growth of the church. This strategic plan will evolve from surveys and studies of your church and your community. It also emerges as you uncover your church's strategy for growth. The vision and the expertise of the leadership team and the design team also play key rolls in the development of this plan.

The goal of every strategic master plan needs to be the successful uniting of your church's mission and ministries with your property, facilities, and resources. All of these elements need to be woven into your strategic master planning process. Your mission and ministries are the driving forces in the master plan. Once defined, these become the standards which are used to determine the property and facilities required to meet your church's mission and ministries. As you work to develop your church's master plan, remember that this is the fundamental step required to keep your planning priorities in the proper perspective. Property and facilities are not the primary concern of your church's master plan, but they can become the only focus if not properly and effectively linked to your mission and ministry.

PROCESS THREE: STRATEGIC MASTER PLANNING

Strategic Focus Activity	Progressive Stages of Process	Tactical Focus Activity
DEFINE Mission Ministry Vision Goals	**3.1** God's Call on Your Church	**COMMUNICATE STATEMENT OF:** Mission Ministry Vision Goals
GATHER Growth data Program data Financial data Worship data	**3.2** Church Historical Analysis	**ESTABLISH** Church growth Programs Finance Worship
GATHER Growth data Demographic projections Population projections Social/Economic projections	**3.3** Community Demographic Analysis	**ESTABLISH** Community Growth changes
GATHER Zoning requirements Neighborhood issues Surrounding land uses Sub-surface data Boundary survey Topographic survey Utilities survey	**3.4** Site Capacity Analysis	**COORDINATE** Site Zoning Neighborhood issues Boundary Topography Sub-surface conditions Utility availability/location
ANALYZE Worship attendance Nursery attendance Preschool attendance Youth attendance Adult attendance Seniors attendance	**3.5** Worship Balance Analysis	**GOALS FOR** Worship attendance Nursery attendance Preschool attendance Youth attendance Adult attendance Seniors attendance
ANALYZE Fellowship attendance Preschool attendance Christian education Recreational goals Community outreach Senior adult ministry	**3.6** Weekday Program Requirements	**GOALS FOR** Fellowship Preschool Christian education Recreational Community outreach Senior adult ministry
ANALYZE Human potential Financial potential Facility potential Property potential	**3.7** Resource Analysis	**DETERMINE** Human potential Financial potential Facility potential Property potential
SYNTHESIZE	**Prioritized Planning Synthesis**	**PRIORITIZE PHASING**

The goal for every master plan is to also provide a balance of the requirements for parking, worship, education, fellowship, administration, and recreation. By the time you have developed a strategic master plan, you should begin to see the proper relationship emerging in the process. The leadership team also should have a comprehensive understanding of God's call on your church, along with your church's history of growth and ministry; the demographics of your community; the analysis of your membership, facilities, and site; a sense of your church's growth potential; the ministry programs of your church; and a preliminary resource analysis. Pulling all of this information together is the hard work of strategic master planning, yet without this information in hand a successful strategic master plan is almost impossible to complete.

The goal for every master plan is to also provide a balance of the requirements for parking, worship, education, fellowship, administration, and recreation.

Your leadership team needs a thorough understanding of your church's existing balance of ministries. They also will need to be able to project these needs into the future so your church will be able to continue to grow. This is the real benefit of the strategic master planning process—to provide a strategic plan to meet all of your needs, and to devise a method of meeting these needs with a phased development plan using the resources available to the church. Through the use of the strategic master plan, your church can make an informed decision on the current priorities, and be confident that the future priorities can be constructed as additional resources become available.

PHASING A STRATEGIC MASTER SITE PLAN

Think of your strategic master plan as a pattern or road map for the long-term development of your church—a map to be used in charting the course of all of your future development. It is a tool to be used to divide your church's long-term dream into manageable phases so that its leaders can pace its development and adapt to changes in its future ministry needs.

Here is a checklist to use as you prepare to develop your strategic master plan:

• Review the needs of your church and explore the path that you will need to travel in order to provide a solution for those needs.

• Seek guidance from leaders and committee members from other churches.

   Ask them what was fulfilling and insightful about their journeys.

   Ask them to share with you where they took wrong turns so you can avoid making the same mistakes.

- Gather books and guidelines to help you organize and plan your journey.

- Gather as much information as possible! The resources you need for a successful journey are best gathered before you begin. The completion of a successful journey depends more on what you prepare to take with you than it does on what you encounter along the way. You cannot always predict, but you can be prepared.

- Commit this project to prayer—seeking wisdom, guidance, and courage for the entire journey.

- Take as much time as required to prepare for this journey. The time you spend in preparation will produce huge dividends once you set out.

The distance from your present realities to the possibilities in your future is likely so great that many church members would become overwhelmed by the challenge of planning for the long-term development. The development of a phased master plan provides the bridge required to communicate with your church—a comprehensive phased plan developed to reach your long-term ministry goals. The phasing of your master plan allows you to create "bite-sized" portions of the dream. It also allows you to present your long-term goals to the congregation in a well-thought-out and non-threatening manner.

A new church with 300 people in worship may have a vision and see an opportunity to impact its community, and possibly have an attendance of 2000 people within the next 10 years. Its master plan is a working document providing it with certain milestone markers that indicate the multiple phases of construction required in order to provide the facilities needed for future growth.

Of course, this plan will need to be reviewed and updated at each phase of the church's development. There will be times when it will need to be adjusted to reflect the changes that have occurred since the initial analysis. This includes any program changes which are required to meet the church's ministry needs. Nevertheless, a strategic master plan is a road map and a tool for the church to use in every step of its journey.

Finding a way to balance the needs and current resources of your church is one of the key benefits to the strategic master planning process. As each phase of the strategic master plan is developed, the church must continue to balance the needs and the resources available for the development.

Finding a way to balance the needs and current resources of your church is one of the key benefits to the strategic master planning process.

As part of the master planning process, you will need to rank all of your needs by priority, and then balance your resources with your top priorities.

If your church tries to provide more of your needs than you can adequately fund in one phase of development, the problem of inadequate resources will frustrate the entire process. As part of the master planning process, you will need to rank all of your needs by priority and then balance your resources with your top priorities. The critical decision required at each phase of your church's development is to provide the space for your continued growth in worship and education—either with program changes such as adding additional services, or by providing additional capacity.

During each phase of development, the strategic master plan must balance space needs for buildings with parking and green space requirements. As churches find more efficient ways to use their facilities, parking requirements increase and consume larger portions of their property. Many local regulations also require a certain percentage of the property be retained for green space. These requirements influence the entire development of your site and must be designed into the initial master plan.

Keeping all of these issues in balance during each phase of your development will require well-informed decisions and careful advance planning at each stage of your development. Make sure that the design team has completed all of its duties, including all of the related site requirements, before your strategic master plan is fully developed.

IT'S OKAY TO MAKE ADJUSTMENTS

A properly designed strategic master plan should not be developed and then blindly followed without further evaluation. The master plan is designed to be a working document that should be carefully studied and reevaluated prior to each new journey or phase of development. New analysis and information should be brought into this evaluation every time you build. As the master plan is developed, the church should continue to gather data and to develop an improved perception of the trends and conditions that could be only vaguely understood when the strategic master plan was originally developed.

Every strategic master plan will need to be adjusted as future phases are developed. Therefore, the master plan is never completely finished, but remains a work in progress. However, the plan must be firm enough to provide your church with true guidance and direction, and flexible enough to allow for modification to accommodate changing conditions and circumstances. One key to a successful strategic master plan is the proper solution to vehicular and pedestrian circulation systems. Adequate access to the site is a critical aspect to the plan. It is also important that the overall pedestrian circulation be well-thought-out and adequately connect each phase of the strategic master plan. The plan also should be adaptable to allow for minor adjustments in overall capacity as needed, and where feasible, the sequence of phasing should be flexible as future circumstances dictate.

A fundamental building block of the strategic master plan is the overall space allocation for your church. Based on the existing ministries of your church and the ratio of the current attendance for each of these ministries, you can determine an existing space allocation and then develop a proposed space allocation for each phase of your growth. If you determine that an average of 20 percent of the worship attendance is in the nursery each week, and you plan to increase you worship attendance by 40 percent, you need to make sure that you provide additional capacity for that area or you will find that your nursery space will become a roadblock to future growth in worship attendance.

The same logic holds for all of the requirements of the strategic master plan. If you find that you have one car parked for every two seats in your worship center, you will need to provide additional parking along with the increased worship attendance, or you will need to have a plan in place to provide the additional parking as soon as the existing parking areas become full.

An often overlooked but very important aspect of the strategic master plan is the determination of the requirements for other facilities that may be necessary to meet the ministry goals of your church. For example, it is becoming more common for churches to plan for the development of day care centers, schools, athletic complexes, retirement centers, retreat centers, counseling centers, and even entire communities as a part of their overall strategic master plan.

While the master plan is being formulated, take time to discuss and decide about any additional facilities that the church may want to provide as a part of this process. It will be much more difficult and probably more expensive if the planning for these facilities is not done concurrently with the rest of the planning for the development of your church.

Once again this is the time when everything is open for discussion. If a need, idea, or dream does not become a part of the master planning process now, the insertion of it at a later point may have a negative impact on your master plan and require you to redo the entire plan before it is implemented. The more you can settle at this phase, the more accurate and useful the master plan will become.

TAKING CARE OF YOUR PARKING NEEDS

The ultimate capacity of your site and the size of your church's worship attendance are determined by the number of parking spaces you provide—either on the church's property, on adjacent property, or with the use of shuttle vehicles. The space dedicated to parking consumes considerably more property than most people realize. One useable acre will generally provide parking spaces for between 110 to 120 cars. If a ratio of one parking space to every two seats in the worship center is required, a church with a seating capacity of 1000 will need to allocate almost 4.5 acres for parking.

Many churches do not realize it, but sooner or later, parking becomes a limiting factor in the master plan. If visitors and members cannot find parking places, they cannot be expected to continue attending your worship services. Another factor to consider is that if you do not have a visible parking lot with approximately 20 percent of the spaces empty on Sunday morning, you will have a hard time attracting new members. Adequate parking is more important than adequate facilities. If you only have provided enough parking to accommodate 750 people, a new sanctuary designed for 1000 people will never be filled to capacity on a regular basis.

During the analysis phase of your journey, this actual ratio for your church should be determined. Get someone to count cars and divide the number of people in the worship service by the number of cars counted. This count should be made for several Sundays and averaged to determine the ratio of parked cars to people in worship. Your ratio will depend on how many services and educational options you have on Sunday morning. As you grow, a simple count like this one can be used to predict the parking requirements. However, your final number will shift if you add or subtract worship services, especially while developing your master plan. The proper ratio for planning purposes will probably be between 1.5 people and 2 people per car.

Do not make the mistake of using the local code requirement of one parking space for every three to four seats in the worship center for your planning purposes. These ratios are *unrealistically low* for today's dynamic, growing churches and only will restrict your growth. The goal of this analysis is to

The space dedicated to parking consumes considerably more property than most people realize.

provide adequate parking to support your church's programs and not just to provide enough parking to meet code requirements. Remember, if people cannot find a place to park, more than likely they won't return to your church. This is why I advise people not to inadvertently build in a roadblock to the growth of their church by underestimating the actual number of parking spaces required to support the programs.

The demographics of a congregation can alter parking needs dramatically. Churches with a large number of high school students, single adults, or senior adults will need to provide a higher parking ratio than a congregation made up of predominantly young families. Another factor that affects parking requirements is multiple services. Scheduling two sessions of Christian education or two morning worship services will proportionately increase your parking needs. Those attending early services may not have exited the parking lot before those attending the next service arrive. Separating the services by 15 or 20 minutes will not completely eliminate the problem.

The only practical solution is to provide more parking, probably a ratio of one parking space for every 1.5 actual seats in the worship center. Often, the added vehicular congestion created by multiple services requires expanded driveways and passenger loading and unloading areas. Every active church has a high volume of traffic arriving and leaving within a short span of time. This is often a 15-minute problem, and it creates the need for well-planned site entrances and exits so that the traffic flow will be at a tolerable rate. Exits need to be spaced so traffic will not block the flow from nearby exits.

Generally, exits to the street should not be within 150 feet of each other. Whenever possible, exits should be provided to more than one street to help decrease traffic congestion. Traffic also should also be routed in such a way as to avoid making left turns across lanes moving in the opposite direction.

The demographics of a congregation can alter parking needs dramatically.

Ideally, parking should be located all around the building and not clustered into just one or two specific areas. Many churches like to plan for a significant amount of parking on the front of the property, so those who pass will see evidence of activity. If the parking area and entry drives are well designed and include attractive landscaping, this is a good idea. Increasingly, local codes require at least a minimum amount of landscaping in all parking areas. This helps to provide appropriate screening for the adjacent property owners. If properly

designed, landscaping will create an attractive and inviting entry for the church.

Do not forget to provide special areas for visitor, elderly, and handicapped parking. There are code requirements for handicap parking spaces, but not for visitor or elderly parking spaces. Your master plan needs to address all three of these special parking needs as you plan for the phased development of your church. These parking areas also need to be close to a main entrance near an area provided for passenger loading and unloading. They should be designed so that they do not block other traffic during the loading or unloading process.

Paved walkways connecting the parking areas and the buildings are also an important aspect of the master plan. They should be carefully thought out and designed to conform to normal paths of pedestrian traffic. To assist the visually impaired, the surface material for the walk should be changed where the walk crosses a driveway. Large, paved areas near major entrances should be designed to provide space for gathering before and after services, as well as for special celebrations such as weddings.

One or more areas should be provided where passengers can unload with sheltered access to the buildings.

One or more areas should be provided where passengers can unload with sheltered access to the buildings. These should be designed for one-way traffic so passengers can exit on the passenger's side of a vehicle next to the building entrance. The sheltered area should be large enough to cover an entire car. The height must be carefully planned to provide for emergency vehicles, but not so high that blowing rain will sweep across the entire entrance.

Driveways located between buildings should be situated to discourage significant pedestrian traffic flow for safety reasons. Be aware that there always is the chance that a child will dart out of a door. Therefore, there should be a safety zone between the exits and the path of moving traffic.

ADDRESSING YOUR CHURCH'S LANDSCAPING NEEDS

Your church should not wait until the building is completed, parking lots and walkways paved, and exterior lighting installed to consider a landscaping plan. In fact, a master-landscaping plan should be established during the early stages of the master planning process. Creating a master-landscaping plan will enhance the entire master plan and bring harmony to the entire site development plan. It also can highlight major entrances and facilitate traffic flow.

Planting islands can help direct traffic and define and buffer parking areas. Landscaping also is a valuable asset for developing energy efficient building designs. Once the overall landscape plan is developed and coordinated with the master plan, you can begin to implement the landscape in phases and plant smaller trees in areas where they can mature and add continuity to the future phases of your development.

Appealing landscaping is one of the ways you can draw people to your church. This is because attractive, well-designed buildings and grounds offer visitors an inviting scene. They indicate the church's interest and concern for its environment and community. In contrast, inadequate landscaping and poorly kept grounds can have a negative influence on the very people you are trying to reach. Plantings can also be used to screen unattractive surroundings and to frame the church property. They can provide additional privacy for neighbors whose property is adjacent to the church. In many communities, codes now require buffer screening for churches. Even if it is not required by local codes, screening is a thoughtful gesture churches can make towards their neighbors.

It should be noted here that in today's regulatory climate, it is impossible to predict the changes to the regulations over the next several years. However, it is *possible* to assume that regulations dealing with the site development near wetlands and streams will become more stringent and will cause this property to be more difficult to develop. Also we can assume that in most areas, the land dedicated to tree save areas and landscaping will increase and that neighborhoods will continue to have even more influence over what can be developed on the land adjacent to their houses. These are influences that, although not completely definable, must be factored into the development of every church master plan.

Appealing landscaping is one of the ways you can draw people to your church.

Well-designed-landscaping is both attractive and functional. When properly achieved, it will provide a unity to your phased master plan. If it is implemented early, landscaping can be developed over time in an economical manner. Planting smaller materials in areas of future development can be a great investment in the overall development of your master plan. Identifying your property boundaries with planting or fences is often a good investment in roadway growing areas where neighborhoods may be developed after the church has been established.

PLAN FOR EXTERIOR LIGHTING

When used to emphasize architectural features and landscaping, well-planned lighting is a very successful design tool. It gives the church significant visibility at night and provides an important aspect of security. Parking areas, walkways, and entrances should be well lit to ensure that there are no dark areas. Parking lots are usually lit with pole-mounted fixtures that spread light over the entire area. Walkways, entrances, and steps can be lit with either low-mounted fixtures installed at the sides of steps, or louvered lights in walls along the edge of walks. Mounting accent lighting fixtures on the building can provide an additional level of security.

If large trees are available, special lighting effects can be designed through the addition of fixtures placed 20 to 25 feet up in the trees and directed onto the area needing light. An alternate method is to place fixtures around the base of the tree and focus the lighting into the tree so it is reflected into the area. Both these methods of tree lighting have a soft moonlit quality that provides illumination without creating harsh light.

All lighting must be designed to minimize any light spilling off your site and onto your neighbor's property. Today's computerized lighting design programs can graphically show the amount of light spilling onto surrounding property. These studies are called *photometric studies*, and are often required as part of the development agreements with local officials.

There are several commercial lighting fixtures that are designed to eliminate light pollution and are specifically designed to limit the light from the parking lot from spreading light onto adjacent property. Photoelectric cells and timers can be used to control the hours of operation for the lighting, providing light when needed for security reasons and limiting the light when not needed. These devices conserve electricity, extend the life of the lamps, and help control the concerns of adjacent property owners.

If your church finds that it cannot afford to install all of the exterior lighting desired as a part of its current building project, you should plan to install empty conduits to provide power to those areas in the future. This will allow your church to add the lighting later at minimum expense. By planning ahead, your church will avoid additional installation costs that would be incurred to dig up the parking area and install the conduit after the parking lot is completed.

Walkways, entrances, and steps can be lit with either low-mounted fixtures installed at the sides of steps or louvered lights in walls along the edge of walks.

FINDING THE RIGHT PLACE FOR SIGNAGE

For many visitors, the first introduction to your church will be your exterior signs. An attractive and adequate system of exterior signs is a vital communication tool for your church that should not be overlooked. They should be designed to complement the architectural style of your church building. This is your first opportunity to tell the visitor who you are, when you meet, and where to park. Do not underestimate the importance of a clear, concise message to those entering your facility. As churches continue to grow and minister to their communities, it has become more important to clearly identify points of entry and places of destination.

As you prepare your strategic master plan, think through the circulation pattern you are creating from a visitor's point of view. How do you find your way to the proper parking area and into the proper designation within the facility? It is very easy for someone working on the plan for a long time to lose sight of how others view the facility, and how they might need to find their way from the road to the nursery. The solution to solving this problem is obviously an entire system of signs. Remember, however, that the need for clear signage starts when visitors first enter your church site, and only ends when they have successfully made their way to your worship center.

As with several other aspects of your master plan, the development of the exterior signage will probably be regulated by several local codes. Most areas have strict criteria for size and location of signs. Part of your planning must include checking with your local city code departments before designing or installing an exterior sign.

Many churches make the mistake of cluttering signs with too much information. Again, consider the sign from the point of view of the person reading it. If the sign is intended primarily for passing motorists who are driving down an interstate highway, it will look very different from a sign that needs to be read by those entering the church campus. Therefore, make sure that you limit the information placed on your signs and that each one is appropriately designed for its location.

A good rule to follow is this: the information on the sign should be brief enough to be read at a passing glance. If the sign is intended primarily for pedestrians, more information may be included.

Many churches make the mistake of cluttering signs with too much information.

SERVICE AREAS

Thoughtful attention to the location and provision of service areas is another fundamental step in the master planning process and must be considered early in the process. These areas require special requirements and relationships to properly support your facility. Consider the following in your planning:

1. Kitchen and food service areas

    a. Provide for convenient delivery of paper goods and groceries.

    b. Give attention to and devise a plan for garbage and trash removal, including provisions for washing garbage cans and screening the service area.

    c. Find storage for gas-powered equipment away from buildings where people meet.

2. Maintenance and delivery

    a. Provide for delivery by large trucks.

    b. Give good service accessibility to mechanical rooms and utility equipment.

    c. Provide access for special equipment used in the worship center for special events and performances.

    d. Screen equipment located on the ground and provide security fencing for equipment susceptible to damage or posing a hazard to children playing in the area.

Thoughtful attention to the location and provision of service areas is another fundamental step in the master planning process and must be considered early in the process.

Many churches need to provide a building on the property where they can store mowers and other equipment used to maintain the grounds. Without special building design considerations, an oversight in this area could result in creating a fire hazard, as well as violating fire codes and insurance company policies. Many churches combine the need for storage and the need for a bus or van garage into one building located off the main circulation artery.

PRESENTATION TO THE CONGREGATION

In most cases, it is helpful for the design team to assist you in presenting the preliminary master plan to the congregation. The presentation should include the established space allocation needs, proposed site development plans, preliminary floor plans, building sketches, and a preliminary project budget. Members of the design team can often field and answer questions about the study in a more objective way than members of the church. One exception would be the discussion of the possible means and sources of financing the project with the understanding that the final project budget is not definite at this point in the development. It is always better to have a member of the church talk about the funding requirements. Some discussions need to be lead by a respected church member, and this is certainly one of those discussions.

Many people do not like to speak up in a large gathering, so ask for feedback from the congregation on a short questionnaire. Respond to and share the comments by publishing the compiled results and, where possible, revise the master plan in response to any common concerns. Prepare answers to concerns that cannot be met in the master plan, and once this process is completed, finalize the master plan and present it for final approval.

Nehemiah was in a position of leadership, which led to an opportunity of development and future hope for the city he loved. While God had given him the vision for the project and the emotional energy to see the task through to the end, he did not overlook those who were working beside him. You and your congregation are partners on a journey of great blessing. Therefore, take time to explain all that needs to be conveyed to those who are traveling with you. Be willing to listen and enjoy the entire process of reaching the goals your church has set for the future.

It is always better to have a member of the church talk about the funding requirements.

LESSONS LEARNED

Over the last 25 years, I have had the blessing of working with many dynamic, growing churches. Most of these churches have continued to grow and to impact the communities around them. Typically, they can be grouped into three basic types:

- The classical or traditional church with a steeple and columns

- The transitional church that looks like a church when you drive by, but has many of the more contemporary interior features

- The church that does not want to look or feel like a traditional church and wants to have the type of atmosphere that attracts people who did not grow up in a traditional church environment

I have worked with all of these models and have seen many of them become very successful churches—successful by any way you choose to measure their impact. They all have had steady growth in attendance, programs, and resources. What I have learned from working with these various churches is that there is no set formula for growth. The things they have in common is that they know:

- Who they are

- What their mission is

- How to meet the needs of their communities

They also know the people they are seeking to reach. They do not try to be all things to all people. However, whatever they do, they do very well. These churches have a solid plan for growth—a plan they review and monitor consistently. They also are completely committed to getting the proper staff in place to handle the growth before it occurs.

One of the most important functions of the strategic master plan is to uncover the roadblocks to the growth in your church and to devise a way to remove them as soon as possible. Whether they are caused by programs, by staff, or by facilities, removing these are the only way your church will meet its full potential. Finally, make a commitment to develop a process to stay ahead of your growth and to monitor your plan on a regular basis. Also, be willing to make the inevitable adjustments that will be required to keep your church growing.

PROJECTED PHASING FOR SUNDAY CAPACITY

Space	People	SF / Person	Phase 1	Phase 2	Phase 3	Phase 4	Phase 5	Summary
Youth Worship	**400**	**18**	**400**					
Youth Education	400	20	400					
College/Single Worship	400	18	400					
College/Single Education	400	20	400					
Nursery	75	40	75					
Administration	12	225	0					
Total People			**1,675**					
Phase 1 Total			**1,675**					**1,675**
Interim Worship	2,800	18		2,800				
Seniors	725	20		725				
Adult Education	750	20		750				
Elementary	800	25		800				
Preschool	200	40		200				
Nursery	125	40		125				
Total People				**5,400**				
Phase 2 Total				**5,400**				**7,075**
Final Worship Space	4,500	18			4,500			
Worship Support	250	25						
Seniors	440	20			440			
Adult Education	500	20			500			
Elementary	525	25			525			
Preschool	130	40			130			
Nursery	130	40			130			
Administration	75	225						
Total People					**6,225**			
Phase 3 Total					**6,225**			**10,500**
*Phase 4 Total						**0**		**10,500**
Chapel	375	18					375	
Brides Room	12	35						
Reception Room	400	15					400	
Total People							**775**	
Phase 5 Total							**775**	**11,275**

Phase 4 is the FLC and has no impact on Sunday activity.

PROJECTED PHASING FOR SUNDAY CAPACITY

Space	People	SF / Person	Phase 1	Phase 2	Phase 3	Phase 4	Phase 5	Summary
Interim Worship	2,800	18	50,400					
Senior Adults	725	20	14,500					
Adults	750	20	15,000					
Elementary	800	30	24,000					
Preschool	200	40	8,000					
Nursery	125	40	5,000					
Total Net Area			116,900					
45% Net to Gross Factor			**52,605**					
Phase 1 Total per Hour	**5,400**		**169,505**					**169,505**
Youth Worship	400	18		7,200				
Youth Education	400	20		8,000				
College / Single Worship	400	18		7,200				
College / Single Education	400	20		8,000				
Nursery	75	40		3,000				
Administration	12	225		2,700				
Total				36,100				
45% Net to Gross Factor				**16,245**				
Phase 2 Total per Hour	**1,687**			**52,345**				**221,850**
Final Worship Space	4,500	18			81,000			
Worship Support	250	25			6,250			
Seniors	440	20			8,800			
Adult Education	500	20			10,000			
Elementary	525	30			15,750			
Preschool	130	40			5,200			
Nursery	130	40			5,200			
Administration	75	225			16,875			
Total Net Area					149,075			
45% Net to Gross Factor					**67,084**			
Phase 3 Total per Hour	**6,550**				**216,159**			**438,009**
3 Court Gym with Track						20,000		
Rock Climbing Wall						500		
Aerobics Room						1,000		
Weight Room						1,500		
Meeting Room						1,200		
Craft Room						1,000		
Pool						20,000		
Locker Rooms						3,000		
Game Room						900		
Administration						1,500		
Total Net Area						50,600		
45% Net to Gross Factor						**22,770**		
Phase 4 Total						**73,370**		
Total								**511,379**
Chapel	375	18					6,750	
Brides Room	12	35					420	
Reception Room	400	15					6,000	
Total Net Area							13,170	
45% Net to Gross Factor							5,927	
Phase 5 Total per Hour	**787**						**19,097**	**530,475**

STEP EIGHT

Prepare a Financial Plan and Project Budget

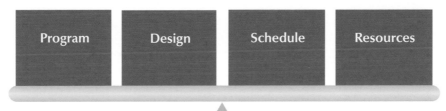

Program	Design	Schedule	Resources

These four must be balanced before you move on with your journey.

STEP EIGHT

Prepare a Financial Plan and Project Budget

Nehemiah made sure that he had the right paperwork, plan, and goal for his journey. He did not hesitate to ask King Artaxerxes for help, and God provided greatly through this man. He also made plans for the direction that he would take once the building process was underway. He knew the effort would be ongoing with many challenges, but he was committed to the entire journey.

Even before he left for Jerusalem, he made preparation to purchase some of the material that would be used for the project. In order to buy the timber for the reconstruction effort, he needed a letter from the king addressed to Asaph, who was the keeper of the king's forest. In it would be the explanation of his mission, need, and goal. However, the most important part was the signature of the king.

During his time of preparation, Nehemiah determined what would be needed and took the appropriate steps to gather the right materials. His up front preparation, research, and willingness to incorporate capable people into his project were the beginning of success. The same can be true for you and the project you are undertaking.

Because the gracious hand of my God was upon me, the king granted my requests.
—Nehemiah 2:8

UNDERSTAND THE EXPECTATIONS

As you prepare a financial budget for your journey, it will be very important to ask the right questions about every area of your ministry. Does your leadership team really understand what the church staff is expecting—new computers, a new computer network, new furniture, new musical instruments, or special production facilities? As you begin this journey, realize that everyone has unexpressed expectations.

Managing these expectations can be difficult; not understanding that they exist is worse. Expectations can add up and ultimately undermine the entire project. An interesting fact about these expectations is that they are very difficult to detect until later in the journey. The best way to manage this potential problem is to set a budget at the very beginning and monitor it closely as you continue on.

Without a reasonable target budget, these expectations will continue to grow. The very fact that many cannot be set early will be difficult to deal with later.

You will find that the most difficult issues to deal with will be the management of ever-changing expectations. As the journey progresses, people not previously involved will come forward. These new people, people outside your team, will often try to add new expectations. Your goal should be to try to establish a realistic project budget as early as possible.

At this stage in planning, it is time for everyone to put everything into the project that he or she has been thinking about for years. No church has the money to build everything it needs—let alone what everyone wants. The sooner you separate the needs from the wants, and begin to prioritize the needs, the better the journey will become. Almost everyone understands the need for discipline when it comes to budgeting, and most will understand the real priorities of this project.

Involve the church staff in your quest to include all that is truly needed. Take time to visit other completed projects and review the level of design finishes and furniture used. If they can view something completed, most people get a better understanding of the expectations being set for the journey. Many people have a very difficult time looking at drawings and pictures and understanding what the completed project will look like. We all learn in different ways. Therefore, make every effort to communicate the destination of this journey in a way that everyone involved will understand. Once again, a little extra time spent at this point will accrue huge dividends later.

The final project will not be fully known until you have completed your planning and budgeting. However, that is not a reason to delay dealing with the project budget as early and as realistically as possible. Once the budget is

The sooner you separate the needs from the wants, and begin to prioritize the needs, the better the journey will become.

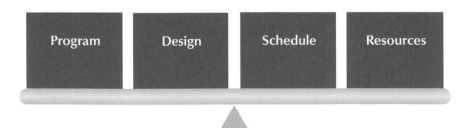

These four must be balanced before you move on with your journey.

established, it can be modified as more accurate information becomes available. The good thing is that you will have it available and can use it as a tool to balance everyone's expectations.

MAKE SURE YOU HAVE A PROPER BALANCE

At no other point in the journey is open and honest communication more important. Most of the unsuccessful journeys you have heard about started here—with a budget, a program, and a design that did not match. Every *successful* project must have a realistic balance between the expectations for the program that will be set up, the design that will be implemented, the schedule that will be kept, and the budget that will be maintained. Moving forward without having reached a proper balance among these issues will mean continued compromise and struggle. Again, these decisions will not get any easier, and the potential for an unsuccessful journey will only increase if you move forward without dealing with everyone's expectations.

The first important task for your finance team is to establish a preliminary estimate for the total resources that will be available for the proposed development.

At this step, it is imperative that you begin to balance the program expectations and the project budget. It also is critical that everyone understand that the resources will be available for the needs that are required to fulfill the church's mission. If the leadership team does not make hard decisions at this point, it will find itself struggling for the rest of the journey.

You can have a great plan, a great design, and a great site—yet without proper financial planning, all of your work may be unrealized. Start early researching your church's financial resources and capabilities. Be realistic about how much you can afford without limiting God's plan to bless you and your church.

At no other point in the journey is open and honest communication more important than at this one.

It is difficult to know the true potential for raising funds within your church, but you must use the best information you can gather to make an informed estimate. The analysis, planning, design, and construction for your church must go hand in hand with your fund-raising efforts. The project budget must be in balance with the fund-raising goals in order for you to have a successful journey.

The first important task for your finance team is to establish a preliminary estimate for the total resources that will be available for the proposed development. Ultimately, the finance team and the leadership team will need to establish a balance between how much the proposed building expansions will cost and how much money the church can actually afford to spend without hurting other ministries.

A design team experienced in working on this building type will be able to help you establish a reliable preliminary construction budget for the proposed building. However, during the preliminary budgeting estimates, the budget for the site development cost is much more difficult to establish and to manage. It can only be established using historical data from similar projects. Therefore, the finance and building teams will need to help establish budgets for several other costs associated with the building program. When you add up all of these associated costs and combine them with the building construction and site development cost, you arrive at the project budget.

The building construction cost is only one item in the overall project budget. The finance team will need to ensure that the church can fund the entire project budget and not just the construction cost. If the project cost is too high, then the design team and leadership team must work together to discover ways to phase the building construction or to defer some portion of the other costs and modify the project budget to match the available resources. After the project budget is set and the capital fund campaign is completed, you must once again balance the expectations with the resources before you can begin construction.

As a rule of thumb during a capital building program, your church should be able to raise funds equal to 1.5 to 2.5 times your annual operating budget. These funds are usually collected over three years, and history shows that you probably will collect about 90 percent of the amount pledged. Also, as a general guide, a lending institution will lend a church an amount equal to two to three times its annual operating budget.

Many churches today do not want to borrow on a long-term basis for building construction. However, they will plan to borrow on a short-term basis to allow the construction to proceed while the pledges are being collected—normally over a three to five year period.

I am not saying that there is a right answer or a wrong answer to the question of church funding or finance, but I am saying these options must be discussed and decided upon before you can continue planning for the growth of your church. The leadership team cannot continue on in a meaningful way and have any expectations of a successful journey until these fundamental financial decisions have been finalized.

I always urge a leadership team to be realistic. When you fail to take time to realistically prepare a total project budget for all of the expenses involved, you will introduce another element of concern to the entire partnership for the remainder of your journey.

There are two budgets that must be monitored during this process. The first is the *project cost*, which is the summary of every cost required for the project. The second is the *construction cost*, which includes only the items required for the construction process. The project cost will be approximately 18 percent to 24 percent higher than the construction cost. When communicating about the budget with the congregation, it is imperative that the total project cost is discussed and not just the construction cost.

Many leadership teams have caused themselves undue heartache because they have lost control of the project cost, resulting in additional expenses which later surprised them. This is why it is extremely important to prepare a master budget for the total project cost and monitor it at each and every step of the way.

The discipline required to manage the overall project budget may be unfamiliar to many people chosen to serve on the leadership team. If necessary, enlist the help of someone on the finance team to help you monitor the project budget. Then, from time to time, you can ask him or her to give you the information you require to make proper, informed decisions along the way.

Regardless of how well every team member estimates his portion of the work, the project cost will continue to evolve and change throughout this journey. Knowing this, you need to prepare the most accurate estimate possible with the information you can gather. As more accurate information becomes available, continue to refine the project budget and make the necessary changes to your project as you continue on in your journey.

LESSONS LEARNED

Developing an initial project budget is a fundamental requirement to successfully managing the outcome of your journey. Your committee will not have all of the information required to develop the final project budget, but you must begin to assemble all of the budget elements that will be required. These budget elements will be different for every church, and your leadership team must make sure you have spent the time required to identify the elements that your team will need to monitor.

It is extremely important to prepare a master budget for the total project cost and monitor it at each and every step of the way.

Depending on the type of construction and complexity of a project, the building construction cost may vary from as little as $80 per square foot to well over $150 per square foot.

This first project budget is a preliminary road map of your journey. By establishing the budget elements to monitor, your team will have a tool that can be modified as required. Remember to put everything required to complete this journey into the project budget. Even if you do not have all the information required to set the correct budget amount for a specific element, the project contingency can be reduced and these funds can be allocated to the changing requirements. The following guidelines are provided to help you begin to establish your initial project budget.

BUILDING CONSTRUCTION COST

Construction cost is a large portion of the project budget and can be difficult to estimate, but with the right design team, it is possible to make early projections that will be very close to your final building construction cost. This cost should be determined early in the design process. Trying to establish these costs without the assistance of an experienced team member is one of the worst mistakes that your leadership team can make. For example, depending on the type of construction and complexity of a project, the building construction cost may vary from as little as $80 per square foot to well over $150 per square foot.

At this point, the cost of renovating an existing space is even harder to define. Renovation costs can range from the cost of repainting a space to the cost of installing completely new systems, and can often cost as much as new construction. Once again, the goal at this stage of the journey is to try to estimate as closely as possible the expectations and the budget for this work.

With the potential for such a great variation in the square foot building cost, your design team will be an invaluable help in establishing your expectations and providing an accurate building budget for the building costs to match your expectations. Beware of taking estimates from other professionals who are not associated with your project. It always seems like everyone else is building for less than what you are being asked to budget. However, my experience is that others tend to leave out some critical costs associated with their projects, and it is very difficult to make comparisons unless you are intimately involved in a project.

I do not mean to indicate that there is any intention to mislead you. It is just human nature for someone to seek to make a project he is involved with look as good as possible. If you have selected the right design team, and they have been good guides in your journey, trust them with this aspect of the project budget.

You still need to ask questions until you are sure you understand the projected building costs, and try not to listen to others who are not completely informed about your project.

SITE DEVELOPMENT COSTS

In addition to the building construction expense, the cost for the development of the site must be considered. The site development cost cannot easily be quantified with square footage figures due to the wildly varying conditions that exist with different sites and any special conditions that may exist within the property. Early budgets can be established using the number of parking spaces to be developed and the number of acres to be disturbed. It is not uncommon for the site development cost to range from $12 to $20 per square foot of new building construction.

This initial estimate will work for very preliminary budgets. However, the sooner the design team establishes the scope of the site work and prepares a more refined and accurate site development budget, the more accurate the project budget will become. This is the most difficult portion of the project budget to manage. It is very difficult to cut money from this budget, especially if the overall project budget exceeds the church's resources. Unforeseen site conditions and local jurisdictions can add substantial cost to this area of the budget, and there is little that can be done to reduce these costs. This is an area of the budget where the potential to spend unexpected funds is the greatest. This also is where most of the contingency budget is usually spent. There will be a collective sigh of relief as the journey moves past this phase of the construction.

LANDSCAPING COSTS

Landscaping costs can vary from a few thousand to several hundred thousand dollars. More and more local jurisdictions are imposing tree replacement and landscape buffer requirements on any development, including churches. At this point in your journey, it is wise to try and establish a budget for the anticipated landscaping cost.

In the past, many churches would wait until the end of the project to establish the landscaping budget. With the current trend of mandated landscaping requirements, this can cause a major budget problem if it is not addressed in the initial project budget.

You can develop a master landscape plan as part of the master site plan. It can be implemented in phases. Often you can plant smaller landscape material in

Unforeseen site conditions and local jurisdictions can add substantial cost to this area of the budget. This is where the potential to spend unexpected funds is the greatest.

It is not unusual today to put a sound-board or projector into a new project that was not even available when the project planning was started. For this reason, I recommend that a separate fund be set aside to manage this area of the project.

areas of future development and let this material grow for several years before you develop this portion of the site. This will save your church money and allow you to develop a unified landscape plan in phases that match your master site plan. When you have completed your master site plan, you will have the benefit of several years of growth and a more mature look to your site than is possible without the use of a master landscape plan.

AUDIO, VIDEO, AND THEATRICAL LIGHTING

The impact of technology on today's church cannot be ignored. The expectations have never been higher, the technology never better, and the changes never more rapid. It is not unusual today to put a soundboard or projector into a new project that was not even available when the project planning was started. For this reason, I recommend that a separate fund be set aside to manage this area of the project.

Once the preliminary expectations are identified, you can establish a preliminary fund in the project budget for these items. While planning the initial project budget for a worship facility of approximately 1000, I normally recommend spending approximately $140 per seat in a worship facility for the sound system, approximately $70,000 for the video projectors, and approximately $100,000 for theatrical lighting. Obviously, these amounts can wildly vary depending on expectations and size of the worship facility, but this line item is becoming more and more important to the master planning of new church facilities and should be thoroughly discussed, established, and monitored as a separate line item.

FURNITURE, FIXTURES, AND EQUIPMENT

An often forgotten expense is furniture and other items such as chairs, tables, pews, kitchen equipment, telephone systems, security alarms, and computers—all necessary if the new facility is to function properly. This list of items can be very lengthy depending on the type of facility to be constructed, and should be developed early and reviewed as the project progresses to ensure that the list is accurate. Items included in this category are not generally part of the construction cost because they are not a part of the actual building construction.

There is usually no reason to include these items in the general contractor's cost, but they are part of the overall project budget and must not be forgotten. Rely on your design team to help establish this line item in the project budget and work together with the church staff to make sure everything is identified when budgeting for items in this category. When the initial project budget is set up, the usual range for this category is 3 to 5 percent of the construction cost.

CONTINGENCY FUND

No matter how well the partnership works together, one part of the construction process that cannot be avoided is dealing with unforeseen circumstances and changes. There will always be situations that will require a change in your journey. These changes may be something that the church wants, or changes required by the code officials, even though they may have already approved your plans. While digging the footings for the facility, the construction team may uncover something that needs changing or removing, such as unexpectedly poor soil or rock. Removal of these items will require additional money. The contingency fund is there to pay for these essential changes in the work without destroying the project budget.

No matter how well the partnership works together, one part of the construction process that cannot be avoided is dealing with unforeseen circumstances and changes.

The contingency fund should not be used to increase the construction budget; it is established for unanticipated or unavoidable changes. When the initial project budget is established, the contingency fund is usually allocated as a percentage of the construction cost and should be approximately 6 to 8 percent. The contingency for additions and remodeling work should be approximately 8 to 10 percent.

As the construction process continues, a portion of the funds can be released for other uses, such as upgrades in the finishes, furnishings, or equipment. Remember that this fund is established to cover items that are unforeseen and unexpected. Every construction project will have unforeseen circumstances, but they should not be unexpected, because they will occur no matter how well you plan. Build this into your planning and set this fund aside to provide the funds needed to deal with these expected circumstances.

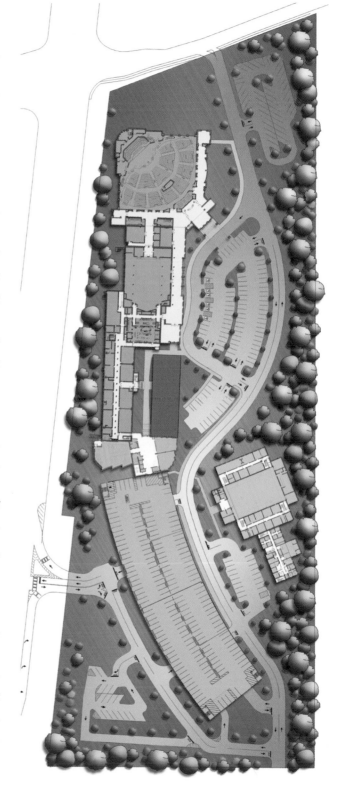

MISCELLANEOUS COSTS

These expenses are usually separate from the architect's fee and are paid directly by the church. When the initial project budget is set up, these costs are usually set up as approximately 2 to 3 percent of the construction cost. Examples of miscellaneous costs are as follows: site surveys, soil testing, construction material testing, interest on the construction loan, legal costs, and insurance costs. There are also several types of environmental investigations that might be required by local governing agencies, or possibly even by your lending institution.

A site environmental investigation, also called a Phase One Investigation, is often required. This investigation is for the purpose of looking for hazardous materials that may be buried on your property, and for recommending a method for their removal. Existing buildings that are going to be renovated may contain hazardous materials such as asbestos and lead paint. If hazardous materials are found, they can turn into a major expense and add additional time to the construction. This is not a problem if you are aware of it early on in the process and have a plan to overcome it on your journey. Testing to verify their presence is usually completed during the preliminary portion of the master planning process to ensure that an adequate budget is set for their removal.

Before your design team can provide an accurate master site plan, they also need a boundary and topography survey.

Before your design team can provide an accurate master site plan, they also need a boundary and topography survey. During the construction process, these surveys will provide the design team with information that is invaluable about your property during the design process, and will eliminate many potential additional costs and design problems. The cost of these surveys will depend on the size of the property, the vegetation, and the severity of the slope of the property. The cost could range from $1000 to over $1500 per acre.

Subsurface soil investigations are often required by the design team to determine the qualities of the soil and the bearing capacity. These investigations will also determine the presence of any rock that could interfere with the proposed construction of the building. The costs of these investigations are dependent on how many boring tests are made. A preliminary report usually ranges from $4000 to $8000.

To ensure overall quality control on the construction site, the soils, concrete, and steel will be inspected and tested by specialists to determine that they meet the level of quality outlined in the construction documents. The cost of these tests is usually paid for by the owner to ensure impartial testing results.

FUND-RAISING AND FINANCING COSTS

The cost of fund-raising and project financing should be calculated into the project budget. Today, most churches try to keep long-term borrowing to a minimum. Even then, there may be some expenses associated with short-term construction loans. Therefore, I suggest talking to several lenders for help in calculating financing and interest costs. Ask about closing costs and fees. Many churches decide to hire a professional to assist in the fund-raising.

During a capital funds campaign, these specialists usually more than pay for their expenses by significantly increasing the amount of money that is pledged. Also consult with several professional fund-raisers to obtain estimates of their fees and expenses. While calculating the preliminary project budget, set up this category as 1 to 2 percent of the construction cost. Another associated cost with this portion of the budget is the cost of the preparation of the information and printing of the material used to communicate with the congregation.

SPECIFIC PROJECT NEEDS

This line item is not always used, but many projects have special items that need to be a part of the project budget and tracked separately. Examples of this are stained glass windows, special musical instruments, special chancel furnishings, and special athletic equipment. It is not difficult to budget for these items, but they need to be identified early in the budgeting process and monitored as you move from one step to another.

DESIGN TEAM FEES

The method of establishing the architect's fee is typically based upon a percentage of the construction cost or a lump sum basis. (For more on design team fees, see information in Step 3.) Remember, many services that are standard to one architect may be additional services for another. For preliminary planning purposes, assume the architect's fees will run anywhere from 6 percent to 9 percent of the construction costs. For larger, multi-million dollar projects, the fees may range as low as 6 percent to 7 percent of the construction cost. In addition to these fees, there are other services that you may need from your design team that will incur additional expenses. These services usually do not include models, videos, brochures, travel expenses, and printing.

Many services that are standard to one architect may be additional services for another.

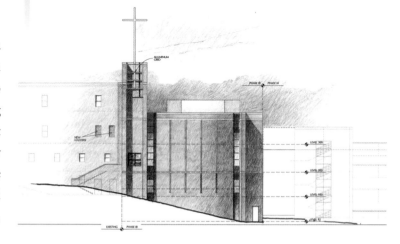

LAND COST

Your first large expense may be the purchase of new or additional property. Include all costs associated with the land purchase, such as the sale price for the land, financing costs, taxes, and any realtor expense. If you own the land already or you do not need additional land, then this item can be left out of the project budget. The master plan study will determine your present and future needs for additional land. During the initial project budget, the land cost is usually set up on a cost per acre basis.

Initial Project Budget Allowances
Based on a Percent of Construction Cost

Percent of construction cost:

Architect and professional fees	6 to 9 percent
Furnishings	3 to 5 percent
Landscape	2 to 3 percent
Contingency	6 to 10 percent
Construction loan financing	2 to 3 percent
Financing closing costs	2 to 5 percent

Hard construction costs will usually be only 70 to 80 percent of total building budget. The remaining costs are called *soft costs* and will be 20 to 30 percent of the overall project cost. Remember, when communicating about this project use the project cost, not just the construction cost. Many leadership teams have caused themselves unnecessary difficulty because the congregation thought that the construction cost was the project cost, and felt that they had been misled.

SAMPLE SUMMARY BUDGET

Phase One Construction		Phase One	% of Total
	New Construction	66,000	
	Average Cost / SF	$135	
A.	**Building Cost**	**$8,910,000**	**65.8%**
	New Parking Spaces	510	
	Cost per Space	$2,200	
B.	**Parking Cost**	**$1,122,000**	**8.3%**
	Cost per SF	**$17**	
	Stage Equipment		
	Theatrical Lighting	$150,000	
	Audio / Visual	$550,000	
	Video Production	$250,000	
C.	**Technology Total**	**$950,000**	**7.0%**
	Cost per SF	**$14**	
D.	**Sub Total Construction**	**$10,982,000**	**81.1%**
	Cost per SF	**$166**	
E.	FFE at 3.0%	$329,460	2.4%
F.	Prof. Fees at 6.5%	$713,830	5.3%
G.	Seating	$90,000	0.7%
H.	**Target Budget Amount**	**$12,115,290**	**89.5%**
I.	Contg. at 8%	$878,560	6.5%
J.	Misc. at 5%	$549,100	4.1%
K.		**$1,427,660**	**10.5%**
L.	**Total Project Cost**	**$13,542,950**	**100%**
	Total Cost per SF	**$205**	

Note : All of these prices are based on 2004 construction prices.

SAMPLE ITEMIZED BUDGET

Phase One

A.1	**Building Cost**	**$4,160,000**		**E.**	**Owner FF & E**	**3%**	**$ 124,800**
	Level 100	20,000			Phones		$ -
	Level 200	12,000			Computers		$ -
	Area	32,000			Security		$ -
					Stained Glass		$ -
	Average Cost / SF	$130.00			Musical Instruments		$ -
					Playground Equipment		$ -
A.2	**Renovation Cost**	**$ 175,000**			Furniture (By Owner)		$ -
	Level 100	2,500					
	Level 200	2,500		**F.**	**Contingency**	**8%**	**$ 392,400**
	Area	5,000					
				G.	**Administrative Costs**	**2%**	**$ 98,100**
	Average Cost / SF	$35.00			Legal Fees		$ -
					Material / Soil Testing		$ -
A.3	**Demolition Cost**	**$ 55,000**			Reimbursables		$ -
	Level 100	5,500			Site Survey		$ -
	Level 200	-			Moving Costs		$ -
	Area	5,500			Insurance		$ -
					Fundraising		$ -
	Average Cost / SF	$10.00			Promotional Material		$ -
					Interest Costs		$ -
B.	**Project FF & E**	**$ 140,000**					
	Audio / Visual	75,000		**H.**	**Professional Fees**	**7%**	**$ 343,350**
	Theatrical Lighting	50,000					
	Fixed Seating	-		**I.**	**PROJECT COST**		**$5,863,650**
	Signage	15,000			Project cost / SF		$ 183
	Furniture (By CDH)	-					
	Food Service	-			Building SF Before Phase		38,599
					SF Added During Phase		32,000
C.	**Site Cost**	**$375,000**			**Total Campus SF**		**70,599**
	Site Development	200,000					
	Landscape	25,000					
	Parking Spaces..............	150,000					
D.	**CONSTRUCTION COST**	**$4,905,000**					
	Construction Cost / SF	$153					

STEP NINE

Establish the Architectural Program and Preliminary Design for Phase One

STEP NINE

Establish the Architectural Program and Preliminary Design for Phase One

Nehemiah's heart resided within the walls of Jerusalem, but he had been forced to live in another city. Therefore, when it came to asking the king for permission to return to his homeland and for help in reconstructing the city walls. Nehemiah had little trouble conveying his heart's desire. Our churches can have the same effect on us. We enjoy the various activities, church programs, and Bible studies, and our heart's desire is to be with others who want to worship God.

There is an essential sense of community within the church. It is where we go to find spiritual refreshment when we are weary, hope when we are discouraged, and enlightenment when we need a word from God. Within the walls of our worship centers we can sing, worship, and mature in ways that we could not in other settings. This is why many people long to have a church home. Once they have experienced God's love through the church, they want to return over and over. Nehemiah wanted to return to the city of God, and he wanted to build for the future.

> *The king said to me, "What is it you want?" Then I prayed to the God of heaven, and I answered the king, "If it pleases the king and if your servant has found favor in his sight, let him send me to the city in Judah where my fathers are buried so that I can rebuild it."*
>
> —NEHEMIAH 2:4-5

DEALING WITH NEEDS

As the planning process continues, I usually ask church leaders the following questions: "What is the single most pressing need of your church? What needs must be met to allow your church to grow?" The reason to ask these questions is because during this critical step, you must finally establish the most pressing needs of your church, along with refining and finalizing the project program, budget, and schedule. Your leadership team has been working to develop a strategic master site plan for the long-term development of your church. Now you need to make the difficult and final decisions required to balance all the information you have gathered with the resources your finance team feels can be committed to this next step in the development of your church. It may help to know that very few churches have the resources to build all of their needs, let alone all of their wants.

This is why it is so critical to establish your true priorities and to rank them according to your resources.

The key to working through this step of the journey is to begin balancing your budget and your priorities. As you begin this step, you should have a preliminary project budget number to work with; this will allow you to begin establishing the size and quality of this phase of your strategic master plan development. The options available to you in order to keep this phase of development and your preliminary budget on track are to balance the size of the building and the level of quality within the building and the schedule for the start of your construction.

As this discussion works its way to a conclusion, you will need to depend on the design team for valid information. It is important that everyone on the leadership team has a good understanding of the consequences of the decisions made at this point of the journey. For example, it is often difficult to understand the quality level of interior and exterior finishes at this point, but the budget and the scope you set as your target will determine these and other final outcomes. If the balance between the size and the quality is incorrectly set, the remainder of the journey will be a continuous struggle.

It is often difficult to understand the quality level of interior and exterior finishes at this point, but the budget and the scope you set as your target will determine these and other final outcomes.

Before you move on, take the time to question the design team until you feel that you have a good understanding of the project expectations. Visit some completed projects to look at exterior and interior quality levels, and be sure that your team is comfortable with the direction before you begin to establish the preliminary architectural program. Once the initial program and the preliminary designs are underway, you lose a significant amount of opportunity to control the overall project cost. Changes made after this point could cause additional work and, in many cases, additional design fees.

Developing the strategic master site plan forced your leadership team to make some decisions about the potential phases of your development, and has narrowed down the choices you face. But your team is now being required to decide between several very good options, and to pick the best ones for further development and presentation to the congregation for approval. Now is the time to begin to prioritize your needs and desires. A little additional preplanning at this point in your journey will save your team many roadblocks later.

Unfortunately, many churches make the mistake of drawing up final building plans and presenting them to the congregation before they fully understand the church's real needs and the resources that will be available to meet those needs. This usually proves to be a costly mistake and causes many detours. However, your leadership team will be able to avoid these costly mistakes because the entire team has taken the time to discover the true needs and capabilities of your church. Before spending any of its resources on the development of building plans that are beyond the capabilities of your church, the design team has taken the necessary time to consider what is really important to the project.

Now is the time to begin to prioritize your needs and desires. A little additional preplanning at this point in your journey will save your team many roadblocks later.

SETTING THE RIGHT GOALS FOR YOUR SPACE

Your leadership team's goal at this stage of the journey also is to begin balancing the program, budget, and building design as closely as possible with the information that you have gathered. Your team will need to compile this information into a format that can be presented to your church for approval.

The preliminary building designs need to be developed in response to all of the information previously gathered by your team. The building solution developed in the preliminary design will need to provide a balance between the program requirements, the site constraints, and the budget requirements.

Once your team has reviewed and prioritized these various options, the next step is to begin turning the best of these options into an actual building design with a corresponding building program and more accurate project budgets. Start by getting the design team to prepare several options for your team to review. This step will finally turn all of your analysis and planning into an actual physical building design that can be reviewed, discussed, and finally approved by the entire leadership team.

I know that this is what you thought you would be doing several months ago.

However, it is only now that all of the information has been gathered, reviewed, and approved so that the building designs being developed by the design team will be a response to the real needs and resources of your church. From experience, I have learned that your church will recognize your hard work and will understand why your team made the difficult decisions required to balance the church's priorities before your team authorizes the preparation of the design drawings.

By studying several design options before selecting the final solution for further development, your team will be able to discover the best aspects of each option and craft a single design solution that produces the best balance and meets the needs of your church. Your team should be looking for drawings that translate the partnership's vision into reality.

These drawings need to convey the quality, character, image, and feeling of the project. However, at this point in the project, your team does not need detailed engineering drawings. This is due to the fact that your design team should know how to allow for engineering requirements without needing to spend your resources to have them designed at this time.

A room designed and built for worship is one of those special spaces where everything needs to be perfect—sight lines, acoustics, lighting, video, accommodations for special celebrations, type of seating, placement of sound, lighting console, size of choir and orchestra sections.

If a new worship center is part of this phase of development, your leadership team will need to take extra time and special care to review the designs for this room. A room designed and built for worship is one of those special spaces where everything needs to be perfect—sight lines, acoustics, lighting, video, accommodations for special celebrations, type of seating, placement of sound, lighting console, size of choir and orchestra sections. All of these elements need to be finely balanced and coordinated into one space.

The air conditioning and heating will need to be designed to be very quiet, and the lighting controls needs to be accessible. Everyone in the congregation needs to able to see and hear. Often, these design parameters cause conflicting priorities and can only be coordinated and solved when the construction documents are being completed. However, your design team should be familiar enough with this building type to be able to plan a space that is designed completely enough to be presented to the church for approval before all of the engineering drawings are completed.

PLANNING FOR AN INTERIM WORSHIP FACILITY

If a multipurpose or interim worship facility is to be considered as part of the phasing plan for your church, your leadership team should spend some time reviewing completed versions of this option. It is possible to design a multipurpose room as a banquet hall that is used for worship, fellowship, and occasional athletic activities. It is also possible to have a multipurpose room designed as a gym and use it for worship and fellowship.

This room could be the same size and have the same ceiling height, but be designed to have a completely different look and feel. The final design of the room needs to serve its function and primary use whether it will be used for worship, fellowship, or recreation. The location of this room in the overall strategic master plan also will vary depending upon its first primary and final designated use. Work with your design team to explore all of the options before settling too quickly on the final design of a multipurpose room.

Again the goal here is to present a design and a budget for church approval before your leadership team spends all of the resources required to complete the final construction documents. When designing a space for worship, it is imperative that members of the staff using this space have an opportunity to present their ideas and priorities. After the design team has assembled all of this information, it is often useful to have all of the various staff members review the preliminary design at the same time. This will provide an opportunity for everyone to understand the overriding priorities and decisions that have shaped the room.

When designing a space for worship, it is imperative that members of the staff using this space have an opportunity to present their ideas and priorities.

It is critical that at this point in the journey for the design team to include special consultants in acoustics, video, and lighting. These three disciplines will dictate much of the room design, and this information needs to be incorporated into the preliminary building designs from the onset of the design process.

CONSIDERING KEY DECISIONS

The budgets required to provide for the technology incorporated into today's large worship spaces must also be adequately accounted for in the project budget before it is presented to the church. If your leadership team believes that a new worship space should be included, be sure to pay special attention to the design team you select.

These spaces have become very specialized, the expectations continue to grow, and the design experience and expertise have become even more critical. If the design team that you chose to work with does not have this experience, make sure that the proper consultants are brought into the design process as early as possible. Make sure that these consultants have the proper experience to ensure your leadership team the results you are expecting.

In the design of a church project, it is often the interior spaces that are of most interest to those who will be asked to provide the resources to fund the project.

The one other area where we find it necessary to spend a little more of your resources than normal in this phase of the design process is in the area of interior design. When you prepare this design for presentation to the church for approval, it is necessary to prepare a more complete image of the interiors than for most projects. In the design of a church project, it is often the interior spaces that are of most interest to those who will be asked to provide the resources to fund the project.

The expectations for the interiors of new church projects also continue to grow. It is not unusual to provide nursery and elementary facilities that are designed around a theme. The intent here is to design memorable spaces that make the children feel special and invite them to come back. I often spend several meetings discussing the best way to reach and teach children, and am often asked to respond with designs that are unique to each age group. The entire pedestrian circulation system also is becoming much more important in church design. Again, I am often asked to spend a lot of time designing large, inviting, and comfortable gathering and circulation spaces that connect the major functions of the church.

It takes more time to design these interiors, and it takes more effort to make sure that these designs are properly communicated to the church. However, these are the areas of most importance to many attending church today. Your leadership team should spend some time reviewing your church's expectations and make sure you spend the time and effort to communicate these interior designs to the church when your team presents the building design for approval and for funding. Keep in mind, the building your leadership team is now designing will probably be serving your church for many generations.

When you consider the changes in church design over the last several years, it becomes very clear that you need to provide for as much flexibility as possible so that the building you are now designing can be adapted to meet your church's future program needs. Although your church may not be able to incorporate everything you need in this phase of development, you can provide the infrastructure to add those things at a later date.

Over the last several years, much of our design time has been spent in the search for a design solution that balances our traditional Christian forms and elements with the more contemporary aspects of our culture. Building designs that connect the best of our past with the best of today seem to hold up well over time. These designs seem to be more flexible, and resonate with growing churches.

What you ultimately choose to build will be a reflection of your church, your culture, and your values. Everyone wants to be able to say, "We did our very best. We were good stewards of our time, talent, and treasure." This takes on a different form for each congregation. No longer are we bound by strict design rules and regulations. We must ask, in each case, what the right response is to a particular journey, how we should respond to the blessings we have been given, and how we can best provide for the ministries of the church.

Once the entire partnership has agreed upon the building design and budget, the design team needs to prepare the final information required for the leadership team to communicate the team's work to the entire congregation. Depending on the complexity of the design solution, some form of graphic representation of the entire design needs to be prepared for presentation. This presentation can vary from simple, colored plans and renderings of the project, to a complex computer generated video—which virtually walks the congregation through of the entire exterior and interior of the project.

The goal of the information provided at the end of this step is to help your congregation make an informed decision concerning the future direction of the church.

The goal of the information provided at the end of this step is to help your congregation make an informed decision concerning the future direction of the church. Your membership needs to know where they are going, how they are going to get there, and when they will arrive. The key to a successful transition from this step to the next step is to make sure that all the information you assemble can be clearly communicated to the entire congregation for their approval.

Drawings, informational brochures, computer animations, videos, and small group meetings are all successful ways to make sure that everyone understands the preliminary designs, and that the congregation has an opportunity to get all of its questions answered. You need to explain the message and cast the vision. Be sure that you have communicated with the entire congregation and that you have their permission or approval before you move forward in the design process.

LESSONS LEARNED

As a way to illustrate the difficulties of keeping poor decisions from detouring your journey, I want to share one of my many battle scars. This journey started out as a master plan that led to the decision to construct a new sanctuary and education building. It was a journey that took longer than most—almost five years from the beginning to the end. During that time, several of the initial design expectations changed, the resources to fund the building program were not available, and, during the final phases of the planning, a new pastor began to lead the church!

The committee was led by a very capable leader, had several good members including some with building experience, and a new pastor who was a very strong leader. Yet, as this journey proceeded, and with my full agreement, we made some decisions that caused several significant changes to be made to the project. After several years of planning, a pipe organ was added to the program and the acoustical requirements for the room were revised. Two video screens and projectors were added, the chancel was reconfigured, and because of budget constraints, the building area and seating capacity of the sanctuary were reduced.

At this point of the project, we had spent much of our fee preparing the pricing drawings in order to help the owner, and to keep him from having to pay us for additional design services to redesign the project. We made a few simple reductions in the building and moved forward with completion of the construction drawings.

We started construction, and as the forms on the balcony were being stripped, it became apparent that the sight lines were not going to be adequate. As the construction proceeded, we made corrections to the balcony, the pews, and the chancel platform in order to improve the sight lines.

This was a difficult situation that simply occurred over time. It was the result of several independent decisions; no one decision caused the problem. But the accumulation of several decisions made over a long period did cause a serious problem. In hindsight, I should have stopped the project when we had to reduce the building area, and require the entire partnership to start over and review and redesign the entire project from the very beginning. In order to save the owner a few dollars during the construction phase, we moved on only to discover a serious problem.

You must be sure that you have communicated with the entire congregation and that you have their permission or approval before you move forward in the design process.

I learned a very important lesson and that is this: whenever a change is made, stop and review the entire project—regardless of the point in the journey and regardless of the additional cost associated with a complete review of the project. No matter how strong the leadership, and no matter how good the intentions, it is impossible to adequately monitor long-term projects that have changing expectations and budget constraints like the one mentioned above.

However, I do believe that serious and expensive problems can be avoided when you choose to take the right steps to monitor your journey from its beginning. Again, it is important to have a system in place to keep your journey on track and to review your decisions at regular intervals.

The tendency of long-term, complex projects is for them to veer off course and for the necessary course corrections to be hard to see until it is often too late to be easily corrected. Changes made late in the planning process are the most likely to cause the problems such as the one illustrated here. Take extra time to review any decisions or changes that you make, even if the changes seem to make good sense.

Serious and expensive problems can be avoided when you choose to take the right steps to monitor your journey from its beginning.

We know Nehemiah was a man who had a plan, a purpose, and a mission, but he still took time to evaluate the needs of the people and the city itself. The work he was doing was for God's glory and not his own. Therefore, he wanted it to be done *not only* correctly, but so that everyone could use and enjoy it. He stuck to his plan and completed the task, and you can do the same!

Is your service to the Lord a job or a ministry?
Some people have a job in the church,
while others involve themselves in a ministry.
What is the difference?

If you are doing it just because no one else will, it is a job.
If you are doing it to serve the Lord, it is a ministry.

If you are doing it just well enough to get by, it is a job.
If you are doing it to the best of your ability, it is a ministry.

If you are doing it because someone else said it needs to be done, it is a job.
If you are doing it because you think it needs to be done, it is a ministry.

When you finish a job, people will say, "Well done."
However, when you complete your ministry, the Lord will say,
"Well done, my good and faithful servant," (Matthew 25:21).

An average church is filled with people doing a job.
A great church is filled with people, who are involved in a ministry.

STEP TEN

Gather the Resources for the Journey:
The Capital Fund Drive

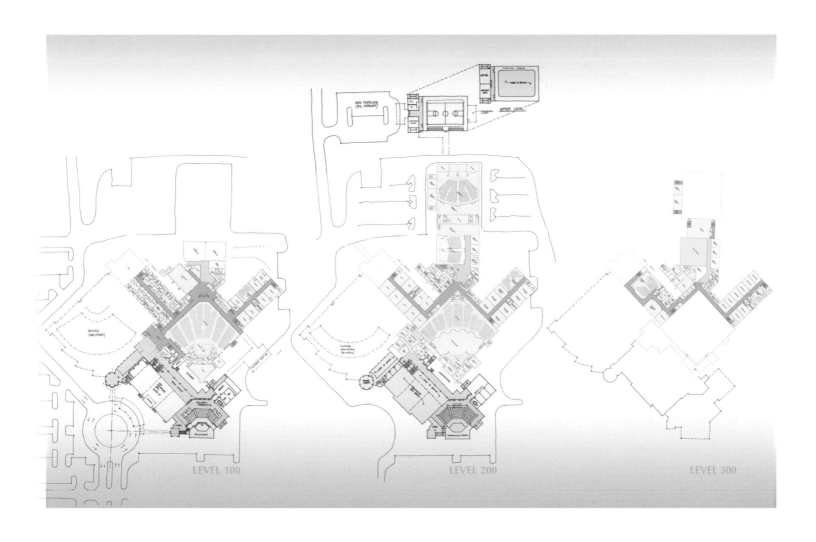

LEVEL 100 LEVEL 200 LEVEL 300

STEP TEN

Gather the Resources for the Journey: The Capital Fund Drive

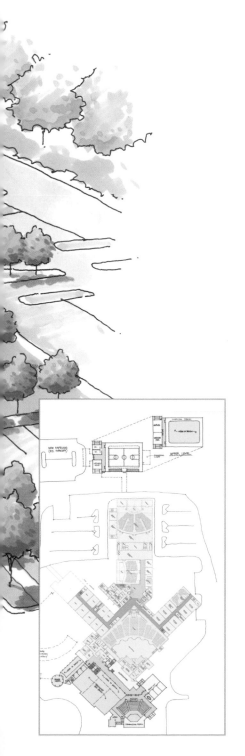

God gave Nehemiah a vision that was captivating. It touched the heart of King Artaxerxes and ultimately the hearts of the people who would help to rebuild the city walls. Once Nehemiah began to share his vision, the resources for construction became available. Then he was able to begin building.

People give to a vision—to a future—and not to a budget or a program. People move into a new house because they have a vision for a better life. Should you consider building for the future or just for the committed members of your congregation? No. The committed will attend in spite of the circumstances.

Instead, you want to build in order to draw the uncommitted and the unbelievers. Also, you build because you believe in the mission of your church and its ministries, and because you believe that the path to growth is to provide for the people who would never hear the truth of God otherwise. Build because you understand that God does not usually provide the resources to do what you are called to do until you step out in faith and begin the journey.

A well-designed capital fund drive—led by either a special team within your church or by a capable and experienced outside professional—is a tremendous asset to the proposed building program. It has the potential to bring the church together with an increased spirit of unity, while strengthening the sense of fellowship in the church.

Properly done, a successful capital fund drive can also dramatically illustrate the strengths and resources available in your church. Just like every other step in this journey, a successful capital fund drive is developed on the basis of defined principles that include a strong understanding of the problems, a well-thought-out plan, and an organized method to provide adequate communication. Most importantly, it is based on biblical giving.

The officials did not know where I had gone or what I was doing. . . . Then I said to them, "You see the trouble we are in: Jerusalem lies in ruins, and its gates have been burned with fire. Come, let us rebuild the wall of Jerusalem, and we will no longer be in disgrace." I also told them about the gracious hand of my God upon me and what the king had said to me. They replied, "Let us start rebuilding." So they began this good work.
—NEHEMIAH 2:16-18

A capital fund drive provides a unique opportunity to grow and stretch the entire congregation in their faith and in their stewardship.

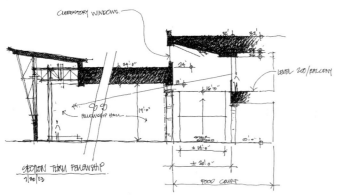

A capital fund drive provides a unique opportunity to grow and stretch the entire congregation in their faith and in their stewardship. When properly presented, this can be a time when many church members who have never pledged to the general church budget step out on faith to help with the new building.

A successful stewardship program often will secure pledges from 60 percent of the families in the church, while the annual budget campaign in most churches may only secure pledges from 30 to 40 percent. A church member who first pledges to the building program and develops a sense of participation in the ministries of the church, has a good chance of maturing into a fully committed supporter of the church. Therefore, during this part of the journey, you should allow an appropriate amount of time for developing a deeper level of understanding for the ministries of the church and the needs that are to be met by the proposed building. This opportunity alone is a sufficient reason for scheduling enough time to conduct an effective capital fund drive.

IT TAKES TIME

It usually takes about six to eight weeks to get organized and prepared to conduct the capital campaign. It will probably take about the same length of time to get all of the material you need to share the vision with your membership. These two components of the journey can be accomplished simultaneously. Usually there is some coordination required between the team handling the capital fund campaign and the team working with the design team to produce the material needed to adequately communicate with the membership.

Another very important reason to schedule adequate time for the planning of the capital fund drive is to allow the proper time needed to prepare the information that will be used to communicate with the congregation. You also need time for your membership to understand, deliberate, and finally approve the plans and information being presented to them.

Some churches only produce brochures, while other churches produce video animations of the project to help in the communication process. The key is to think about the vision that you are trying to cast and match the presentation with your journey. However you choose to communicate this with your membership, it needs to be done properly. Keep in mind that doing it right will take time, and you will need to plan ahead and work around your church calendar.

Detailed planning is essential early in the process of organizing a capital fund drive.

Detailed planning is essential early in the process of organizing a capital fund drive. Most churches have the potential to raise more money for a building project in the months leading up to and during the construction process than at any other time in the life of the church. Since this is the optimum time for fund-raising, adequate allowance must be made in the master schedule for this to be done properly.

A capital fund drive usually involves a commitment day when the congregation makes gifts and pledges to last for a predetermined period of time. Ideally, this commitment event occurs six to nine months prior to the start of construction and at least two years prior to completion of the construction. During the early phases of building, if you can use the funds raised as a result of the capital fund drive, you will minimize the amount of money you need to borrow during construction. Your church will save a significant amount in the cost of interest, and avoid some of its short-term indebtedness.

Just like your leadership team, before they can be expected to reach an intelligent and informed decision, your congregation needs to be fully informed. The church needs to know and understand why the proposed building is required and what areas of the church ministries will be enhanced when the project is completed. They also need to know—

- What kind of space it will provide

- What programs it will support

- What it will cost

- How the church intends to pay for the project

Church leaders who shortcut the process of communicating information often contribute to the confusion and misunderstanding within a church family.

Once again, plan ahead. Do not rush the building program through so fast that you leave some church members feeling confused and left out of the process. If your leadership team has kept the church informed and updated as important decisions were made, your team will have a much easier time explaining the information presented during the capital fund drive.

If your leadership team has kept the church informed and updated as important decisions were made, your team will have a much easier time explaining the information presented during the capital fund drive.

MAIN ENTRY/ PRAYER CHAPEL — FELLOWSHIP HALL — WALKER CENTER

Communication with the congregation is the key to every successful capital fund drive.

INSPIRATION AND INFORMATION

The right kind of communication can inspire your congregation to a greater level of support. This is because it informs and motivates. It also is the key to every successful capital fund drive. There are several tools of communication that can be used: drawings, renderings, models, brochures, and video animation. The use of videos is gaining popularity with many churches. Once you have produced a master video, you can produce still photographs for use in printed material. You also can show parts of the video during group meetings and even produce a special video copy to give every family in the church.

It will take several weeks to produce these required communication tools, and you will need to schedule this in advance with the design team. It is difficult to know exactly what will be needed until after the analysis and preliminary design has been completed. Even with the technology used in today's design offices, it takes many weeks to produce material of the quality that your leadership team will need. After the design team has completed its work on your material, it will take several weeks to finalize the presentation to your church. At this point in the journey, your building design still will not be completed. However, you will have enough material available for congregation to visualize the plan and to understand the design intent. This should be enough to motivate them to support the proposed program.

Imagine the lack of motivation in the appeal of words like these: "We do not know exactly what we need to build, or what it will look like. However, we just want you to give sacrificially because we believe that we need to construct a new building."

Contrast that with a presentation that clearly states, "We want to build a new worship center to seat 1000 people because we already have two worship services and are still nearing capacity. This is the general building design and the way that the new building will look on the outside and on the inside. We will start construction in six months after the completion of the capital fund drive, and we are scheduling the completion of construction 18 months after the start of construction. Of course, all of this depends on your approval and support." The differences in these two statements are remarkable!

Remember, Nehemiah entreated the passion of the king and then of the people. He was able to paint a concise picture of the rebuilt walls of Jerusalem in the minds and hearts of those who would be involved in the project. Once this was done, the people eagerly signed on to the project. You will find that the same is true for your church.

HOW MUCH WILL IT COST AND HOW WILL WE PAY FOR IT?

When you answer these questions, you will provoke comments from the congregation about the anticipated construction costs. Those who aren't in the construction industry are often inclined to think that proposed construction costs are completely out of control.

Take a little time to educate your church on the quality and the cost of your proposed project.

Do your homework and be prepared to answer this question with honesty. Tell your congregation what the leadership team is recommending and why. Take a little time to educate your church on the quality and the cost of your proposed project. If there is someone in your church who is well-respected and knowledgeable about current construction costs, let him or her be the spokesperson to explain this aspect of the presentation.

There are two extreme responses to the financial demands of a potential building program. The first is the church that is overly cautious and conservative and waits so long to build that the window of opportunity for church growth is lost. When this happens, the responsibility usually falls on another church to meet the ministry needs of the community.

The second extreme is the church that fails to do proper planning and rushes to build way beyond its resources. It ends up with a staggering debt that impairs its program and ministries for generations. Fortunately, these are not the only two options available to your church.

PLAN CAREFULLY AND SUCCESSFULLY

Careful evaluation and wise financial planning can transform the financial concerns surrounding a building program into a time of growth and maturity. If your team's financial plans are sound and fiscally responsible, they will serve your church well. It will allow your church to fund this project and to grow and continue to meet the needs of your community. However, if the financial plans that are presented are based on faulty assumptions and flawed financial projections, they can enslave your church and create an enormous financial burden that could curtail the proposed mission and ministry. This is one area of the journey where your team must do everything it can to ensure that you get the best advice possible and that the entire leadership of your church understands and supports the proposed financial plan.

Some two-dimensional graphics do not communicate to people who are not visually oriented. Therefore, extra efforts should be made through videos, models, and other three-dimensional visuals to convey the intended message to every member of your church.

LESSONS LEARNED

The presentation of the plans for the new building to your church is critical and should not be underestimated. This moment sets the tone for the rest of the process. Remember to be willing to communicate your plans and presentation in a clear and concise manner. Often, the design team leader is used to help make these presentations. As an independent member of the process, he or she can often answer the difficult questions and provide the information in a way that is not perceived to be a biased presentation.

Adequate time should be allotted for full and open discussion. Questions and answers should be encouraged. Remember that some two-dimensional graphics do not communicate to people who are not visually oriented. Therefore, extra efforts should be made through videos, models, and other three-dimensional visuals to convey the intended message to every member of your church.

For large and complex projects, there is wisdom in giving the church a week or two to deliberate before asking for a formal vote. At all costs, avoid the impression that the proposal is being rushed, that there is something to hide, or that a decision is required before all of the congregation's questions are completely answered.

Several churches have conducted successful capital fund campaigns based on the idea of going the extra mile. This is when the leadership team presents the project and budget that they feel can be supported by the church, but they also show an additional option that represents more closely what the church really needs to build to remove the current roadblocks. This is presented as a win-win option. If the church funds the project at the first level, the project will move ahead as planned. However, if it funds the projects at the increased level, the project will be enhanced and built with the additional capabilities. Either way, the church does not feel as though it has failed in its capital fund campaign.

I have seen several churches and building programs go down in defeat because the church set unrealistic goals and could not meet them. Be careful to present a campaign in a manner where there is more than one level of expectation. This will allow for a positive approach and a positive outcome. Nothing detours your journey faster than a capital fund campaign that is poorly planned or too aggressive, or one that fails to bring the church together to build for the future.

Six Page Stringer
25.5" x 11" flat
8.5" x 11" folded

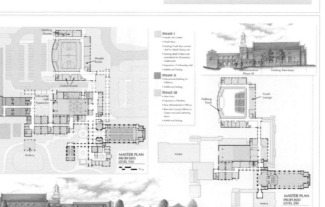

Eight Page Booklet
17" x 8.5" flat
8.5" x 8.5" folded

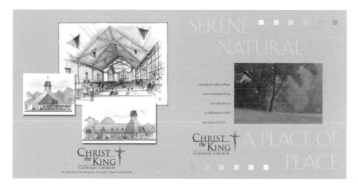

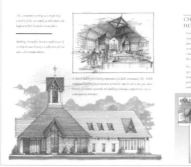

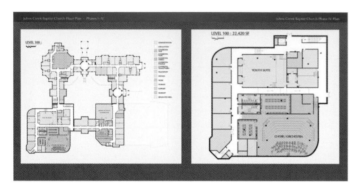

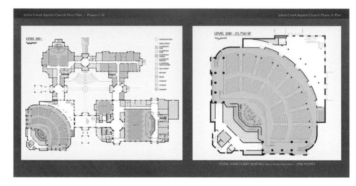

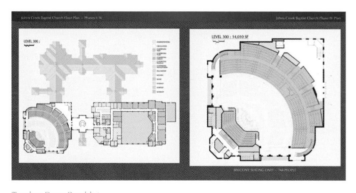

Twelve Page Booklet
17" x 8.5" flat
8.5" x 8.5" folded

STEP ELEVEN

Prepare the Final Program and Design Development Drawings

STEP ELEVEN

Prepare the Final Program and Design Development Drawings

Humility of heart and a teachable spirit were two of the characteristics of Nehemiah's life. He was a man who wanted only to be used by the Lord. He also was a person who willingly listened for God's instruction and was determined to obey. When we honor God with our time, talent, and finances, He sets us on a course for tremendous blessing. As you begin to finalize your plan for your project, think about why you are doing what you are doing. Then consider how God will be able to use your church within your community and perhaps in other parts of the world. When you begin to see your project from His perspective— containing the potential for success that only He can give—all the time you have spent in planning and preparation will become even more meaningful.

O Lord, let your ear be attentive to the prayer of this your servant and to the prayer of your servants who delight in revering your name.
—NEHEMIAH 1:11

PULLING TOGETHER THE DETAILS

It is now time to prepare the final detailed building program. By now, you have completed the space allocation analysis, the strategic master plan, the preliminary program, and preliminary design drawings. The capital fund drive is over, the church has set the resources available for this phase of construction, and your final project budget has been set.

During the past 25 years of working with churches, I have found that it is very difficult to get the leadership team to finalize the program and the building design without the discipline of having the final project budget firmly established. There always is hope that enough resources will be made available to fund just one more important aspect of the plan for your church. We are people of faith, but this is the time to firmly establish the final destination for this journey. It also is the time when the leadership team decides which aspects of your ministry requirements will need to be saved for another journey.

We are people of faith, but this is the time to firmly establish the final destination for this journey.

BALANCING THE WORSHIP AND EDUCATIONAL GROWTH PROVISIONS

By this point, most leadership teams realize that the correct balance of worship, educational space, and parking is crucial to continued growth of their churches. Therefore, a planning strategy that allows for growth in each of these areas becomes essential for the development and growth of your church. Churches that fail to understand this relationship and concentrate their efforts in developing a strategy that provides for growth in only one of these areas will fail to maximize their full growth potential until balance is provided in a future phase of development.

One of the most difficult problems encountered by a church planning for relocation is the decision of which facilities to provide in the first phase of their construction. Many people within the church insist that a significant worship center be built first. They believe that this facility will be the key to providing for growth.

Others within the church who share an understanding of the importance of a strong educational program will insist that adequate space also be provided for Christian education. The dilemma is that most churches cannot adequately provide for both of these needs in their first phase of new development.

The financial demands of providing a building to accommodate both of these needs is probably more than the church can support. Therefore, the challenge becomes finding the balance required to develop the first phase of construction so that the building project will support a growth strategy for both worship and Christian education.

This does not mean that the capacity of both facilities must be identical. It simply means that the leadership team must have a workable plan for growth in both worship and Christian education.

Dual worship services or dual educational sessions may be a part of the overall strategic master plan for your church. One option would be to build a first unit for 900 people in Christian education and only 500 in worship. During its first growth phase, this plan would be based on the church having dual worship services to bring the worship potential to 900.

Another church may decide to build for only 500 people in Christian

One of the most difficult problems encountered by a church planning for relocation is the decision on which facilities to provide in the first phase of their construction.

education and 900 in worship. This plan is based on having dual Sunday schools until a second educational unit could be built. In either situation, the growth would slow when either the worship or Christian education space becomes saturated. At that point, the church should have a plan in place to provide some additional space or additional services.

When facing relocation, many churches overlook this critical point in the planning and the design of their first building. The tendency is to either overbuild the worship space or underbuild the educational space, without properly planning for dual use of their first building.

As a result of this lack of planning, the church only grows to its capacity in the smallest area and never fills the larger capacity in the space provided for the other programs. A lack of worship or Christian education space may not be the only reason these churches reach a plateau. We usually find this to be a significant factor in their lack of growth and a problem that can be predicted and planned for in advance.

Your leadership team and church have a responsibility to make sure that your facility adequately provides for the safety of all who enter.

BUILDING CODES AND SAFETY

Both your leadership team and your church have a responsibility to make sure that your facility adequately provides for the safety of all who enter. The building codes that govern the design of your church are designed to provide a guide to follow as well as establishing the legal requirements for the protection of the public safety in your church.

In recent years, these codes have become increasingly stringent and the regulatory agencies have increased the enforcement of the adopted codes. Every church facility in the United States falls under the jurisdiction of some form of building code. Some local jurisdictions are not as persistent in code enforcement as others. Regardless of the location, your church should make every effort to go the extra mile to make sure that you are meeting the current code requirements and to ensure the safety of everyone in your church.

Prior to January 2000, each local and state municipality chose to follow one of the building regulations outlined in the National Building Code (as published by BOCA), the Standard Building Code (as published by SBCCI), or the Uniform Building Code (as published by ICBO). Recently, a national effort to consolidate all of the governing codes into one all-inclusive code—called the

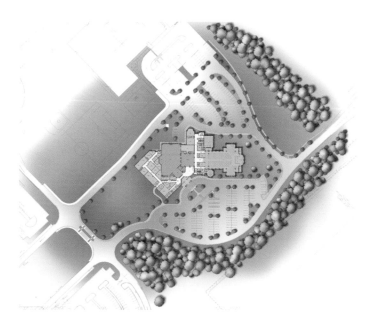

International Building Code (as published by ICCI)—has taken hold, and this code is currently being adopted throughout the United States. The intent of this initiative is to provide order and to simplify the complexity of having various independent guidelines. I believe it is a step in the right direction. However, you need to be forewarned. State and local agencies continue to author amendments that supplement the International Building Code.

These amendments can be very specific and can go as far as defining the exterior building materials and color schemes permitted in your area. A second code guideline that's been adopted throughout the entire country is the Life Safety Code (as published by the National Fire Protection Association). This is usually enforced by a separate agency—normally associated with the local or state fire department.

It also is important that if your church is planning to have special programs that require state certification, such as a day care or preschool facility, that you advise the design team of this intent as early as possible. Generally, both state and local agencies have an additional set of guidelines that define rules and regulations governing the specific requirements for classrooms and support spaces required to secure licensing. The combination of all of these code requirements will have a great impact on church design and construction of your church.

The impact of all of these various building code requirements must be addressed early in the design process. These codes affect everything from the width of your corridors and doors, to the construction type of your stairways, to the type of interior and exterior wall construction you use. Once your building is under construction, the correction of any code violations can be extremely expensive and will often impact the entire construction schedule.

For example, a church built a new worship facility with the intention of adding and finishing a balcony area in a future phase of its development. During the construction, it paid to install the balcony's platform. However, the access stairs to the balcony were not built wide enough to handle the additional occupant load. Therefore, the church was unable to finish this future portion of construction without incurring additional cost. It did not find this out until it was ready to begin construction on the additional seating in the balcony.

Another church started construction on its new facility with the understanding that the county did not require any review process or construction permit.

State and local agencies continue to author amendments that supplement the International Building Code.

However, during the construction, a state inspector drove by and stopped to review the work in progress. He realized that the project did not have a State Fire Marshall construction permit. Therefore, he halted the work until the project was reviewed and all of the state code requirements were met.

Even after they have reviewed and approved the construction documents, it is not uncommon during construction for the reviewing agencies to find items that they want changed. Major problems like those in the previous two examples can be avoided through a careful code analysis during the preliminary design phase and another careful review during the construction document phase.

Building codes are changing constantly, along with the expectations for church design. This often makes it difficult for even highly-trained design professionals to address every issue. Whenever possible, it's a good idea to review preliminary building designs with code officials. This allows early discussion of the design concepts and the life safety plans relative to the building code concerns. Usually this is beneficial to the code officials as well as the church. It not only familiarizes building officials with the proposed project but also allows time for any areas of concern to be addressed early in the design process.

In this way, everyone can work together toward a common goal—the use of the facility for its intended purpose and the safety of its occupants. Your design team should take a leadership role in any code discussions. When this happens, usually all requirements are properly incorporated into the building's design.

HANDICAPPED ACCESS

Provision for the physically handicapped is also required in all new construction and often in the major renovation of existing facilities. Federal, state, and local codes have established minimum standards for these provisions under the ADA (Americans with Disabilities Act). While there are many kinds of physical handicaps, the codes focus mainly on wheelchair access. Although there are many specific requirements, most handicapped accommodation requirements reflect common sense. Most churches want to take the lead in meeting these codes, but often find it difficult to meet the interpretation of the local officials.

These codes often come in conflict with the intent of some code officials who want the church to provide handicap access to every row in the choir and to every level on the platform. Therefore, be sure to take time to review these issues early in

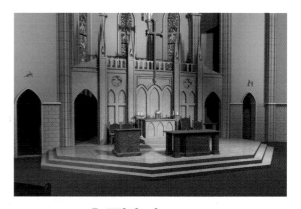

While there are many kinds of physical handicaps, the codes focus mainly on wheelchair access.

As you choose the interior finishes for your new worship center, keep in mind that these elements are extremely important because they will have the most "people contact."

the design process. If you do, you should be able to integrate these elements into the building's design as discreetly as possible. With a little thought, accessibility requirements can be incorporated into the design without causing conflicts and in ways that are beneficial to all building occupants.

DESIGN DEVELOPMENT DRAWINGS, INTERIOR DESIGN, AND MORE

At this point in the process, your design development drawings should be completed. These represent your final building and site design. Once you have reviewed and refined the final project budget, they can be completed. Your master schedule should be refined at this time and reviewed for adjustments.

After the project design has been approved and funded by the congregation, you can proceed. This is the time when all detailed decisions required to move the project forward are made. It also is where you need to make final decisions concerning the building systems required to price your facility—including the structural, mechanical, plumbing, and electrical systems.

In recent years, elements of interior finishes and designs have become very important. The "look" and "feel" of a facility can add or subtract from its overall appeal. Therefore, as you choose the interior finishes for your new worship center, keep in mind that these elements are extremely important because they will have the most "people contact." Interior design is often the one area where you have the most flexibility to save money. However, if the correct amount is not factored into the design budget, you may find that you come up short and do not have adequate resources to meet your expectations for the final project.

Building maintenance is also an integral part of the design development process, and planning for the long-term as well as the short-term maintenance of the completed project should begin very early in the design process. The long-term usefulness of your completed building can only be sustained by having a regular maintenance program, and the cost of this ongoing maintenance should be factored into the decision-making process early in the design. Durability and maintenance expenses are critical factors in the selection of the systems and materials that go into your project. Decisions made solely on initial cost can be very shortsighted and costly over the life of the building.

LESSONS LEARNED

Dr. Walker of Mt. Paran Church of God was the first person I ever heard tell the story about a woman named Virginia. Even during the depression, Virginia was a very wealthy lady. One morning as she returned from shopping for food, her three-year-old daughter ran out to her balcony and greeted her. In the child's excitement to see her mother, she leaned out too far over the railing and fell three stories to her death.

Following the mourning of her beloved child's death, Virginia made a crucial decision. She decided to devote the rest of her days and resources to help the hungry and homeless children of her country.

One day as she was returning home, she noticed a small boy huddled up in a doorway, looking for protection from the cold. This young boy was obviously homeless and hungry. Virginia took him to a restaurant and bought him a good meal. Then she took him to the YMCA where they cleaned him up. Next she took him to the store and bought him new clothes, a coat, and a pair of shoes. As she looked down at the child, compassion welled up within her, and she decided to take him home with her. Upon entering her house, the boy looked up at the tall ceilings, the beautiful furniture, and paintings on the wall, and asked her, "Lady, are you God's wife?"

She answered, "No, but I am His child."

The young lad smiled and said, "I knew you were related!"

Is that not what we all want—to be one of those who are related to God and someone who is willing to share what we have with others? When you begin your church's journey toward growth and expansion, you are taking the first step toward sharing what God has given you with others who need to know Him.

STEP TWELVE

Determine the Method of Construction, Select the Construction Team, and Verify the Construction Cost

STEP TWELVE

Determine the Method of Construction, Select the Construction Team and Verify the Construction Cost

Distractions. We all know the feeling of being on course and then suddenly sensing that we have gotten off track and are wandering along miles of uncharted territory. Nehemiah, however, did not fall for a scheme that had the potential to take him far away from God's plan. When two of his most formidable enemies decided to trick him by luring him away from the construction, Nehemiah refused their offer. There may be times in this process of seeing your new facility take shape, that you will be tempted to go in other directions. This is why you have a master plan, a design plan, and a budget to guide you. They keep you on course and moving in a positive direction.

As I mentioned earlier, there may be times when a short detour is allowable. We can learn a great deal from our mistakes. However, we always need to do what Nehemiah did: have a plan and stick to it.

THE CONSTRUCTION BEGINS

After months of study, evaluation, planning, design, tough decisions, and communication, the time to prepare for construction is finally within sight. Up to this point, the process may have seemed like a series of hard decisions and frustrations. Now that it's time for the construction to begin, your team may feel they can breath a sigh of relief. The dream is about to be fulfilled before your very eyes. But unfortunately, your team cannot assume that from this point forward everything will go according to your plan, schedule, or budget.

The construction process will not be without its own set of unique problems. In fact, some of the major frustrations in the journey usually come during the construction process. Unfortunately, the leadership team cannot simply select a contractor, sign a construction contract, and then wait for the project to be completed. There will still be major responsibilities for your team throughout the

Your team cannot assume that from this point forward everything will go according to your plan, schedule, or budget.

Sanballat and Geshem sent me this message: "Come, let us meet together in one of the villages on the plain of Ono." But they were scheming to harm me; so I sent messengers to them with this reply: "I am carrying on a great project and cannot go down. Why should the work stop while I leave it and go down to you?"

—NEHEMIAH 6:2-3

entire process. So once again, summon your courage and renew your determination for this last major push toward completion and the day that you will begin to use your new facility.

Spend some time evaluating the various options for delivering the construction of your building. Set a goal to become an informed team member, and do not wait until the construction documents are completed before you explore your options for the construction process. Long before you are ready to begin construction, the leadership team should become familiar with the various systems designed to actually deliver a completed building for your church.

In recent years, there has been a proliferation of delivery systems for construction projects. The leadership team needs to know enough about these systems to be able to evaluate the advantages and disadvantages of each, and to match the correct system to the requirements of your project. You will be working with your design team for a long time, and you need to make sure they help you review and understand all your options. The design team has accumulated a lot of experience. They will be able to present the solid options that are available to your leadership team while they continue to work closely with your construction team. Before making a final decision, make sure you listen and fully understand their recommendations.

1. DESIGN-BID-BUILD

The traditional approach to designing and constructing a building usually begins with the selection of a design team, who works with you to develop the final construction documents. The bidding process comes next. This is a time when a group of selected general contractors submit bids for constructing the building according to the construction documents. Based upon the responses of the contractors, the contract usually is awarded to the responsive low bidder.

Advantages to the traditional approach:

1. The church selects and employs the design team that will be directly responsible to the church for the design of the building and for specific construction and administration tasks.

2. With adequately detailed construction documents, contractors do not have to guess at the level of quality and quantity. Therefore, they can submit bids for the construction of the project. Competitive bidding should secure the lowest contract price for the building as designed. The building should be constructed according to specifications and at the contract price.

3. This method also provides significant checks and balances. The architect normally is retained as the church's representative. He assures that the construction documents are followed, shop drawings are approved, all change orders are detailed and credited, and a comprehensive final inspection is conducted.

Disadvantages:

1. During the time that the final construction drawings are completed, early estimates of the construction costs often lack required precision and are very difficult to control. The final cost of the project cannot be known until bids are obtained. If the bids are significantly over budget, it may be a difficult and painful process to revise the plans to bring the cost down.

   Professional estimators are available who, for a fee, will make a cost estimate before plans are complete and with time for changes before bidding. However, these estimators often are not used because they do not have the ability to control changes to the design as the drawings are finalized. Although their estimates can be good tools to check the budget, they do little to establish the discipline necessary to control changes in scope.

2. Since the architect does not know who the general contractor will be until the final bids are opened, the construction documents cannot be developed to take full advantage of the most cost effective systems, materials, and details. Of course, numerous factors interplay in this process, and it is difficult to decide the most economical way to achieve the desired design intent without having the contractor selected prior to the completion of the final construction drawings.

   The design team must keep the overall design intent in mind as the drawings are completed, and must completely detail the project to produce a set of construction drawings to be used in the competitive bidding process. Changing materials or designing alternate methods can have a domino effect. I have found that when one material or detail is changed, this inevitably leads to changes in several other areas of the contract documents. If a set of contract documents is confusing or unclear, the contractors cannot be expected to provide a competitive bid without adding additional money to cover the areas of confusion.

3. The nature of this arrangement often means that the design team, the leadership team, and the construction team bypass significant financial

Both your leadership team and the design team can be kept aware of the financial impact of their decisions before it is too late to make a design revision.

This arrangement brings your leadership team, the design team, and the construction team together as a partnership.

disciplines that could lead them to adopt firm and realistic budget parameters early enough in the design process to keep the project within budget. Therefore, the traditional method does not naturally provide the built-in tools to keep both the design team and the committee from contributing to the development of the construction plans that are beyond the financial capability your church.

Several alternatives to the traditional approach of the design-bid-construction process have emerged. Committees should be aware of these and be able to evaluate the strengths and weaknesses of each.

2. NEGOTIATED PROJECT

One common way to minimize the disadvantages of the traditional design-bid-build system is the use of a negotiated contract. During the design development phase, this approach brings a construction team into the process and draws on its expertise in the many areas that will affect the construction costs. The construction team often can supply firm cost estimates for various alternatives before the design is complete. Therefore, both your leadership team and the design team can be kept aware of the financial impact of their decisions before it is too late to make a design revision. The negotiated contract is a means by which your team, in consultation with the design team, selects a construction team on a negotiated basis. The basis for selection may be either one or a combination of the following:

- Construction costs plus either a fixed fee or a percentage of the cost of construction.

- A guaranteed maximum cost, which includes the contractor's fee, and incentives paid to the construction team for any savings under the guaranteed maximum cost.

Advantages to the negotiated project approach:

1. This arrangement brings your leadership team, the design team, and the construction team together as a partnership. Each member of the partnership has a significant part to play in keeping the project within the accepted budget parameters.

2. Each team member must accept his or her individual responsibility in the process in order to ensure a successful outcome. The key to a successful negotiated contract is the shared responsibility of each team member.

3. If trust is lost between any two of the parties, the process will break down quickly. The entire contract is dependent upon cooperation and trust throughout the entire design and construction process.

4. In this arrangement the design team is still competitively bidding over 90 percent of the project and the leadership team still gets the advantage of competitive bids, but retains the ability of selecting the best specialty contractors for your project. The only items set before the final pricing are the construction team's fee and general conditions.

Disadvantages:

1. It is difficult to maintain the project budget throughout the design.

2. One of the perceived problems with a negotiated contract may be the perceived lack of competitive bidding. During the design phase, this can be dealt with through a process of selecting a qualified contractor. This construction team will consult with your leadership team and the design team throughout the design process to bid out the individual sub-contracts and achieve some of the advantages of the negotiated contract while maintaining a competitive bid environment. In return, these construction teams are given the exclusive privilege of bidding on the project, and the lowest bidder is awarded the contract.

3. DESIGN-BUILD

Another method gaining acceptance is the design-build approach. This approach integrates the two disciplines of the design team and the construction team. The goal is to bring together an architect and a contractor who will work together as one team to provide full services required in the design and construction process. When these two professionals understand and complement each other, significant advantages emerge to produce a well-coordinated project.

Generally, design-build firms work with their clients to determine the broad parameters of the project in the early stages: scope, structural system, mechanical system, roofing system, materials, finishes, and maximum cost. Some limited design-build firms tend to use standard materials, finishes, and structural systems. However, more design-build firms are developing the expertise to provide any building type and any level of interior finish.

When these two professionals understand and complement each other, significant advantages emerge to produce a well-coordinated project.

Advantages to the design-build approach:

1. The church has a single source for the delivery of the desired building and does not have to work with two or more independent firms.

2. Your church will have greater flexibility and more control over cost and schedule.

3. You receive a depth of experience in planning, design, and construction, which are needed to anticipate problems and to react quickly to unforeseen conditions.

4. Relative benefits and costs of various design alternatives can be evaluated more precisely, especially during the design stage, giving the church better information on which to base its decisions. The owner and design-build firm can then make a decision based on complete data.

5. A firm cost is set at the earliest possible time. This, of course, imposes severe restraints upon the owner because the projected cost is tied directly to the established design parameters. Every change made after the budget has been set can increase the cost of the project. However, this is exactly the discipline most churches need in order to keep from over-designing the project and then going through the painstaking process of cutting back on the project scope to bring the project back into budget.

Disadvantages:

1. If a design-build firm is selected that is not led by a design firm then the architect's primary responsibility is to the construction firm and not to the client. For this reason, the design team may not represent the church's interests as effectively as if they were employed directly by the church.

2. Architectural drawings are usually less complete than in the traditional process. This helps to keep costs down, but it also gives the design-build firm more latitude in the final product. The church must be sure it understands exactly what the final outcome will be, so that you get what you expected and produce what you promised the congregation. In addition, the construction-phase services normally provided by the architect are shared with the construction team.

Construction management was developed primarily for complex, multi-million-dollar projects that needed to be coordinated by someone highly skilled in both construction and management.

3. Too much attention may be given to low initial building costs, and true life cycle costing may be sacrificed. This can be a critical mistake that would force your church to pay significant long-term maintenance and operational costs. For example, a focus on low initial building costs can lead to eliminating energy-efficient features that could be very cost effective but would be extremely expensive to add later.

4. CONSTRUCTION MANAGEMENT

Another method to deliver the building is the construction management approach. Construction management was developed primarily for complex, multi-million-dollar projects that needed to be coordinated by someone highly skilled in both construction and management. The purpose was twofold:

- To bring a construction specialist into the design process so that he could work with the architect and utilize his construction expertise in early design decisions relating to construction methods, materials, structural systems, and related issues.

- To bring a person with significant management skills into the construction process for planning, coordination, and execution.

Ideally, by the design-development stage or earlier, a construction manager has been hired. His job is to consult with the design team and to be responsible for managing the construction of the project. The construction manager is not a general contractor. Instead, he is the manager of the construction process.

Advantages to the construction management approach:

1. Both the architect and the construction manager are employed by the church and are responsible to it.

2. Construction expertise is available to the architect and the committee in the design process.

3. Early construction cost estimates can influence the design of the building and contribute to budget control.

4. Competitive subcontractor bidding can help control costs.

Disadvantages:

1. The cost of the construction manager can exceed the savings on a small or medium-size project.

2. Some construction managers and architects do not work well together. This can create conflicts, entangling the committee and complicating the entire process. On some projects, this conflict has pushed the cost of construction even higher.

3. Bonding and insurance arrangements are more complex than with the traditional approach.

Your leadership team needs to be aware that some companies use the term "construction management" in an effort to designate services that differ significantly from those just described. There are many companies that mix some of the concepts from design-build and construction management. In reality, they offer little more than project supervision under the umbrella of construction management. Sometimes, they will have an agreement with an architect to do a minimum amount of design work for the project. The firm then secures bids from subcontractors and sends in a building superintendent to oversee construction.

The superintendent's expertise in construction and management may be limited. These companies do not usually guarantee a maximum cost for the project. They obtain subcontract bids and then estimate other costs. There are times when these firms will talk about a *guaranteed cost estimate*. Many leadership teams hear this term and believe that what they have been given is a firm contract price. However, that is not the case. Usually the contract gives no guarantee that the building will be constructed for a fixed price. For example, one church used a construction management firm and was disappointed in some of the workmanship. They tried to secure adjustments and failed. When they explored their options for legal action, they discovered the contract only obligated the company to consult and advise with the church on the construction project. The committee was surprised to learn that this was the limit of the company's obligation to the church! The committee remembered all the sales talk they had heard and had mistakenly understood the contract on that basis. They had signed a contract without adequate study, evaluation, or even legal counsel.

In the interest of objectivity, committees should note that many churches have used construction management firms and been pleased with the result. However,

Your committee should thoroughly investigate all firms, understand the limits of their proposed services, and submit proposed contracts for approval before signing them.

the advantages and disadvantages cited above for construction management do not apply to all firms who call themselves construction managers. Your committee should thoroughly investigate all firms, understand the limits of their proposed services, and thoroughly review proposed contracts before signing them.

Always remember that the sales presentation is not the contract. Verbal understandings are significant only when supported by specific contractual agreements. The terminology used does not always mean the same thing to everyone using the terms.

5. PACKAGE BUILDER

Another option is the package builder. These are firms that offer a complete building package: design and construction, and perhaps even furnishings and financing. In some respects, these firms are like design-build firms in that one source provides the design and construction work. Package builders usually have an inventory of packages that have been produced for other churches.

They also have a working agreement with an architect to do minor revisions and adaptations. In many instances, the packages are low-cost structures that are produced by cutting corners to reduce the final price. Little or no attention may be given to your church's specific program needs, growth opportunities, long-term master site planning, or projected operational and maintenance costs.

The package builder is a firm that offers a complete building package: design and construction, and perhaps even furnishings and financing.

Package builders offer a variety of working agreements with churches. Some give a firm contract price and bring in their own crews to do the construction work. Others provide only supervision and general administration of the contract and finances. In some instances, the church serves as its own contractor and assumes all the risks usually assumed by the general contractor.

Advantages to the package builder approach:

1. The church works with only one company.

2. Specialization in a certain type of building and sometimes provides more economical construction.

3. Reliable cost estimates of the project are usually available in the early stages of planning. Therefore, if the church limits itself to the package offered, the final cost should be known very early.

Disadvantages:

1. The church gets a standard, stock solution instead of one designed to meet its specific needs. This may mean program needs and future growth possibilities are completely ignored.

2. The architect is secured by the firm and may feel little or no accountability to the church. In many instances, he never goes to the site, never meets with the committee, and has no personal communication with its members.

3. The church may have to assume the same risks as a general contractor.

WHAT IS THE BEST APPROACH FOR YOUR CHURCH?

By now, you are probably thoroughly confused and wonder which option offers the best approach to the challenge of designing and constructing your church building. Don't be concerned. Every owner struggles with this question.

Each of your team members should thoroughly explore the options and evaluate the advantages and disadvantages of each approach, and then determine just what construction risks they are prepared to recommend to your church. Your committee should talk with several churches that have used the various alternatives and look closely at the buildings constructed by the various options.

Your leadership team members need to talk with other leadership teams from churches who have gone through the process that you are now facing. You will want to ask them how their buildings function, along with evaluating the operational and maintenance costs of these facilities. Before your leadership team decides on one option and enters into a contract, be sure to obtain legal counsel to help evaluate the proposed contract.

After doing all this, the leadership team will still need to be aware that no one approach to the design and construction of your building will be perfect and trouble free. During any construction process, there are always frustrations and disappointments. There also will be delays and bottlenecks to face. Regardless of the construction method you choose, each one of your team members will be given the opportunity to remain a model of integrity, love, and grace to the construction team and to all who work on your project.

Regardless of the construction method you choose, each one of your team members will be given the opportunity to remain a model of integrity, love, and grace to the construction team and to all who work on your project.

SELECTING THE CONSTRUCTION TEAM

After you have finally chosen the preferred method of construction, you will need to select a contractor, who also includes his construction team. The right selection in this area will provide your leadership and design teams with the information needed to keep on track, on schedule, and within budget. I also want to point out that construction contracts negotiated with churches tend to change more than those with other owners.

How can you make sure that you have made the best selection possible?

- *Be sure to select a contractor based on integrity.* This is one of the two most important concerns in the process. No matter what other qualifications this person possesses, if he lacks integrity, the committee will likely have to fight one battle after another.

- *Select a contractor and construction team on the basis of competence.* This ranks in importance with integrity. Your contractor and his team should be skilled not only in basic construction techniques but also in cost control. He should possess planning and coordination skills so the project will continue to move forward and meet the various subcontractor deadlines. He also should be able to monitor and control a complex project.

- *Select a construction team with a good reputation.* You want a construction team that has earned respect because of their quality work and sound warranty. The construction team is the key to getting specialty contractors to stand behind their work. In most instances, the church has no formal contract with subcontractors and, therefore, may have little clout with them. However, the construction team is accountable to the church for the work of the subcontractors. They usually have significant clout with them because of continuing relationships in the construction industry. (The exception to the church's relation to subcontractors occurs when the church has no general contractor and in instances of some "construction management" in which the church has direct contract dealings with the subcontractors.)

The construction team is the key to getting specialty contractors to stand behind their work.

Reputable contractors stand behind their projects. They want the buildings be as problem-free as possible.

CHECKPOINTS IN SELECTING A CONSTRUCTION TEAM:

- *Check on the quality of work done on other projects.* This involves not just a visual inspection of those projects but some evaluation from other committees and maintenance personnel. Have there been problems in their workmanship or materials? Have there been any problems with maintenance?

- *Check on their track record for meeting schedules and deadlines.* Are they known for keeping a project moving and bringing it in on schedule? If your project is not a large one, will they push other projects in ahead of yours? If a deadline is critical for your church, consider the possibility of writing a penalty clause into the contract. This imposes a monetary penalty for every day's delay beyond the scheduled completion date.

- *Check on their reputation for monitoring and controlling costs.* Even if your church has a firm contract with the construction team, cost-control skills will be important. If the costs begin to exceed the bid, they may start to look for places to cut corners, which can lead to problems later on in the process. One thing is for certain, this can certainly affect the quality of the building.

- *Check on the reliability of their warranty.* Reputable contractors stand behind their projects. They want the buildings to be as problem-free as possible. They will schedule return trips to make needed adjustments or repairs. However, do not expect the construction team to assume all the responsibility or liability for any trouble that may occur. In some instances, this may be the responsibility of the equipment manufacturer, or it may have been the result of faulty material or design. There are times when the design team, the construction team, and a manufacturer's representative may have to resolve a problem together.

PERIMETER CHURCH YOUTH CENTER
SCHEME A
1"=20'   L.300

The selection of the construction team is a vital milestone. Without accurate construction input, your journey could take the wrong path. Sadly, you may not discover this until late in the process, which might cause you to take a major detour.

However, if you have an experienced design team, you can build the first preliminary project budget without the input of the construction team. The design team can provide the information needed to make appropriate basic decisions concerning the master plan. This will provide all you need in order to present your findings to the congregation for their review and approval. Once this step is completed, the leadership team will need more accurate information.

Selecting the construction team early in the planning process also allows the leadership team to have more input in the selection of the finishes and specialty contractors used on the project. After all, you are building a church, and your goal is not to end up with a profit at the end of this project. Instead, it is to make sure that you invest every dollar as wisely as possible, and to know that those on your team have been good stewards of every resource allocated by the church.

HANDLING CHANGES ON YOUR PROJECT

Your leadership team should have a contingency fund established for those unforeseen but not unexpected conditions. As you move through the construction process, these funds can be freed up to provide for better finishes, upgraded building systems, and additional equipment. However, you always need to remember that any change can lead to alterations in the construction contract.

If you make these changes without having a good construction team member on board, they can become very difficult and costly to negotiate. I always remind members on the leadership team that when it comes to the design and construction of churches today, they need to look ahead and realize that changes are a part of the process and should be negotiated in the final construction cost.

RESPONSIBILITIES CAN CONTINUE FOR CERTAIN TEAMS

At the end of your journey, you want to be sure that you were treated fairly by each team member. You also want to know that you did not pay more than necessary for any part of the process. However, the cheapest way to build a building is not always the most economical way. The bitterness of poor quality lasts much longer than the sweetness of a low price. Often, the low bidder is not around when you have a problem that must be fixed before the next Sunday morning. At times like this, you want a construction team who not only takes pride in their work, but one that will be there to take care of any problem for you.

From the very beginning, your leadership team should seek to establish a strong relationship with the contractor. Whenever he and his team are brought

on board, he joins forces with your leadership team and the design team to create a partnership. If the contractor is chosen on the basis outlined in this step of the project, the relationship should be initiated in a positive way. In some of the early meetings, your team should emphasize the mutual commitment and responsibility you feel is necessary.

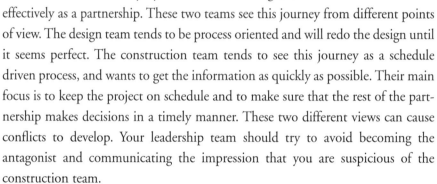

Your team may need to appeal to the design team and the construction team to work in a spirit of unity. You also may want to ask the design team and the construction team to discuss ways you can all work together effectively as a partnership. These two teams see this journey from different points of view. The design team tends to be process oriented and will redo the design until it seems perfect. The construction team tends to see this journey as a schedule driven process, and wants to get the information as quickly as possible. Their main focus is to keep the project on schedule and to make sure that the rest of the partnership makes decisions in a timely manner. These two different views can cause conflicts to develop. Your leadership team should try to avoid becoming the antagonist and communicating the impression that you are suspicious of the construction team.

In other words, don't allow a "you verses us" mindset to develop. Instead, spend your energy on selecting the right construction team for your projects, and on keeping the partnership emphasis in the forefront.

BUILDING A PARTNERSHIP

Agree at the outset that a selected team member will be the only person to communicate with the design team and the contractor.

One of the ways a team relationship is cultivated is by designating a person on your leadership team to work with the design and the construction teams. Once this is done, all other members of the committee should channel communication through this team member. A sure way to create division and a communication nightmare is for several members of the leadership team to go to the job site and tell the contractor what the leadership team expects. Therefore, agree at the outset that a selected team member will be the only person to communicate with the design team and the contractor.

As you begin this partnership, come up with ways to affirm the construction team and compliment them for their good work. Let them know you expect quality work and then recognize and compliment it. Positive feedback allows you to develop a much more constructive relationship than negative comments. Sometimes work is done improperly and inadequately and must be done over. There will be times when your committee representative will have to be confrontational. When this is needed, your leadership team should ask for corrective action. They also should rely heavily on the design team for recommendations according to terms of the construction documents. At times, a spirit of negotiation and an attitude of give and take will be required in order to maintain a sense of partnership.

The key to this is remembering that each person is important to the success of your project. Without the contractor and his subcontractors, your new building will not take shape. I always remind leadership teams that these men and women are committing their resources to your effort. I also have found that a good construction team develops a sense of pride and appreciation for the buildings they construct.

I believe that what you decide to build is as important as how you build it.

BEGIN YOUR PROJECT WITH A CONSTRUCTION CONTINGENCY

Every church needs to begin the building process with a construction contingency. This is to be used to fund unforeseen construction conditions. However, as your project moves forward, you may realize that the entire contingency fund is not required. If this is the case, it can be used for upgrades to the finishes or to buy additional furnishings. Hiring a trusted construction team— one that will make you aware of every opportunity that is available to you—will be the key to making these types of decisions.

As a side note, I want to say that when your team reviews the comments concerning the selection of construction delivery methods, you probably will find that there are several options that fit your church and project. My experience indicates that neither the hard bid option or the package builder option work for most of churches contemplating a building program. Above all, I believe that what you decide to build is as important as how you build it.

I have been on several campuses where the church has outgrown phase one of its master plan quickly. As new leadership team members talk through their areas of concern, I am usually asked to explain what happened. Sadly, in many of these cases, I find that the church decided to build a low-cost building and got exactly what it paid for.

Although your church may not realize what it is purchasing now, it will one day. Therefore, wisely consider your options, along with the potential for future growth and your church's mission. Then make a decision to proceed. This is exactly what Nehemiah did. He did not waste the money that was entrusted to him, but he also knew that he wanted the reconstructed walls of Jerusalem to remain for years to come. So, he purchased wisely and chose team members that would be steady and confident.

Every contractor is going to pay the same thing, within a few pennies, for the brick, block, concrete, steel, and labor. What you are looking for is good management—someone to be your trusted advocate during the construction process. In closing this chapter, I want to remind you to make sure that your contract with the construction team allows you to review and understand the true cost of all materials and labor. Then you can choose the best team based on their fees and overhead.

LESSONS LEARNED

On one of our projects, the leadership team wanted to select the contractor without our input, which is often the case and usually works out without too much difficulty. However, in this situation things turned out differently. The leadership team selected three construction firms to be interviewed—two were very well qualified and one was clearly not qualified for a project of this size and complexity. After the interview process, we were informed that the contractor that was not qualified was selected. We were surprised, expressed our concern and hesitation about using this firm, and asked why it was selected.

The leadership team explained that they had been split in their decision. All had voted for one of the two qualified firms. Both of the qualified firms had the same number of votes. However, when it came down to making a final decision, no one was willing to change his vote. The only way an agreement could be reached was to select the third construction firm—the one that was unqualified and the one that no one had selected initially! Due to this decision, the project became a struggle for all involved.

I realize that it can be difficult for some committee members to select a construction team. They realize that

they will have to stand before their congregation and explain their choice. However, solid decisions must be made—ones that will be in the best interest of the church and the success of the project.

I usually recommend that a leadership team complete the pricing drawings. Then the team should select three qualified contractors to price these drawings and make a presentation, which covers the estimated construction cost, schedule, and their method of working with the church and design team. I also urge churches to be open to potential ideas from the construction teams interviewed on how a project can be improved.

The leadership team can then make a selection of the construction team with the knowledge that they have had a competitive review of the drawings and the construction cost. Of course, there always is risk involved. By this point, your leadership team has made several decisions that will affect the cost of your project. They also have set certain expectations in the minds of church members.

Realize that during the review process, some decisions may be altered depending on the information received from the contractor and the construction team. However, if your leadership team chooses a qualified firm with an excellent reputation and experience, you should have accurate information in order to establish an excellent budget.

ADVANTAGES	*Project Delivery Methods*	DISADVANTAGES
Assurance that the best price was obtained	◄ **1** **DESIGN-BID-BUILD** ►	Poor early budgeting opportunities Poor value engineering opportunities Poor team building opportunities Little control over sub-contractor selection Potential for more change orders Difficult to negotiate change orders
Good potential to resolve complex problems Opportunity to value engineer budget Good opportunity for sub-contractor selections Good early conceptual budgeting Good team building opportunity	◄ **2** **NEGOTIATED BID CONTRACT** ►	Unsure you obtained the very best price Poor early budgeting opportunities Can be difficult to select construction team
Early fixed contract amount Greatest cost and schedule control Single contract for design and construction	◄ **3** **DESIGN-BUILD CONTRACT** ►	May not be the best choice of design talent Contract drawing is not usually as complete Sometimes too little attention to program
Competitive subcontract pricing Good early cost control Can provide church with management skills Architect and Construction Manager contracted to church	◄ **4** **CONSTRUCTION MANAGEMENT CONTRACT** ►	Can add costs on small to medium size projects Bonding and insurance arrangements more complex Construction Manager not always a team player and can cause conflicts
Usually very competitive construction costs Reliable early cost information Church has one contract	◄ **5** **PACKAGE BUILDER** ►	Usually standard or stock plans Architect works for builder and has little accountability to the church Church may assume additional bonding or contract risks Church may not be able to customize building and still realize cost savings

STEP THIRTEEN

Complete the Construction Drawings and the Building Construction

- Complete all construction documents

- Complete all construction pricing

- Complete permitting process

- Begin construction

- Coordinate all construction activities

- Obtain certificate of occupancy

- Deliver all maintenance and warranty manuals

- Follow up on warranty items

- Six-month inspection

- Year-end inspection

- Yearly follow-up inspections and reports

STEP THIRTEEN

Complete the Construction Drawings and the Building Construction

Can you imagine how Nehemiah felt looking out over the completed walls surrounding the city of Jerusalem? His heart was overwhelmed with a sense of gratitude to God. While the workers had been faithful, he knew that it was the Lord who had given them the ability, courage, and strength to complete the task.

Where there had been brokenness and destruction, there now was strength and stability. Nehemiah could travel the circumference of the walls and never see a gap or a place where enemies could enter. A safe boundary had been established and the people of the city could now begin to rebuild their lives. They also had a fresh desire to worship the Lord. Often, this is the result of a construction effort, especially when God is the One who is leading the project and guiding all who are involved. Renewed hope and vision for the future lift the hearts of many.

ESTABLISH THE FINAL CONSTRUCTION COST

One of the key aspects of the project that Nehemiah had to address was financial accountability. The financial discipline established by having the final construction cost and the final project cost set should not be underestimated. There will still continue to be many good ideas for things that need to be added to the project. A certain portion of the congregation will support each of these good ideas, and all the supporters will be working with good motives. The truth is that all these ideas represent relevant and valid concerns. As I mentioned earlier, if your church is like most, it probably cannot afford to build everything it needs to build, let alone build everything it wants to build.

The only way to bring any sense of order to the inevitable increase in the scope of the project is to have the final construction budget established. This will need to be reviewed and approved by the construction team and by the church. Once this is done, your team's real work of setting the final priorities will begin. This is usually the hardest task the leadership team will accomplish. After all, who wants to be the one to choose a portion of the children's ministry to be built over an

> *So the wall was completed on the twenty-fifth of Elul, in fifty-two days. When all our enemies heard about this, all the surrounding nations were afraid and lost their self-confidence, because they realized that this work had been done with the help of our God.*
>
> —NEHEMIAH 6:15-16

> *The only way to bring any sense of order to the inevitable increase in the scope of the project, is to have the final construction budget established.*

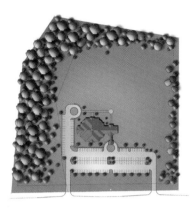

element of the music ministry, or certain parking requirements over additional seating in the worship center?

As you move from the design development drawing to the final construction document, this is exactly what needs to happen. The design team cannot proceed without this final information. It will take a lot of time and money to produce the final documents, but it could cost your church even more to change its mind after the design team completes this part of the process.

Therefore, your leadership team should be very careful not to set expectations that cannot be met. Remember, up until this point there has been an opportunity to revisit previous decisions or to add just one more small detail.

COMPLETING THE CONSTRUCTION DOCUMENTS

A design team familiar with the construction process should be able to guide you through this step, give you the information you need to make an informed decision, and keep this journey on the right path.

Upon the final approval of the design development drawings and the approval of the final project budget, the leadership team can authorize the design team to move forward with the construction documents for the project. There are many decisions left for your team to make. The design team will begin to select the final mechanical system and the security system, and coordinate the actual structural system with the rest of the building elements.

It may appear that most of the decisions required by your team have been made. However, there are many more that the design and construction teams must make before they can prepare a final construction contract for signature. This is a point where decisions about the method of construction, the types of systems, and the construction details can make a great impact on the construction budget. This also is a time in the process where many people are working on the project at the same time. If not properly coordinated, the project can veer off course before a partnership between the teams has been formed or realized.

At this stage, all of the various consultants who make up the design team will be working on this project. A decision made by one consultant ultimately affects the work of the others. Also, you may have a situation where one consultant cannot complete his work until another completes what he is doing.

The electrical portion of the project cannot be finalized until the mechanical engineers size all of their motors, and they cannot do this until they have completed all of their energy calculations. This series of steps may seem to make the process long. However, this is the only way to properly complete and

coordinate the construction documents, especially for a custom building designed to meet the special needs of a church like yours.

The decisions made during this step are ones that will communicate all of the other decisions to the construction team. Your team will need to review these documents and provide feedback on these systems before the final contract is signed with the construction team. I have found that during this part of the process, some projects become simpler and easier, while others become more complex, difficult, and expensive. A design team familiar with the construction process should be able to guide you through this step, give you the information you need to make an informed decision, and keep your journey on the right path.

No matter how many similar and successful projects your design team has completed, there always will be new problems to confront and solve. My advice is to stay in contact with the design team, ask for three or four reviews, and ask questions—especially when you do not understand something.

This point in the project is complex and involves many different engineering disciplines.

The best building projects come as a result of an active and participatory partnership. Even after you have spent a great deal of time with members of your design team, never assume that they understand every aspect of your church's mission and have the same desires for the project.

This point in the project is complex and involves many different engineering disciplines. It is best to remember that your church's project is unique because it is being constructed to meet your personal needs. I always encourage leadership team members to take the necessary time to review the drawings and to understand "what you are buying and building" before you sign the construction contract. Most design teams welcome this type of review and are interested in making sure that there are no surprises during the construction process. Understanding what is taking place during this process will help you know when to ask for a review and when your team needs to provide the input required to keep this journey on schedule.

Giving input too early can lead to the need to review and change what is being done, especially if you do not have all of the information you need to make an informed decision. Providing input too late adds time to your working schedule. This portion of the process can be difficult to manage due to the individual consultants working on the project and because one consultant's work is dependent upon the work of others. A design team that is familiar with this step in the project is extremely important to your leadership team. It helps if this team has worked together on previous projects.

Also, as part of the final coordination, you need to review the interior design selections made in the design development phase. During this step of the process, the interior design construction documents, including any provisions for any furniture procurement, are finalized.

Make sure that the construction team you have hired is planning to construct the same facility that your team has promised the church that it would build.

What you will "see, feel, and touch" in your new building is extremely important. The interior design drawings show all of the special finish elevations and details required to complete your building. Also, any special ceiling or wall treatments should be "shown" and detailed. Be sure to take time to review and to understand each one of these drawings. They represent the "look and feel" of your new facility. More than any of the others, these drawings set a tone for your project. They also are an important factor in determining how your church will respond to its new facility.

As this project takes shape and becomes a reality, watch out for any surprises that may surface. You can do this by making sure that the desires of your leadership team have been correctly communicated, understood, and translated into the information on the construction documents. Make sure that the construction team you have hired is planning to construct the same facility that your team has promised the church that it would build.

It is almost a certainty that some modification to the original design will need to be made. No design team can foresee the coordination needed to meet the requirements of all of the special consultants. This is the reason construction documents are developed. However, the design team should keep your team fully informed of any required coordination changes. This way, you will have a good understanding of the project and can approve the changes that are necessary. The difficulty is not that many small details will change—this is inevitable. The problems come when these changes are not reviewed with the leadership team. Some may not seem very important until there is a problem on the construction site and everyone is upset because of a misunderstanding about some aspect of the project.

COORDINATING PRICING AND EFFORT

As your leadership team continues to gather accurate pricing information from the construction team, you may need to have the construction documents modified to meet the church's required project budget.

It will take time and a concerted effort to review the drawings and interior finishes, but this is much easier and less time consuming than trying to solve a misunderstanding about the design during construction. Most misunderstandings are not caused by anyone making a mistake but rather by miscommunications. So, be steady and don't quit. Remained focused on the task at hand and spend the necessary time to completely review the drawings as they are finished. If you do not understand an aspect of the drawings, ask questions! This is your building project, and it is your responsibility to be informed before you make a final decision.

Once these steps are completed, your leadership team will want to make sure that final construction documents are ready for final pricing, for submittal to the permitting agencies, and for construction. In order to obtain a building permit, the city, county, or state building and fire marshal's offices must often review and approve your construction drawings. These agencies have the authority to require additional changes to your plans, either because of differing code interpretations or often to meet requirements dictated by codes that have changed since you began planning for construction.

Prior to issuing a permit, and as a means to control many environmental and life safety issues, the local review agencies are requiring church facilities to meet more construction requirements than ever before. Regulations almost always equate to higher construction costs. Therefore, these agencies must be involved during the planning and design process.

Regulations almost always equate to higher construction costs. Therefore, these agencies must be involved early during the planning and design process.

If you get input from these groups as early as possible, the final permitting process will be easier and contain fewer surprises. It seems as though many jurisdictions are creating new regulations as a way to slow down new construction and limit growth in their communities. Your design team should be familiar with the time it takes to get through the permitting process and should be able to help your team schedule accordingly. As always, communicate your progress with your congregation by giving them updates along the way. They will appreciate the information and encourage you in your effort.

Usually, the design team will prepare the initial contract for review by both your team and the construction team.

FINALIZE THE CONSTRUCTION CONTRACT

Once the construction documents are completed and the construction team has provided the final construction cost, it is time to enter into the construction contract. Usually, the design team will prepare the initial contract for review by both your team and the construction team. One crucial point of decision is the requirement for a performance and payment bond to protect the church in the event of the contractor's default on the project.

The bond will provide for the completion of the building, including contractor performance, labor, and materials. It should also cover extra work by the architect that is often required when a bonding company must take over a project. Even large and reputable contractors have been known to have serious cash flow problems leading to the default of a contract. The performance bond is basically an insurance policy that stipulates that the church will obtain the completed building at the original contract price, if the contractor defaults on his contract.

If your church does not have these bonds and the contractor defaults on the contract, the church will simply have to pick up the pieces, find a new contractor, and negotiate for the completion of the building. Generally, the original contract price would no longer be guaranteed. If the construction process is properly monitored and your leadership team has selected a good construction team, the actual risk to the church can be minimized. However, there always are risks that cannot be completely controlled, and your team needs to understand these before it assumes responsibility for the construction.

The cost of the bonds can be broken out of the base bid as an alternate. Even if the church elects not to require bonds on the project, there is wisdom in stipulating that the bonds become a part of the contractor's bid. Surety and bonding companies establish premiums on the basis of the perceived risk factor and past performance of the contractor. Therefore, your team can learn some important aspects about the construction team through examining the certified written quotation from the surety company. This might even alert your team to some unknown problems or potential risks involved with a particular construction team.

Making sure that the construction team has adequate insurance is one of the duties of your team. Along with that, your leadership team should make sure that the performance, labor, and materials payment bond are identified in the contract documents and presented in review along with the contractor's final pricing.

If your team decides to hard bid your project, bonds should be required. However, if you select a qualified contractor and negotiate the contract price for your project, this will probably not be required. The general contractor should bond all of their major subcontractors. This will give you the protection you need for most negotiated construction projects, and you probably do not need additional bonds for the general construction, unless your financial institution requires it. Many financial institutions will waive the bonding requirement for contractors that have a strong financial history.

In addition to the payment and performance bonds, it also is important that your church has proper coverage in each of the following areas:

- Liability

- Builder's risk

- Workman's compensation

- Fire and casualty

- Property damage

Builder's risk insurance coverage may need additional explanation. This type of interim insurance covers the building as it is being constructed. It also protects the contractor and the church against loss until the building is completed and insured. In order to be certain there are no needless duplications and that no area is being overlooked, be sure to discuss this insurance coverage with your design team and the agent who normally handles the church's insurance. Once again, work with your design team to determine the proper coverage for your specific project.

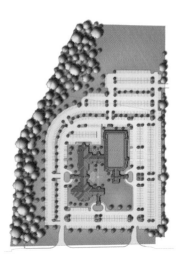

The contract will usually specify the coverage the general contractor must provide. In most instances, this includes liability, builder's risk, and workmen's compensation insurance. Other delivery systems present varying degrees of complex insurance coverage because the lines of liability and financial responsibility are not as clearly drawn as with a general contractor. Some of these delivery systems place all of the responsibility on the church. Your leadership team should be certain that adequate coverage is provided for the church. During this critical time, the liabilities and risks are too great to cut corners and leave the church unprotected.

It also is important that your church has proper coverage in liability, builder's risk, workman's compensation, fire and casualty, and property damage.

Give careful attention to the type of contract used for the construction project. Your church should try to use a standard contract developed by either the

American Institute of Architects or the Design-Build Institute Association. These contracts represent industry standards, have clear legal language, and hold no hidden clauses or bias.

If the contractor you have selected objects to either of these contracts and insists on using his own standard contract, the leadership team should view this development with concern and caution. You need to *insist* on extensive legal scrutiny of the proposed contract. Any modifications to either of the other contracts should also be subject to legal review before the document is signed.

The design team should be commissioned to visit the site on a regular basis to observe the construction and to prepare site status reports.

Negotiating and executing the contract with the construction team should not be taken lightly or done in haste. Review the entire contract with your design team to make sure that your team really understands the contract that will be executed. If your committee is going to err in this process, let it be to the point of being overly cautious and legally judicious.

MONITOR THE CONSTRUCTION PROCESS

Construction administration is the term usually given to this step. During the actual construction, there will still be many important decisions to be made and several meetings will be required to review changes dictated by unforeseen conditions. The design team should be commissioned to visit the site on a regular basis to observe the construction and to prepare site status reports. During these visits and meetings, they also should provide the coordination that is needed between your leadership team and the construction team.

The main focus of the construction team is to coordinate all of the work and the materials used so that the project will be completed on schedule. Sounds simple enough, but this is a very complex task. Every decision and change affect the schedule and all of the construction team's coordination. Therefore, they want the plan to be complete and consistent in order to avoid changes. They also know that they need the submittals returned promptly so every problem will be resolved as soon as possible. If the construction team has any hope of finishing on time, their focus must remain on the project coordination and schedule.

At this point, the design team's main focus should be set on getting everything coordinated and finding the best solution for the project. This may take longer than first thought, but patience always pays off. As owners, you also will be focused on getting everything right—the brick and mortar, the paint color, the carpet selection, and the position of each piece of furniture.

During the construction process, the fundamental conflict becomes the different focuses of the construction team, the design team, and the leadership team. In order for the contractor to have a successful project, he needs information on time and according to his schedule, or things get out of sequence and the construction process becomes off balance, behind schedule, and, finally, litigious. A good design team, however, will realize this fundamental conflict and will work with the construction team to maintain the contractor's schedule, even if they have to push the leadership team to make some decisions quickly.

The tension that can build between these teams should not be overlooked or ignored. If the partnership is going to work, the leadership team and the design team must be willing to make the decisions required to keep the project on schedule. By now, most of the fundamental decisions required to bring the project to a point of reality have been made, and the real work of actually building your new building lies ahead. Your design team will spend many months of intense effort to coordinate your construction project, and your construction team will spend every day coordinating and scheduling each aspect of the project. Many hours also will be spent working with subcontractors, making sure that as one completes his assignment, the next can begin his.

The leadership team and the design team must be willing to make the decisions required to keep the project on schedule.

Over the course of the project, the design team should keep your leadership team informed each step of the way. This is why regularly scheduled meetings are recommended to review the construction process, the budget, and changes to the work. It is the intent of these meetings to keep everyone informed and to solve coordination issues before they become large problems.

Set regular periodic meetings with the design team on the construction site to review the progress of the construction, and to discuss any construction problems or changes the church would like to make during the construction process. The meetings also can be used to answer any questions that the church might have concerning the building.

The timing of these meetings depends on the size and complexity of the construction project. At a minimum, these meetings should be held on a monthly basis. For larger projects, it is normal to meet on a weekly or biweekly basis. The design team should prepare *change orders* for alterations in the scope of the work. They also should review the shop drawings and submittals from the contractor—along with reviewing and approving the contractor's applications for payment.

There is usually an independent company hired to perform the testing required to ensure that the specified quality level is being maintained. Invoices from this company normally go to the design team for approval before the church pays them.

No matter how much time the leadership teams spends looking over the drawings, there will be some aspect of this project that you will want to revise—it may be as simple as the location of a door, or as complicated as the redesign of a room. Remember, revision is a part of the construction process. While each team member will do everything possible to minimize changes, these will happen. The sooner these changes are identified, the more economical they are to make. Even simple changes affect several subcontractors and will take a lot of effort to coordinate.

COORDINATE THE OWNER SUPPLIED ITEMS

Most of these projects include some furnishings or equipment that will be purchased directly by the owner and included in the project. This is most often pews, kitchen equipment, computer networks, telephone systems, security systems, athletic equipment, or furniture. The design team will usually help to coordinate the required delivery dates for any of this equipment or furnishings.

They also will coordinate and schedule the deliveries with the contractor to ensure that the overall construction schedule stays on track. Kitchen equipment requires more coordination than any of the other owner furnished items; the effort required to coordinate the proper connection of this equipment is significant. In spite of everyone's efforts, it is common to have problems with the hookup of the kitchen equipment. Therefore, my recommendation is to have the construction team purchase and coordinate the kitchen whenever possible.

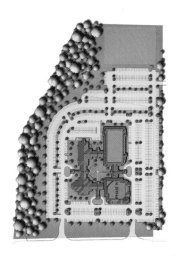

Have the construction team purchase and coordinate the kitchen whenever possible.

CLOSE OUT THE CONTRACT

As the construction process finally comes to an end, make sure that all the training necessary in order to use your new facility is completed, all of the warranties are processed, and everything is ready for the building dedication. Develop a final list of corrections for the contractor, meet with your design team to make a final inspection of the building, and list all *punch list* items to be corrected. When this list is completed, make the final payment to the construction team and design team.

The post construction and follow-up portion of the project often is misunderstood. When the construction finally is completed, your church will be ready to celebrate. To your surprise, many in your church may be ready to move on to another new challenge. However, the partnership you have shared with the other teams is not over yet. There is still a little distance to be covered before your journey is completed. This is because the end of the construction process is not the end of your involvement with the project.

After the building dedication, the design team will make sure that any warranty items are resolved. After six months, a meeting should be set to review the entire project and to discuss any part of the project left undone. At the end of six months and then again at the end of a year, the leadership team and the design team should inspect the project to ensure that all the systems are working properly. Each of these inspections should be followed up with a written report for your records.

You also need to—

• Make any final arrangements necessary with the loan company for permanent financing.

• Contact your insurance agent to secure appropriate insurance on the new building.

• Present a final report to the church members from the leadership team to address any final actions taken by your team.

After six months, a meeting should be set to review the entire project and to discuss any part of the project left undone.

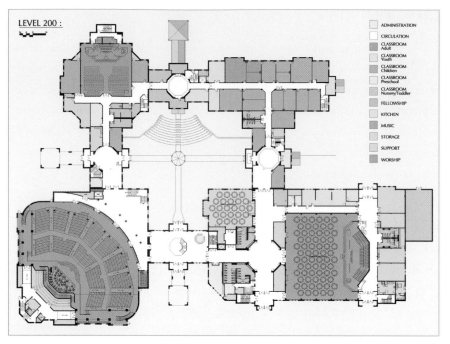

LEVEL 200 :

Your building dedication is a time of true celebration. It also is a time to review the journey you have just taken and to look forward to the impact your church will have on its community and beyond.

• Be sure to document in writing the decisions and actions made by the leadership team for reference by future leadership teams.

• Prepare for your building dedication service.

DEDICATE THE BUILDING

The time leading up to your actual building dedication also can be a time of very special celebration. Once we dedicated a new worship facility where the congregation read through the Bible from Genesis to Revelation within 72 hours. This was followed by 24 hours of music and by 48 hours of prayer. Over 144 volunteers were involved in a celebration that began at 8 A.M. on a Monday morning and ended at 8 A.M. the following Sunday morning, just before the worship service!

This was a great way to prepare for the first service—a service of dedication, which was really the continuation of the week's commitment of each of those volunteers. I want to underscore the need to be creative and quick to involve your congregation in this time of celebration. Also, do everything possible to focus the successful conclusion of the project on the mission of your church.

When the walls surrounding the city of Jerusalem were completed, Nehemiah made a point of calling the people together for a time of dedication and celebration. He was quick to remind everyone involved that God was the One who completed the project. The priest Ezra read from the Law of Moses and "the people assembled as one man in the square before the Water Gate" (Nehemiah 8:1). It had been a long time since they had heard God's Word being read. Therefore, they began to weep. However, Nehemiah told them, "This day is sacred to our Lord. Do not grieve, for the joy of the Lord is your strength" (v. 10). By the end of chapter 8, we find that the people had celebrated for seven days! On the eighth day, they stopped and worshiped the Lord and recalled all that He had done.

Your building dedication is a time of true celebration. It also is a time to review the journey you have just taken and to look forward to the impact your church will have on its community and beyond. Remember, you are dedicating more than bricks, mortar, steel, and glass. You are dedicating a place of worship to God and ministry. In a sense, you also are rededicating yourself and your congregation for God's work. Your church is a place where men and women, along with your youth, will be trained, encouraged, and taught to live the lives God calls them to live.

Don't miss this truth because it is the reason that you began your journey of expansion and new construction.

The real work of the church begins with the benediction of your worship service. Each Sunday morning, you will leave for one week of mission work. As you go, you become actively engaged in the work of your church—the work of its mission, which is to speak out, to speak up, to call others to change, and to join in the good fight as you seek ways to bring others closer to God.

LESSONS LEARNED

Before I close this chapter, I want to encourage you to schedule several times when your pastor will visit the job site and share with the workers just how God will use your new facility. He needs to thank them for the work they are doing. Workers and laborers are the often the forgotten teammates of a project. The truth is, you could not finish your new building without them, and they need to know that you appreciate their work.

Schedule several times when your pastor will visit the job site and share with the workers just how God will use your new facility. He needs to thank them for the work they are doing.

A young pastor was concerned about the workers building an addition to the church where he served. Each morning as he walked to his office, he noticed their efforts. Finally, he decided to stop and speak to three brick masons, who were building one of the walls of the new worship center.

The pastor asked the first mason what he was doing and without much emotion, the man answered that he "was building a brick wall." Somewhat taken back by the man's comments, the pastor continued on to the next mason and asked the same question. This man looked at his watch, turned to the pastor, and said that he was "working until four o'clock."

As the pastor approached the last mason, he could feel hesitation rising up within him. However, he pressed on and asked the question once again. This time, to his delight, the answer was completely different. This man's voice contained a definite sense of excitement as he explained, "I'm working on the most important project of my life—a church, and I can't wait until it is completed so I can bring my wife and children here to worship."

Each of us have known people like these three men—some just do their jobs, some just "put in their time." Yet, others understand the potential of what they are called to do and are looking forward to a time when they can share the finished results with their loved ones. At times, all of us have fallen short. We have watched the clock and have done only what was needed to get by. In short, we lost sight of our commitment. However, this does not have to be the case. We are God's workers—chosen by Him for a good work. Therefore, remember that whatever you do, however you do it, your work will end up in the hands of our Lord. So be diligent and be faithful.

We are all builders. We take the days that are given to us-hour by hour, day by day-and with them we build our relationships, our reputations, and our lives.

The way we conduct ourselves seems to have more to do with what we think about our calling than on what we are called to do. When you have to make a hard choice, when you need to speak up and don't want to, when you just want to finish this journey and move on, recall the words of the third mason: "I'm working on the most important project of my life." When you do this, it will help build courage for your journey and strength enough to carry you through the project.

STEP FOURTEEN

Review and Prepare for the Next Journey

STEP FOURTEEN

Review and Prepare for the Next Journey

I was not in Jerusalem, for in the thirty-second year of Artaxerxes king of Babylon I had returned to the king. Some time later I asked his permission and came back to Jerusalem. Here I learned about the evil thing Eliashib had done . . . I also learned that the portions assigned to the Levites had not been given to them . . . So I rebuked the officials and asked them, "Why is the house of God neglected?" Then . . . all Judah brought the tithes of grain, new wine and oil into the storerooms.　　—NEHEMIAH 13:6-7, 10-12

Nehemiah was faithful in every way because he had believed and trusted in the Lord. Just as he had promised, the walls surrounding the city of Jerusalem were rebuilt and completed on schedule. Then he returned to Babylon where he reassumed his position as a cupbearer to the king.

However, even though he returned to his place of service, Nehemiah did not view the project as behind him. He knew there could be future work, and there was. At a later point, he went back to Jerusalem to review the project. What he found surprised him. This time the house of the Lord was in need of repair—not just physically, but spiritually. Once again, Nehemiah took up the challenge and would not let anything prevent him from completing his task and glorifying God.

PREVENTING FUTURE ROADBLOCKS

Close to the end of the project, you may find yourself wondering if you will ever reach your goal, but you will! Then comes the exciting part—when you begin to enjoy your new facility. At this point, planning to return to review and evaluate the journey is an often overlooked part of the project. The time of completion and celebration is a high point in the life of any church. It is great to watch the congregation taking full advantage of its new facility and to see the church's programs operating and growing as expected. This is when you probably will realize that the project consumed more of your time, talent, and treasure than you

If your strategic master plan was successfully developed, you will be able to predict the next blockage and take the right steps to avoid it.

had planned. Certainly, everyone understands that you need to get on with life. So, why would it be necessary to continue to meet, plan, and evaluate the work that has been done?

If your project has been successful, then you will want to remove any roadblocks that may prevent your church from growing in the future. If your strategic master plan was successfully developed, you will be able to predict the next roadblock and take the right steps to avoid it. In all of this, you will find that you have learned to be pro-active and to plan ahead.

Once this journey is completed and you have been using the new facility for six months, take time to get the team back together and review the project and the assumptions you used to develop your strategic master plan. Do they still seem valid? When it comes to your new facility, be sure to take note of what is working as planned and what has surprised you about the completed project. After you have been in the new building for 12 months, repeat this process once again. Also, review the growth and ministry milestones that were set at the beginning of your project. Then be prepared to make the necessary changes to the assumptions you used and, if necessary, revise your master plan.

Before you begin to build again, you may need to recall just how long it took to finish the last project and begin planning ahead. One of the many advantages to having a strategic master plan is the evaluation and modification process. There is no need to start over and create a new plan. Instead, make a commitment to a periodic update of the plan so that your church stays ahead of the growth curve and avoids reaching a plateau or being stopped by another roadblock.

For example, you may have built a new worship center, but only had enough resources to provide parking to meet the building codes. There are not enough spaces available to truly allow the worship center to be used to its fullest capacity or for multiple sessions on Sunday morning. However, a well-developed strategic master plan should provide the information you need to predict when an increase in your worship attendance will require additional parking to sustain your growth. Or, perhaps, you were able to provide all the necessary parking in order to support your worship center, but only enough nursery space and children's space to meet the needs of three-fourths of the people who attend your Sunday worship service. Once again, using your master plan, you should be able to predict when this need will occur and plan ahead before you find yourself in a crisis.

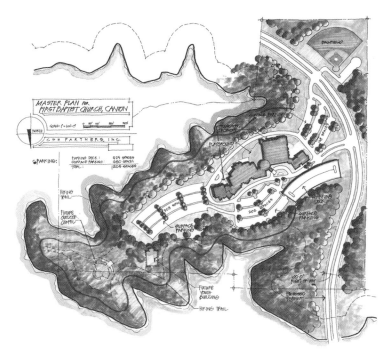

Ultimately, the strategic master plan must address the successful balance of all the elements of your church's ministry.

THE NEXT CRITICAL PART

The next critical part of a strategic master plan becomes the identification of any major roadblocks that need to be removed so your church can continue growing. Ultimately, the strategic master plan must address the successful balance of all the elements of your church's ministry. Initially, most churches center their focus on the areas of worship, parking, children, youth, and adults. This mix will be dependent upon the demographics of your church and new members.

I can't emphasize this enough: the fundamental key to providing successful, sustained growth is found in having a well-thought-out strategic master plan. This is a plan that addresses the final, overall balance of each ministry and their relationships to each other as identified by your church. It also includes a preliminary phasing plan so that the entire congregation understands the priorities of the established or proposed construction sequence. As long as they know that there is a plan in place, and that the existing conditions are not expected to be permanent, most church members will put up with the construction process, the temporary shortages of space, and the need to continually provide the resources necessary to sustain the growth.

The process that you use on your journey to expand, along with the growth you experience will help you know the right questions to ask concerning the future. These also provide key insights into how you need to plan, prepare, and discover the solutions to the future roadblocks that will come your way. Actually, this part of the process is never really complete. Some church leaders try to ignore the subject of roadblocks. They simply wait for another crisis to force them into action. However, sooner or later they will need to deal with the many good problems associated with sustained growth.

Roadblocks such as lack of space and limited parking will not go away. They will slow the growth of a church until they are removed. The good thing about these problems is that sustained growth should provide the necessary resources to take care of them. There are many churches that have problems which are not so easily solved, and most would love to have the problems associated with a vibrant, growing church.

In closing, I want to encourage you to remember Nehemiah and:

- Ask how things are going.

- Seek help in solving the problems you find.

- Commit yourself to the task and develop a plan.

- Refuse to be afraid of detractors.

- Celebrate when the task is completed!

Also, after the project is completed, come back to review the work and correct any problems you may find. Most importantly, pray and seek God's guidance for

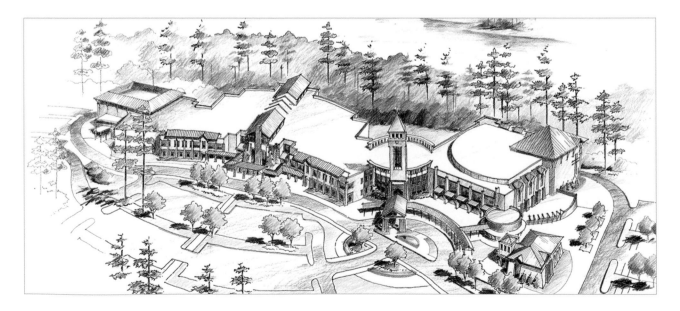

The journey that your church will take is made up of many interrelated but dependent steps.

every step in your project. The journey that your church will take is made up of many interrelated but dependent steps. You may not realize it at the outset of the process, but every decision made by the leadership team will have future consequences. Some will be small and others will have major consequences for the life of your church. It is my prayer that, through strategic planning and preparation, your church will be used by God in a mighty way and that it will enjoy His blessings for years to come.

LESSONS LEARNED

A very wealthy man called a longtime friend who was a builder. This man had a very good reputation for building high quality houses but had never made a lot of money. The wealthy man showed his friend a beautiful new building site that he had just purchased and gave him a set of plans for a large new house that he wanted constructed on this site. Then he told the builder that he would be out of the country for the next nine months and wanted to know if the house could be ready for occupancy when he returned.

The builder was delighted over the opportunity and promised that he would meet the deadline. As the builder started work on this project, he began to see this as his chance to make a large profit and decided to cut some corners. He used second-rate materials and did the very minimum required in every area of this house. He knew that paint and carpet would cover most of his shortcuts and rationalized that his friend had lots of money and could afford to maintain the house.

Nine months passed and the wealthy man returned from his trip. The first thing he did was to call his builder and go right to the new house to look it over. He was pleased with what he saw and turned to the builder and said, "You have been my friend for many years, and I wanted to have this house built for you. It is yours. Enjoy the fruits of your labor. This house is a gift from me to you."

Most of us can guess the ending to the story: the builder, who thought that he was going to make a lot of money, spent the rest of his life replacing poor building materials, repairing the second-rate workmanship, and continuously having to maintain something that was constructed with compromises and shortcuts.

We can learn a great deal from this story. The resources provided for your new facility come from your friends, and they trust you to do your best with what they have given in faith. Your church will be living with the results of this journey for a long time. Only you and God will know if you did your very best.

I would like to thank my Lord, who has called me to this profession. Also, I would like to take this opportunity to thank my family who has supported and encouraged me, my colleagues who have worked alongside me, the teams of people who have learned how to take the *Next Step* with me, and the many congregations who have chosen to take the *journey!*

—Bill Chegwidden

Remember me with favor, O my God.
— NEHEMIAH 13:31

PROJECT HISTORY *and* IMAGE INDEX

YOUR JOURNEY

First Baptist Church – Winder, GA

First Baptist Church of Winder was located in a downtown section of an older city, had outgrown its facility and was landlocked by its location. There was limited parking and no place to expand. The congregation of this well-established church voted to relocate.

Included in the first phase of the master plan of this traditionally designed Baptist church is the construction of a temporary sanctuary that converts into a fellowship hall. The worship center also contains office and educational space. A lake located near the rear of the site provides an inviting environment for family gatherings and a focal point for the development of the church's campus. Future phases include the construction of additional educational space, a new sanctuary and chapel, and a family life center.

Square footage: 60,000 – *Phase 1*
30,000 – *Phase 2*
50,000 – *Phase 3*
10,000 – *Phase 4*
20,000 – *Phase 5*

STEP ONE

Mt. Pisgah United Methodist Church – Alpharetta, GA

CDH Partners Inc. designed a new worship center for Mt. Pisgah United Methodist Church. Phase one includes a 3,000 seat sanctuary, day care center for 250 children with a secluded playground and two children's theatres. The lobby is a two-story open area with two grand staircases and it is used as a gathering place. Exterior spaces include a prayer garden, baptismal pool, and exterior patios. An integrally colored split face block was produced to match the cast stone which is complimented by two exterior brick colors and detailing.

Square footage: 125,430

STEP TWO

First Baptist Church – Gardendale, AL

The master plan for the new Gardendale Baptist Church is sited along a ridge with an orientation for maximum visibility. This relocation is a phased process and will relocate the youth and singles to the new site first. Later phases complete the move of the entire campus. The church is three levels and is recessed in to the hill of the site. The parking is distributed on three sides of the campus. A series of round glass atrium spaces mark the main points of entry into the church facilities. Primary exterior finishes are stone, brick, split face block, precast concrete, an exterior stucco product, and glass. The second level's main entry is located on the north side of the church campus, and is built in phase one. This level provides the main access to the various theaters, the main fellowship hall, and the main worship center and the chapel.

Phase one contains two theaters, each with video capabilities from the main campus. A café and and educational space, designed for youth, college, and singles classes will support each theater. Phase two reunites the entire campus on the new site with a 2,800 seat worship center and the required education space for senior adults, adults, elementary, preschool and nursery age groups, and provides the administration space required for the church. Phase three houses additional support and educational space as the church's ministry grows. Phase four is the final 4500 seat worship center. Phase five is a family activities building.

Site development plan: 200 acres

Square footage: 62,000 – *Phase 1*
170,000 – *Phase 2*
65,000 – *Phase 3*
175,000 – *Phase 4*
74,000 – *Phase 5*

STEP THREE

St. Brigid Catholic Church – Alpharetta, GA

The master plan for St. Brigid Catholic Church includes this Gothic Revival style sanctuary, designed to accommodate 1,100 people. Also included in the plan is a chapel that seats 150 people, a parish hall with a kitchen, an administration area, and classrooms. The exterior facade consists of two colors of brick, cast stone detailing, fiberglass shingles, and a copper steeple. The church is accentuated by a generous array of stained glass windows.

Square footage: 51,125

STEP FOUR

Christ the King Catholic Church – Pine Mountain, GA

Christ the King Catholic Church is a relocation master plan. It integrates trees, shrubs, and flowers with outdoor places for worship and meditation. The church is positioned on the high end of the property providing presence and visibility.

Phase one of the master plan includes the construction of a parish hall that serves as a space for worship, class-rooms, and fellowship gatherings. Phase two consists of the construction of the sanctuary. This building incorporates natural elements such as stone and wood. Stained glass was added for an awe-inspiring setting. Large windows on the north side of the sanctuary provide generous views of the surrounding woods and outdoor chapel. The seating design is a mixture of surround and traditional. Future phases include the construction of a gym, a recreation area, and a new rectory.

Site development plan: 20 acres

Square footage: 14,193 – Church building
16,742 – Edu./admin. building
9,319 – Parish center
1,414 – Chapel
12,109 – Gym building

STEP FIVE

The Cathedral of St. Philip – Atlanta, GA

The Cathedral of St. Philip Episcopal Church is situated on a historical site with a major, commercial thoroughfare on one side and high-end residences on the other. Most of the previous construction was completed in the 1940's and 50's.

Phase one of the master plan included a 42,000 square foot educational building. Phase two included a 77,000 square foot renovation and enclosing an existing exterior courtyard with a skylight to create an enlarged gathering space. Later phases include family life center, and a parking deck. Heavy wood paneling, crown molding, and various custom touches successfully blend the old with the new to maintain the beauty and grace found in one of Atlanta's most visible landmarks. An existing exterior courtyard will be enclosed with a sky-light to create an enlarged narthex/gathering space.

Square footage: 42,000 – *Phase 1*
77,000 – *Phase 2*

STEP SIX

Free Chapel Worship Center – Gainesville, GA

Church leaders for Free Chapel expressed a desire for the sanctuary to have the look and feel of a concert hall rather than a traditional worship space. CDH designed a spacious sanctuary to reflect the church's contempo-rary and progressive style of worship with such elements as open rafters and exposed ductwork. A large tower with a rotunda at the entrance of the sanctuary keeps the flow of this massive structure fluid and inviting.

The wedge shaped 3,500-seat sanctuary with on-site parking contains a theatrical stage that was designed with acoustics in mind. Phase one of the master plan also includes the construction of educational space, a theater and game room for the youth, and a fellowship hall, and preschool. In phase two, the seating capacity in the main auditorium will be expanded to accommo-date 5,000 people. Future phases expand administrative offices, provide a youth center, gymnasium, and a chapel.

Site development plan: 150 acres

Square footage: 91,000 – *Phase 1*
60,000 – *Phase 2*
144,000 – *Phase 3*
50,000 – *Phase 4*

STEP SEVEN

The Church of the Apostles – Atlanta, GA

CDH did not take the obvious route with this project by placing the worship center at the rear of this space-limited track of land. Instead, the sighting of the new sanctuary required an aggressive approach. The master plan called for the footprint of the sanctuary to be located in the front of the property. Today, The Church of the Apostles, with its gothic-styled campus, is one of Atlanta's most visible landmarks.

The sanctuary is a warm transitional space where slate floors, regal stained glass windows, traditional pews combine with open space, clean design, and light-reflecting colors for an intimate yet vibrant worship setting. Special design considerations were taken for the technical equipment used by the church's audio/video production and broadcast ministries. An existing building was extensively renovated for classroom and multi-purpose use. The last two phases of the master plan includes a five-story educational facility and a new chapel.

Site development plan: 9 acres

Square footage: 156,275 New space
92,227 Renovation
1616 Space Parking Decks

STEP EIGHT

Mt. Paran Church of God (Central) – Atlanta, GA

Mt. Paran Church of God is a rapidly growing congregation with a progressive style of worship. The location of the church campus presented serious space limitations. It is situated on a corner lot with a major thoroughfare on one side, and high-end houses on the other. Therefore, considerable time was given to meeting city zoning regulations and neighborhood covenants.

The first phase of the master plan called for the construction of a parking deck and a 300-seat chapel with educational space and elevators. This new facility serves as a transitional space that is connected to the existing buildings. In the second phase a new 2,400-seat sanctuary will be built in front of the existing worship center. The current sanctuary then will be renovated into a fellowship hall with a kitchen. The final phase includes the construction of a new educational facility.

Square footage: 85,000 – Existing Unchanged
27,400 building – *Phase 1*
303,000 parking deck
81,000 new – *Phase 2*
15,500 renovation
35,000 – *Phase 3*

STEP NINE

The Cathedral of The Holy Spirit – Atlanta, GA

This is the first phase of the master plan for the development of this site. This facility provides sanctuary seating for 625, fellowship/ recreation hall seating for 300, and day chapel seating for 100. In addition, the building contains seventeen classrooms and four multi-use rooms. The Parish's desire to unite the existing, contemporary facility and the new worship center in a unified, traditional composition, is accomplished through the use of an architectural style similar to the late nineteenth century Romanesque Revival. A new tower serves as a beacon to the surrounding community and accentuates the main entrance to the worship center.

Site development plan: 32 acres

Square footage: 27,000 – *Phase 1*

STEP TEN

Mt. Paran Church of God (North) – Marietta, GA

Mt Paran North undertook a master planning effort with the goal of maximizing their existing site. After a thorough analysis, the church set out to complete a four phase master plan. The first phase included the complete renovation of the existing building, including the addition of three age specific theaters, Phase two will be the additional of a youth building and a fellowship hall, including a new main entry, Phase three will include a new teaching theatre and production studio, and a new gymnasium, Phase four would add the final worship center and additional educational space—when this final phase is complete the original worship space will be renovated into a youth center and production facility.

STEP ELEVEN

St. Peter Chanel Catholic Church – Roswell, GA

The focus of the 1,484 seat sanctuary, designed in a traditional latin cross plan, is the chancel. The rear docil wall is constructed from marble and features a marble high altar that supports the tabernacle. A stained glass skylight is located above the chancel area at the crossing of the nave and transept and underneath the copper steeple.

The exterior of this new facility is accented by cut stone veneer and cast stone accents and windows. The roofs for the Sanctuary and Chapel are finished with slate.

Other distinguishing features include a copper steeple which is located at the sanctuary's crossing.

STEP TWELVE

Perimeter Church – Norcross, GA

The master plan for this mega church includes the incorporation of the original sanctuary along with other existing buildings. Church leaders believe that youth programs, small group studies, and an effort to strengthen the family are catalysts of a healthy, growing, and active church. Therefore, instead of being a "church on a corner," church leaders sought to develop a campus that was a perfect place for worship, discipleship, community outreach, and recreation. The addition of a lake and thoughtful development of the church's 100 acres has achieved this goal.

Phase two of the campus included three-story educational and church community facilities where twenty-five foot wide corridors along with murals that include streetlights, awnings, park benches, and trees provide a park-like feel for the educational space. The third phase of the master plan was the construction of a 400-seat children's theater with stepping aisles, a split thrust stage, and completely outfitted audio and video production environment. A cobble stone street flanked by various township facades leads up to the facility, which also contains a turn of the century 1800's box office. A senior high area houses a two level theater, rock climbing wall, game room, half-court basketball courts, café, and offices.

Site development plan: 100 acres

Square footage: 114,709 – *Phase 2*
                65,300 – *Phase 3*
                Future phases TBD

STEP THIRTEEN

Johns Creek Baptist Church – Alpharetta, GA

The campus for this traditionally designed church includes the construction of an interim 500-seat sanctuary, a nursery, and space for administration offices. In phase two and three larger educational facilities were constructed. The chapel was renovated, and its auditorium was reduced in size, additional classroom space was also added. Included in the construction is a 1,000-seat multi-purpose room which serves as a fellowship hall. This phase houses additional educational rooms, a full kitchen, an executive meeting room, new administrative offices, and temporary music suites.

The fourth and final phase of the master plan is the construction of a 2,400-seat sanctuary. The central focus of the complex is a beautifully landscaped inner courtyard that contains an amphitheater. During the final phase of construction, the courtyard will be enclosed.

Site development plan: 23 acres

Square footage: 27,000 – *Phase 1*
34,700 – *Phase 2*
77,500 – *Phase 3*
61,400 – *Phase 4*

STEP FOURTEEN

First Baptist Church – Canton, GA

The concept of an arts and crafts theme of the master plan and Phase one was the approach taken to address the client's request to create a retreat-type campus. This relocation allowed for such an opportunity since the location is adjacent to a proposed 300 acre city-owned lake.

The completed phase one of the overall master plan is a multi-purpose facility with a temporary sanctuary of 1100 seats that will serve as a future fellowship hall. Also included in this phase are educational facilities, three theaters and a the final kitchen serving the fellowship hall.

Site development plan: 74 acres

Square footage: 77,200 – *Phase 1*
31,400 – *Phase 2*
Parking Deck – *Phase 3*
102,000 – *Phase 4*
6,000 – *Phase 5*
6000 – *Phase 6*

The projects illustrated in this book were completed by the team members of CDH Partners, and are reflective of their great passion, energy, talent, and hard work. I would like to take this opportunity to offer my thanks to all of my partners, especially Tom Smith, who worked alongside of me with our firm's designers, engineers, and construction specialists. Today, over 100 people work at CDH, and there is no way for me to give the proper credit or express my gratitude to each individual for his or her contribution. However, I do know that without each person's involve-ment, these projects would not have taken place, and I would be remiss if I didn't thank Ernest Pullen and David Brown for encouraging me to begin and for prodding me to finish this book.